Junior Watson is a singer and song writer, youth adviser, teacher, public speaker, manager of the YouTube channel "Gold Nugget – Jaw_success", and author of *Smorgasbord* & *We Want You to Fly*. Outside of his core belief in others, he echoes the motto, "To be successful one must take systematic and calculated steps in the presence of risks". He is determined to make a glass of lemonade out of every lemon life throws at him. Born in Kingston, Jamaica, in 1974 and a graduate of the University of Technology, Jamaica, he now resides in the UK with his wife Natalie.

Dedicated to the ones we have love and lost. To them we say, "Just know that we have loved you, died, and rose again," but above all to the ones who say us in the ashes and refused to let it be our grave. Love you Jman (Jahle-el), Mom and dad, and a church family and co-works out of this world – PGT.

Junior Watson

SEPARATION, A BITTER PILL TO SWALLOW

Be prepared...read this before "I do"

AUSTIN MACAULEY PUBLISHERS™

LONDON * CAMBRIDGE * NEW YORK * SHARJAH

A CIP catalogue record for this title is available from the British Library.

ISBN 9781786936301 (Paperback)
ISBN 9781786935854 (ePub e-book)

www.austinmacauley.com

First Published 2021
Austin Macauley Publishers Ltd
Level 37, Office 37.15, 1 Canada Square
Canary Wharf
London
E14 5AA

Synopsis

This book was born out of a failed marriage and as such it was my original intention to name it *The Reasons I Did Not Die When She Left*. However, I decided on *Separation, a Bitter Pill to Swallow* in the end. Somewhere along the way of writing this 200-page book, my perspective and message had changed. I realise that I had learnt many valuable lessons from the failed attempt at being one with another person and so I wanted to help others, using the lessons I have learnt. There is more to life than listening to people's 'sad sack' stories. In essence, I did not want the sadness of a broken heart to be its principal theme. This is why although the truths found in this book are blunt and somewhat hard to swallow, I did my best to cover them in a good measure of wisdom.

So, this book is far more than a story about my separation or why I did not self-capitulate, it actually helped me live. And as such, it contained valuable instructions and advice to those considering marriage. I wanted to focus on such a lesson as, knowing your own self, choosing wisely, loving wholeheartedly, the purpose of marriage and making a decision to live when it falls apart. Well that is if after you have paid attention to the lessons and it still does fall apart.

Please note that this book is full of unadulterated truth about my life and my experiences, all geared to stimulate your mind and force you to ask the important questions before the big day or if you have passed the 'I do' stage, why you should determine in your heart to stay put where you already are.

This book will highlight the issues that can lead to separation. It also presents the mind-set of a person going through this experience. Hence, you will get a close look at how one contemplates 'how to survive separation?' after being cast aside for nor valuable reason than 'I have made a mistake'. Therefore, you will also see how I battled against depression and suicide when my marriage bonds were broken.

I know others have shared similar experiences and I am certain that they too understand that when the love bond breaks, the river of fury runs rampant and self-destruction seems the only door of possibility. A door many have taken. The ordeal certainly is a deep and murky river called grief and shows itself as a bitterness that engulfs everyone in its path, destroying homes, separating families and turning friends into enemies. What may have started out as a misunderstanding or an inconsiderate expression grew to become a raging flood of denial, anger isolation, pain, regret, bargaining, depression and eventually acceptance of a love lost. One in which although we have accepted the inevitable still carries with it something that grabs at our hearts. The lingering mood swings that creep up on us without warning, especially during specific seasons and special events, seems to be like quicksand or an eternal prison from which we cannot escape but one from which we eventually rise. So, this book is a meaningful attempt to help others recover by sharing the six reason I did not die when she left.

I must admit that it does take a whole lot of grace and favour to overcome some of life's uncertainties and although separation might be the likely ending to a long line of problems, it is not the end to a productive life and future, in itself. It is what we do afterwards that is. This is where many of us need a little help and guidance, as we can become so overwhelmed with the separation that we forget that life goes on or it is not the end of the world.

Preface

What makes life exciting is that it comes with varying opportunities for us to learn many lessons. Each lesson acts like a guiding star, taking us to the ultimate place where we belong. Sometimes this journey can quick and pleasurable and at other times it can be long and very eventful. Whatever the case, many times the essence and truth we gain from each of the encounters we have had, we only understanding after we have failed the test. Ultimately, in the end, we can only bless the many crushing paths we have travelled after surviving and discovered that each trial made us much better for travelling them.

Therefore, although failure is never our intention when we start anything, the wisdom we gain from failing is priceless and gives merit to our experience and sharpen our outlook. It makes us wiser 'If I may say so myself'. I took an examination in matrimony and failed bitterly. However, I dare to share the lessons that I learned, so that you might benefit from them. I am not sure if you will not have to make some bloopers yourself. However, if you are considering making a trip to the altar, never forget:

1. Marriage is a learning institution in itself. In some instances, it teaches lessons through pain, sacrifice, tears, loss and a whole list of endless possibilities.

2. 'For better or worse' was not said by the 'Vows' themselves, it was said by life. Hence, there will be low moments, sick feelings, times of emptiness and loneliness, times of insufficiencies and regrets, etc. That is what makes life, life. So, if you are not willing to be someone else's covering during these times, do not get into a relationship; much less marriage.

3. Marriage is a glorious institution but only for those that court genuine love, respect and an unwavering commitment to compromise with and for their intended spouse.

4. Marriage is never about whether we want someone now. It is about whether we will want them later on when the dark times come, as the hand, we should always want to hold in the murky waters of life; is the one we want and love.

5. The largest fear of marriage is, 'How much of me will I have to give up and how much can I expect to receive in return?' To overcome this fear, one must make giving up 'selfishness' a priority.

6. It is never about winning for we all can handle winning; it is but how we behave when we lose or did not get my way.

7. Do not knock marriage until you have been through it! When you have, you will either develop a great reverence for it or yell, 'Never again!'

8. It is not an 'If' or a 'But'; you will hurt each other. Decide now on how you will guard each other's feelings thereafter. So, before entering, learn how to apologise genuinely.

9. When you have disagreements, both of you will seek to justify your actions and so at the end of it all, one will be left to wonder, *What had I done wrong?* In many instances, this is the hardest question of them all to answer.

10. The left brain of the man and right brain of the woman do not become one until after enduring the pain of the next person dealing and coming to grips with their own self within the context of marriage. This is a process in itself and though counselling is received before the 'I dos', nothing outside of being married can properly prepare you for it.

11. Human nature is 'funny', we all in one way or another want to win. However, in marriage, above all, who is to win is never apparent, no matter how clear the answer is.

12. If you live in fear of offending your partner, then you are immature and your partner is too thin skinned. Your marriage will not work, for it takes two mature individuals to make a mature – peaceful and fruitful – marriage as you will offend each other. There is no doubt about that.

13. In the low times that will come and when you do not have the resources immediately to get you both to where you want to go, serve each other.

14. No matter how correct you are, quit pushing each other over the edge, for if ones go down; both go down. Also, remember most of all, if you quit on each other before you both come out of the hole that learning

how to deal with each other will place you in, suffering is not a word, for none of you will make it out.

15. Never forget that 'Who' owns what, in a relationship is important. We always want the next individual to hold down their end, as there are specific responsibilities for each person in the marriage. Learn them. To ask the other person to hold down our ends for us consistently, will be disastrous.

16. Balancing priorities is one of the biggest tasks of marriage, few know who or what should be the order before the 'I do' and even fewer seek to make their spouse their priority afterwards. So, before you wed, ask yourself, 'Who or what is and will be my priority?', for to survive being married, you will need to prioritise.

17. Marriage is the perfect place to learn inclusivity in diversity and submission despite of passion, possession and position, as you will never always want what your partner wants or even at the time when they want it. You also will not always have their support or see eye to eye on all issue but in the end, oneness must prevail.

18. When having a conversation, if you are waiting on the cue to pounce or jump to an already predetermined conclusion, you will not even hear or receive a sincere apologies when it is given. Therefore, never stay stuck on what you want to hear, listen for what is being said from the heart.

19. A wife is different from a bride, one is for a day, the other is made overtime. A groom may look nice on the day but to become a husband takes time. The good ones I have learnt; take longer in the furnace.

20. This wisdom of a women generally clams the pride and arrogance of a men but the strength and tenacity of men is what makes a woman fruitful. Hence, respect each other's strength and capacity to be real, honesty and open.

To this day, I do not think my wife realised how she tore my heart to shreds when she went out of our home. When she walked out, she expressed that a vow can be broken and that no divine ordinance should keep two people together, if one or both do not want to stay together. The pain of this utterance left me standing alone, hurt and scared. At first, I did not think I could make it or even if I wanted to make it. I did not want to live. At this time, the grave reached out to me. Somewhere deep inside I wanted to answer its call. We took the vow

'Until Death Do Us Part' but something died and I wanted to follow. I did not know what it was but something told me that I was the one who had died and that I should make it real. Yet, somewhere along the journey of putting of the feeling and fighting to keep my sanity, I learned that I could survive. In my pain, I finally realised that God had me. He held me in His arms, for without Him and by His grace, I would not have survived. Now I have picked up the pieces and I am able to give you a simply message.

To give you this message, however, the question: How does one live or love another, after being convinced that they had found the one person in the world that completed their life and even with the odds against them, they courted that individual until they said, 'Yes,' then that person distanced them self and leaves?

Devastation!

How do you survive?

How do you survive this death sentence, this feeling of betrayal?

You give yourself time to become someone new. You grow. You reach out.

The act of a beloved leaving hurts but time is the salve for every wound. Eventually, we turn a corner, then another, until the pain lessens to a dull ache. Then, if we allow ourselves, healing takes place in the deep tissues of our heart and vibrant colours return to our lives. Not to mention our face! We will then be able to rise like an eagle and soar on the winds of our newly found grace.

Introduction

'Fools rush in where angels fear to tread. Read this, before you get married.'

The lingering mood swings that creep up on us, without warning, especially; during specific seasons and special events, makes us moody and without consciousness sometimes snappish. The inability to reconcile how 'good we have been' compared to how we have been tried seems to be like quicksand or an eternal prison from which we cannot escape but one from which we eventually rise. So, this book is a meaningful attempt to help others figure out the 'It is not you, it's me' schizophrenia of another person's inability to remember why they opened up to us in the first place.

Looking in, from the outside, those who are not in this position, can sit back and say, 'I would never have done that if it were me!' or ask, 'Why did he or she had to kill the individual? Only a fool would do that. All it proves is that they never loved the person in the first place. How can you say you love someone and turn around and kill them?', 'I don't love anyone but God more than me, so that could never happen to me!', 'Why didn't they just separate, divorce and find someone else? Look how many other individuals are in the world. You cannot tell me they could not have found someone else!' Those who speak this way do not really understand the war that goes on in our minds when a breakup takes place. Thy do not understand that there is nothing that further obscures an already thin line between sanity and dementia; like a broken heart. Love cost and when it does not cost, it hurts. All of us would rather pay the cost than stand the hurt.

Yes, it is a sin to kill another or to commit suicide and indeed it shows selfishness, weakness and irrationality when dealing with one's pain but how else does one quench the flames. On the other hand, when you are losing the one you love, all rationale goes. You become preoccupied with thoughts of whether the person truly loved you. 'How could they betray me like this?' lingers constantly in our minds. Often, we do not see ourselves as being guilty of any misdemeanour and so we placed the blame elsewhere. For many, the extent of their love is even unto death, so they would rather die and take the other person with them, than to face life without them. 'If I cannot have you, no one else can.' Jealousy is as cruel as the grave and a partner with nothing else to lose will choose such a place. Perhaps, this is why sanity goes through the door and irrationality comes flooding in, when our emotions become stirred by any form of loss.

The loss I am speaking of is not the one relating to death, for as grievous as that is, it is expected and we do find a way to live. I am also not speaking of the loss relating to duty, for working away from home many times have beautiful endings. Neither do I speak of a loss by a couple who came to getter for an objective. When such a couple separate, there is no 'love lost', they simply go their separate ways when the honey runs out of the moon. The objective I had is met, 'I got what I wanted. Good bye.' The loss I am speaking of is the one where the couple have gone through three phases of incompatibility. These I call: self-expression, ravaged and quit. I will explain these phases later. When I do, you will see that these phases are the corrupted versions of what was meant; originally, to be a genuine part of the expression of love and appreciation between two individuals.

You will also understand why separation means ruin for so many. You will see that it is devastating, because both parties had invested their time, effort, emotions and money with a desire for a greater return but is ultimately rewarded with 'irreconcilable differences' and hopelessness. You will see that it is devastating because expectations were not met, dreams died in the process and instead of gaining love, companionship and respect; they are rewarded with loneliness, anger, emptiness and more questions than answers and sometimes a child or two to continue bickering over.

Understand this that in matters of the heart, what is important is the quality of time shared with the object of the heart and not so much the length of time spent overall. It is the time spent in each other's presence, the connectivity of heart and soul, which makes the two becoming one. For in truth, two individuals could have just met or known each other for a short time but in the shortness of the time spent with each other, their lives became so intertwined that it becomes difficult for one to be without the other. The length of time they knew each other had nothing to do with it but something happened in the spirit realm that caused a knitting together of souls. They became kindred spirits.

When this occurs, it happens because purpose is going to be established. The meaning and essence of that couple's life; will be augmented to a greater level.

Moreover, despite their pain and test, they learn to prefer the company of each other rather than living life alone or with someone else. Life became an, 'I would have chosen you again and again, despite it all' moment.

Note, I am not saying that each individual in a union will invest the same amount of time, effort or emotion over the life of the relationship. Both might do so at the start or in the early years but as time progresses, both will not sustain it. Anyone who expects it to be otherwise is fooling himself or herself. With relationships, at some point, there is going to be an imbalance. Roles, responsibilities, strength and body changes as well. As such, one party will feel the strain of the demands on the relationship more than the other will. When this happens that party will start to think that the other person is not pulling their share of the weight. This is in turn taken as: he or she does not love me as much as they did before. How could anyone still love me and allow this to happen to me? Here is where heartbreak can occur, for imaginary or otherwise, when external pressure rises, love is one of the first things we question and when the interrogation is over, what was found not to be genuine love will be frustrated and discarded.

Understanding and interpreting this truth means that this book is not about a one-night stand. Neither is it about two undeserving people. This book is about two people that went into a relationship, with the intention of 'Forever' but somehow ended up saying 'Never again'. Also, this book is neither about two people that were not brave enough to do the godly and honourable thing; that is, getting and remaining married but it is about two individuals who prayed, 'Lord, your will be done,' but still got burnt. What went wrong? You might ask. We separated! If you should ask, 'Why?', what you would get as your answer is something that will 'save face' but hides a strain of bitterness and regret deep inside.

Separation and divorce are indeed bitter pills to swallow. I say this because, if a spouse dies, it is almost easier to accept the loss of that individual than to be separated from the one you love or think you would have loved 'until death do us part'. Death offers closure and a sense of finality. If you were inclined to move on, there would be fewer emotional entanglements. Yes, it hurts and you grieve for a while but after the grieving subsides, you then analyse the position in which you now find yourself in and then make a decision whether to go into another relationship again or to stay single.

When separation occurs from your spouse and you know that that person is still somewhere alive but you cannot have him or her, this makes you feels as though you have been cast into an abyss to fight mental wars. This is even worst when it occurs because of betrayal or adultery. It is painful.

Death is painful, yes but separation carries a different kind of hurting. It feels like there is a hot muffler inside your heart. Bike riders know what I am talking about when I say this. Burns take forever to heal or so it seems and even so, a grotesque scar is usually left behind long after the wound has healed to remind us where we have been.

When an individual leaves, we do not hurt because they choose to leave but because of why and how they left. The reason can sometimes seem insignificant or an excuse for not honouring their commitment. 'I just need a break!' or it can be as large as suffocation or abuse. 'Your family hates me and you are not doing anything for my peace of mind or to help the situation!' Whichever the case, when we love and they leave, a piece of us leaves with them. Whether they took it, accept it or not, they took a part of us and because they took it, no matter what excuse they give, we will still hurt.

However, since excuses or reason for leaving can be many it is hard to say which one will hurt us more. Nevertheless, I would hasten to say the worst one I feel is the time when no reason at all is given. To me, this is even more devastating than I am leaving because 'we no longer see eye to eye'.

In our minds, even arguing and fighting all the time is not a reason to leave, much less leaving without saying why. As such, we are bewildered with many unanswered questions: 'Are they lying?', 'Is there someone else?', 'Is this a copout?', 'An excuse?', 'Am I so evil?', 'Is this the work of a demon?', 'Can they not find a way or discover themselves with me in the picture?' or 'What is so wrong with me?'

Owing to the fact that these questions cannot be easily answered, we further wonder, *How will others see me now?* and can I tell you, depression often sets in when we experience the callousness of others. It might even seem as if no one cares about our plight and some people might seem unfeeling and judgemental. This then reinforces our sense of inadequacy and we begin to feel shame and self-pity. We fall prey to irrational thoughts and ungodly ways of escape.

Death!

So then, with all of the books that have been written on the topic of marriage and separation, why write another book? Why contribute to the plethora of information that already exists? Alternatively, what new perspective can I bring to such a much talked about subject?

Well, in all the books that I had read, all the conversations and counselling sessions that I underwent, I found that none of them directly related to me. I could not find a solution to my situation in them. They did not adequately advise the fundamental issue of how to move on with my life or shake the feeling of rejection. I never felt as though they understood the depth of my sadness. 'Maybe the writers did not have a personal experience', I thought. Those of us that have been through the fire, we can tell the difference. There is a distinction between speaking from theory and research than from writing about our own experience and recovery.

I know, not all things must be experienced, in order to give the best advice or a relevant opinion. When it comes to matters of the heart, however, there is no substitute for experience. As the Bible says, 'The mouth of the righteous speaketh wisdom and his tongue talketh of judgement.' Putting succinctly, 'Experience speaketh wisdom,' and I will say, 'Every fool who will learn from the mistake of his or her past is made that much wiser.' I will also say, 'The one of the biggest mistakes we can ever make in our life is not to learn or be able to teach others the lessons we have learnt from the biggest mistake we have ever made in our lives.'

Therefore, the theory becomes real after it has happened to you. This is my findings. In fact, believe me; healing will manifest in your own heart when you are helping others and showing them your passion by sharing what you have learnt from your ordeal.

This book is my way of reaching out.

My message, 'Don't die! Live!'

I must say this before moving forward, during my separation, I was looking for reconciliation with my wife. I had hoped and longed for it passionately. During that time of longing, I struggled. Consequently, when restoration did not come, I began seeking sympathy and help. When there was a shortage of that I gave in to the voices that attacked my mind. I sought deliverance from all the wrong places. When there was none, I felt despair deep down in me. At this point, my thoughts were self-destructive. I punished myself. I tried to pay penance for my sins by keeping so busy that I became numb. There were days I was on autopilot. I ate sparingly. Slept minimally and wrote feverishly. Still I entertained the hope that she would return. Instead, she grew more distant and acidic in tone. In reverse, I justified my self-defence and eventually I became her enemy.

I do not know of any person that handles being 'dumped' by their wife or husband well. I certainly did not! It led me into depression and suicidal tendencies. I had to make the decision to live for my son. I am sure that there are many individuals like me, who will come to that point. This book is for such a one.

Even the best of marriages can fail. Failure here, however, does not mean condemnation or finality. In some instances, yes, it does mean permanent separation. In others, separation is temporary. It will take work. In either case, we need to know what to do. I did not. I only felt my way though. I hope you will learn from me.

I have come to learn that there are three ways to handle a situation. 1) We can choose to live with it, which means we can endure the pain and strain of it or at least subject our minds and will to live with it as it is. 2) We can also choose to change the situation by seeking help and intervention from others. Some things we cannot change by ourselves, we need a mediator. 3) Lastly, we can choose to get out. Simply put. Leave! Regardless of the way we choose to handle the situation, in the end, there will be either an individual change or a positional change.

All relational trails will require us to perform one of three changes: change ourselves, change another person or change where we are. I acknowledge that we cannot change another individual. Why? Firstly, we are not masters of mind manipulation. Secondly, neither is it our right to do so. Therefore, there are only two alternatives available to us. We must either change ourselves or change where we are. These we do by amending our position and stance or changing what is happening around us. Both, although possible, are burdensome. Leaving the familiar self and place is hard. Sometimes, the idea of change is what 'helps' to push us down further in our bewilderment. It leaves us with the 'friends of Job' effect. 'If you weren't so evil, you would not be in this mess!'

This was what some of the books that I read and sessions I attended did. They placed the blame solely on me. Others ignored certain facts. For example, we can speak all the relevant love language that an individual wants to see, hear, feel, taste or even smell but the individual remains unchanged. They can maintain that we were never the object of their love and desire in the first place. They just cannot bring them self to loving us or regarding what we give and do for them as a thing of worth. They will simply continue to ignore and hurt us. I guess this was what Moses saw and Jesus later called 'hardness of heart'. As such, it has nothing to do with irreconcilable differences, whatever that might be.

One more thing I learned in my psychology class at university. I learnt that an individual given the correct stimulant or placed in the right environment does not always choose the most appropriate outcome. I could have told them that Adam and Eve were in the most ideal of conditions and look what happened to the human race as a result of their choice. But why does this happen? It happens because we are not animals. We are human beings and as such, no one can adequately predict what we will do under varying situations. Sometimes even under the best of conditions, we do the opposite of what is expected of us. We do so just because we can or feel like it. Being human means we have to show others that we have self-will and personal autonomy.

I know to some degree that I have made it sound as if marriage is laden with problems but I will be the first to say, 'No, it is not.' Each marriage is different and some might never have some of the problems others face. However, in the ensuing chapters of this book, I will also convey that 'Marriage is a blessing but if you separate, you can survive. You do not have to die.'

Chapter 1
How Did It Happen?

'Out of the blue is not out of the blue to those who are looking with expectancy.'

Why does it appear that the facts and solutions to the problems and issues of life only come after we have messed up, lost the game or found ourselves in some awkward situation? It is as if 'If I had known…' or 'If I had done…' only comes to mind when we have no other way to explain to our minds how mistakenly foolish we have been. For example, I read this note, after separating from my wife: 'Marriage is not by any, to be entered into unadvisedly or lightly but reverently, discreetly, deliberately, soberly and in the fear of God.' Yes, I went to approximately four or five of the premarital counselling sessions that were mandatory for us. Note I said 'I'. Signs can be all along the way but we ignore them. Yes, I made notes about the dos and don'ts of marriage, I even read books on the subject of marriage but nowhere along the way can I remember hearing or reading these words.

After I read this note, I understood things a bit differently. It showed me that my concept of relationships and marriage had been so way off it was not funny. It showed me that having the wrong reasons or concept is the same as having a bad foundation in a building. In looking at the words, unadvisedly and lightly, along with those that followed, has helped me to understand that all the guidance, insight and best wishes, in the world can be poured upon us but still be wasted because we are not open to hear them, much less accepting them.

Let me plunge a little deeper into this chapter with a love note. At least that is what I thought of it when I wrote it. Now, I see it as a well-crafted cacophony of my maddening emotions. These I experienced during the time of trying to communicate my love to my now estranged wife before we got married:

To the One My Heart Desires and Loves,

My heart beats and my pulse races as the blood runs rapidly through my veins, sending boyish giggles and smiles all over my black turned purple face. A strange delight, I can almost taste! I can hardly keep my breath. I gasp for air, just at the mention of your name and when I see you, I do nothing else but stare at you with a lovesick flair.

Oh the many nights I lie awake, just thinking about the sylphlike nature of your grace. Sweat runs down my back and my jaw drops when I think about the fashion of you and the refreshing dew you bring to my wilting soul. I pray and hope that God will keep you just like that a sweet heart and a continuous refreshing spring, a friend straight to the end.

As our relationship unfolds like a rose, even if this is only in my mind, all I can say is, 'Heaven knows, I love the friendship we have.' Although it is a little bit stormy and deserty some days, I know we will find grace. I am so glad we both serve the Lord God and are being held together by His great and powerful arm, in this crazy state. Thus, as I dream of being a gentleman that minister to your thirst. I stand to assure you that even though I am a klutz, for you I will gladly open any door and allow you to walk through it first.

Certainly, my eyes are not blind and I am not unscratched by the bluntness of you speaking your mind but baby even when you insult me, you come across as kind, for I love you all the time: giggling, upset or at a loss for words to express what you feel inside. Babes my friends ask all the time, 'is love blind, why don't you try some other goldmine, for this one is cold and harsh with you all the time?' To them I say love must be, because I will continue to justify all your mistakes until I make you mine.

Truly, I see all your flaws and apparently, you see mine. I see how you try to avoid me at all cost but forgive me if I already love you. I love you with all my heart, my soul and my mind. Yes, you will not even throw me a life-saving line, to let me know that I should still try, yet I find not a cause to go on pause or run away from your beautiful hive. Neither have I lost sight of the noblest of cause that of winning your heart. At this moment, I have nothing to show for all that I have tried and some days I really expect nothing from your side. But in this knowledge I rest patiently for I love you deep inside. Hence, I say, someone will lose but it will not be me, for to see you be mine is not a fantasy but my pungent reality all the time.

Yours for life, if you want me.

– Junior

When I reflect on the words in this note, I realise a fundamental problem in relationships that do not have a successful conclusion. I noticed that they are often one sided. One individual puts out their all and the other remains true to them self. Here I was putting out all the effort to form a relationship with the one I desired. I now wonder, *Why I did it?*

Why did I not realise this back then? Why did I only realise this after she had packed her things and remained true to her convictions, by leaving me? Why am I now seeing what should have been blatantly obvious back then? You know why I am seeing the now. My perspectives have changed. I have been there! I now know that you can use all your power and will to bring an individual to yourself but it will take the power of God, Himself, to keep them with you. Even then, this will only be dependent upon whether they are willing to submit to Him; for if they chose to be defiant, not even He can make them stay. I prayed and fasted until I started getting dizzy spells. It never changed one thing. God will not force those who actively resist Him.

The truth is keeping someone in our lives, who no longer wants to be there is a grave mistake but it pales into insignificance to bringing in someone who does not want to be there or should not have been there in the first place.

So, one of the fundamental mistakes I made at the beginning of our relationship was to not to properly answer the question, 'Does she belong here?' and if yes, 'Why?' We must be willing to question our motives for letting others into our lives. In fact, if a person does not want to come in, do not force them in! We must also stop turning emotional and spiritual 'No' into 'Yes' because 'I LOVE YOU'. It will not work. Hearing 'Yes' when 'No' is clearly stated and seen in the statements and actions of the other persons, will only hurt you more in the end. It is always best to accept 'No' early than to pursuing after someone who does not love you and have to be forced to accept that same no later.

Take it from me, a reason not properly define, will always leave room for errors and the possibility of a distressful outcome.

These types of mistakes appear to be an incomprehensible part of our human expression, when we are trying to woo one another. It is as though we have to trip and stumble through a mountain of molehills before reality hits us. For me, I had no power to refrain from making these mistakes.

I deceived myself!

I was in love.

Somewhere along the way, I became deluded. My emotions controlled me and gave a feeling of emptiness on the inside. I constantly had a feeling that said, 'I would be unhappy for the rest of my life,' if she never became a part of it. So much so that even though there was no encouragement given to bolster the attention I was paying to her, I still projected what I wanted to see and held on to it for dear life. In doing so, I convinced myself that all the stars were in alignments and we belonged together. In the madness of it all, I gave myself reasons to love, even when my 'girlfriend' did not love me. She said it and showed it in so many ways but I could not hear or see it. She was 'so' all the world to me.

As such, I pursued her and made many mistakes. I even made promises that I would not have been able to keep. Oftentimes, we behave like this, out of pure dreaming, speculation, emotionalism and bewilderment. We have faith and think that hope alone solves everything. Thus, we ignore the facts. Those facts that are hidden somewhere in the back of our minds is the truth we do not want to hear or accept. We know that the object of our desire does not reciprocate our feelings but we act as conquerors.

Yet we lie to ourselves!

I lied to mine and it was hard to accept when she left. The sooner you accept the truth; the sooner you start to see the silver lining at the end of the rainbow.

There is a quote by Maya Angelou, 'When people show you who they are, believe them.' I did not listen to this great advice. There were other choices but this one was nice. I could have accepted the proven and tried but when we are love stricken, we see the facts as lying or as something that 'Only wants us to give up our only chance at happiness'. I did not want to give up my one chance of splendour. How could I?

I saw a Harley motor bike, when my girlfriend, back then, had said of herself, 'I am a ten-speed bicycle.' A bicycle is great yes but not great enough for someone who sees them self as deserving a bike.

I then insisted, 'Yes you are that but I can make you better. I can expand your frame, place larger tyres on you, give you headlights and taillights and create an engine that fits you. You will love it! I can make you faster, prettier and more desirable. I can take you places both day and night. Be not afraid. I will make you better. We will be the envy of the world!'

Oh how stupid. It is not our responsibility to make anyone better. Our responsibility is to complement and complete each other in a relationship, not fix each other. If there is any need for change, it must never be a forced change or selfish motive change. It must be one born out of a desire to honour, respect and a personal desire to grow in unity.

Notice in the note, it was all about what 'I will do' and what 'I can do' for her, not together. I wanted to recreate her, because I was not satisfied with the way she was. Beautiful; yes but can be better. 'Why do we think everyone wants to be better or attracted by the offer of being better?'

I thought that this 'hope of being better' would entice her to come and as she came and sew how much better she was becoming, would stay forever. Who am I to insist or force my desire on her? Who told me she wanted to be more than just a 'ten-speed bicycle?' I should have focused on making me better, because if a better me could not attract her and keep her, she would not know my wreath to stay with me.

Yes, it was unfair of me to project myself, my desires or even my hopes of having a Harley on her, when she did not see me as an individual who would be able to handle a tricycle much less a Harley. This should have been the first sign that I was settling for two little or trying to reach too far over my head.

One of the first signs that should tell us, 'Your about to make a mistake' should be the sign of worth. The question of how much do I worth myself, how much am I worth to you or I worth you is of utmost importance. If we do not value ourselves or value the other person before the marriage, we will not do so afterwards. Strength of character is everything.

I know true worth only comes after being together. However, if we cannot have at least a little glimpse of it before we say 'I do', we will not have it afterwards or worst, value it when trouble comes. The depth of people's heart can often be seeing long before we begin to see their other parts. Without knowing what each other stand for; the foundation of our relationship would be built up on future promise. This is because we have little or no substance at the start to grow on. Why we came together in the first place, matters and it is what we should always seek both to maintain and to improve on. Therefore, anytime we have to promise so much at the beginning of a relationship, we are out of our league.

I captured her in a mental prison and refused to relinquish the keys. If I had only taken the time during our courtship, I would have seen that I was the only one sacrificing and giving of myself to create a picture that I alone saw. If I had logically observed the ways in which she was treating me, I would have been, spared the pain I later felt, for then I would have seen her actions for what they really were a desperate cry of, 'I do not want to be made over and if I need to be, it is not by you'.

However, despite the fact that she did not show me any signs that she loved me or would ever love me, somehow, I thought that she would eventually grow to love me or at least after seeing all that I have sacrificed and gone through, she would never leave me! Thinking this way, deceives us to rely on the idea that someone who does not love us, will grow to love us when they see how much we love them or have sacrificed for them. It never normally does and as such, we should never take the exception for the norm.

This type of thinking is all wishful. Human nature holds no loyalty without true connection and the only true connection between human beings is love.

The love, of which I am speaking here is not a one-sided affair but a reciprocal expression that is balanced. Balanced here means it gives as much as it takes. It is a love that ignores cultural norms and practices, yes but one that values virtues, virtues that transcend one's own desires to behave in accordance to what looks like facts. This is so even when the alternative looks more appealing to the eyes or when the facts obscured the truth. I can act and look as though I love you when I do not.

Only real love goes beyond the facade to the heart because love is a decision. I decide that I will value you above all else, not because you have, you are or even will or will be but because I choose to. Hence, this balance expression cannot be one that is non-existent at the start of a relationship that leads to marriage. It must always be there as an undercurrent for at some point, along the way, the two individuals must pledge to each other the highest offering that can be offered in a pledge, 'self'. It cannot be one forcing it on the other. It has to be real from the outset for both. It must be a godly and fair exchange and it has to be a decision made in the spirit of the individuals. It cannot be a feeling but a state of being. If self – one's own life – is not an amicably exchanged, one will not own the other and none will submit during times of change.

Note here that every turmoil; is a time of change. However, only temporal things will change.

The soul, which is our seat of emotion and feelings, will change over time, according to our maturity or as we grow in our likes and dislikes. However, our spirit remains constant for it is the part of us that is everlasting or timeless. Who we are in spirit, we are forever. We get that aspect of ourselves from our Creator, who does not change and is self-existent. We are not self-existent but in love, we extend ourselves. We become a part of someone else and someone else becomes a part of us. As such, we do not know where self begins or where it ends; we simply keep and sustain each other. Simply put, I in you and you in me!

This is what makes our love the way it is, self-existent and unchanging and causes us to know, from the beginning of the relationship, if we are loved or will ever be loved by the other individual. Love is not blind. We know when we are in love and we know when others are in love with us. A spirit connection takes place deep down on the inside. Hence, both feel empty and meaningless without each other. Often times, however, we fool ourselves and tell ourselves that this spiritual connect is there when it is not.

Be honest with yourself!

In your relationship is there a spiritual connection there? I know the emotional connection is. I do not have to ask that and I hope you are not confusing it with love. For love is not emotions, it is sacrifice and we only give ourselves for those who we give our spirit to and expect to get back theirs in return. So, are you making a sacrifice and is it reciprocated?

Believe me, it is a big mistake to allow your spirit to become entangled with someone who does not want a life-long relationship with you.

So let me ask you another question. How is the other person's spirit towards you?

Often in relationships, we tend to focus on the physical aspects and ignore the spiritual. We keep forgetting that it is the spiritual aspects of who we are as individuals that gives meaning to what we do throughout our lives.

A failure then to identify or see a person's sprit, will lead to mistakes, because we will make decisions based on outward appearances or actions only. From the onset, going into a relationship, we must not only be able to see what is said or done to us in the present but we must also gain an insight into how we will be treated in the future. In other words, we know what we will do 'for and to' the other person and we will not change but do we know what they will 'do or how far' they will go for us? It is only by learning or understanding the spirit of each other, during courtship, can we gain this insight. This is way the wedding day should never be planned in hast.

It is when we know each other's spirit, when we say, 'I love you,' it means I love you from the beginning straight to the end and when you say it back to me, it means the same thing. All that exist thereafter is our manifestation; our actions aligning themselves with our spiritual declaration and our daily devotion of become one flesh, for we already share one spirit.

Therefore, because true love is birth in the spirit and played out through our actions, what we do as the years passes by in our relationship is find different ways to express what we have already declared in our hearts. Hence, the gift we give is just a medium of spiritual expression. It is how we get our spirit to be visible or the door we open to our lover to enter into our souls.

Within this context, love that is born in the spirit is never shaken or destroyed by things that are temporal in nature; this is unless we have turned those temporal things into spiritual ones.

How do we make temporal things cross the spiritual divide? You may ask. We make it happen by us paying them excessive attention. We make them our passion. We allow their constant reoccurrence to jolt, pleasure or annoy us. In the process, we fail to see that the same way we strengthen and reinforce love; is the same way we strengthen and reinforce hatred. Hence, we keep seeing and allowing the weaknesses or shortcomings in our partner to get the better of us or we fail to forgive and let go of past hurts. We ignore that love is only strengthened and reinforced by eternal truths, while the certainty of failure and disgrace is magnified by courting folly.

One such foolishness is to tell ourselves, 'What we have is not good enough,' instead of working to grow what we have.

Note, any lover that pays attention to everyone else's love; will not grow. This is so because love – the band between spirits – grows when it is paid specific attention.

As such, to look elsewhere is to fall in love with elsewhere.

No one grows in love without being specific and deliberate. I say this because each new expression of love takes us to a higher level of virtue than the one before. How does it do so? It does so because it takes effort. It takes something that forces us to think beyond the routine and causes us to ask, 'Is there a new way I can express this?' When we answer this question positively, although the new expression we come up with might be a relic of the past, when we do it again, it is always uniquely and intricately different from the time before. This is so, because, its predecessor become stale or expected, which causes its reception to wane and its value to lessen. To keep doing the 'Same old, same old' is to become annoying and burdensome.

Nothing breathes frustration like a lack of variety.

We all can learn to live in a prison because we are constrained to be there but marriage is not a prison where day in and day out the same thing happens. It is a living and dynamic organism that requires new life. A life that is not based upon absolute routine or taking each other for granted.

This is why, in love, we are always reshaping our concept of each other's likes and dislikes, as new information about each other emerges from under the protective shadow we have built for ourselves. Hence, we have to grow constantly in our principles and expression in order to maintain our relationship, not our love. Our words or the tingly feelings we have do not sustain our relationships, it is the spirit behind the words and the depth from which those feelings flow that does.

Hence, love does not grow, it is either we have it or we do not, because love is the knowledge that we belong to each other in servitude. This is not slavery but a reassurance that we have each body, soul and spirit. This is a knowledge we cannot fabricate, for time and trails will prove its validity. If that connection that we belong to each other is not there, the longer we stay with each other is the more we get on each other's nerves and as certain as the sunrise, all manner of issues will come to cause stressful encounters. So, if it is not there, 'I hate you!' will eventually become a part of our vocabulary.

This is why I believe that deep down, from the beginning, all of us get a glimpse into the other person's soul and spirit and we know if we belong there. So, from the get-go, either we are connected to the essence of the other person or we are not and are willing to make the sacrifice necessary to establish and keep that connection going. However, whether we choose to be honest with ourselves or not is another story!

Therefore, in a relationship, we are the ones who are expected to grow in our ability to relate and to connect with each other and as we grow, we find new ways to express our emotions. A loving relationship tests us and there by causes us to become mature and responsible individuals. The more we grow through the various encounters we face, should be the more we come in tune with each other. As long as we can relate, we can communicate, hope, share time and pace and have a meaningful life. As soon as we cannot, we will hear, 'You never belonged to me.' Nonetheless, if we refuse to grow, we will never find new ways to express love and if we grow selfishly, we will only treat the other person as a medium to foster our desires. For we are either a consciously whole individual or we are a feeling-centred being. If we are a feeling-centred being, we will not truly love

28

anyone but ourselves, because to love someone else means we express a definite choice or state of being to do so and as we keep expressing what we have chosen or determined to be, we become perfected or matured in love.

I am not saying that feeling or emotional attachments do not grow, because they do. A matter of fact, we cannot nurture love via any other means except by continuing to inspire positive feelings in others. This is so, because, naturally we think of love in terms of feelings. However, love is not a feeling, it is who we have 'decided' to 'be' in someone else's life: Stable, committed, strong, honourable and honouring, bold, honest, attentive, cherishing, respectful and respecting, submitting, obeying, following and at other times leading, faithful, truthful, patient, tolerant, preventative at times and allowing at others, sacrificial and the list goes on. It is our decision to 'be and do' that enables us to ride out the storms with others, whether these storms be self-inflected or circumstantial, nothing else.

Thus, if I never chose to 'be' or 'do', I will never express true love, for when I say 'I love', these attributes in a balanced way is who I become. I become fixed, yet pliable and for sure, something will always come to test this resolve. Why? It is so because, we become nothing of worth, without being tested. What better way to test our balance or the strength of our resolve than to subject us to issues and crisis in what should be our most secure and helped place 'Marriage'. The place where two cannot walk unless they agree and we both dies if one refuse to fight. Again, this is where we have to endeavour to be specific and deliberate in our resolve to connect, as our decision to work with, respect, honour and cherish the other person must and will always be tried by time and issues. It is never free from that.

Another way of looking at it is that anything we do consistently for another without reservation, fear of others or regards for time and place can be construed as love. For love is what we do because of who we are emotionally, consciously, intellectually and spiritually. It is the decision we make to stick with a particular choice and our course of action that determines who we love and how much we are willing to extend ourselves to show it. Therefore, it is never about the feel good, although that is fine but it is about the conscious commitment to stay true to our decision of been a tributary in someone else's life. This is why I believe, we will only love in parts if our heart alone is used and our head is not in it holistically. Our head is not in it if practicality and sound judgment is not in it and this is so even when it makes us feel good. Emotions cause us to be fickle but love keeps us grounded and stable.

Therefore, because it is the way in which we seek to express our emotions or the joy and remuneration we derive from the individual we express our continued attention to that makes us feel as though we are loved, we use it to justify that our love has grown the happier we feel. This is also, why we can say that someone will grow to love us, because we hope that by causing him or her to be happier and satisfied, the person will in turn make us feel happier and satisfied. This however is a farce, because love is not happiness only, it is sacrifice. Giving and taking and then give and take some more. Hence, if we equate love with been happy, whenever happiness runs out; our love is finish and our desire to remain with each other lessens.

There is no wonder why the statement 'How much do I love thee, let me count the ways' is always so relevant when we want to prove our love to others. Love calls us to answer the question 'How'? It says prove to me that you do! Moreover, since we cannot prove a feeling except by looking at actions or expressions, we have to 'Show' how we love.

This is way, we can also find two individuals who we say that we love and treat both of them exactly the same way but end up concluding that one loves us more than the other or we in the eventually starts showing greater affection to one more than the other. This happens because one gives us the particular feeling we were looking for, while the other did not. In such an instance, our love for the one who did not give us what we expected dies. This is what I call the 'conditionality of love'. In other words, they stop receiving our expression of what we call love.

This classification of our love or the degree, to which we say we love another is based on feelings and emotions – two things that change. This is not based on what love actually is, a choice or decision to 'be' something definite in someone else's life. No one can make us definite. It has to be a personal decision born out of a developed character. This means that unless we develop true personal character, we cannot love anyone in the way true love requires.

Thus, when we love in truth, the truth of that love is built and propagated upon who we are as a person, someone who is stable and true and not upon what words can express. It takes little or nothing for us to say empty word.

The essence of who we are does not change. Yes, who we are can conform to expectations, be repressed by choices made, practice subterfuge to gain the upper hand and play the victim or the victor in a crisis but we do not change. Therefore, all it will take to bring the true nature of most of us to the surface is a delay, some form of need, restraint, stress, strain or the resemblance of danger. The choice or decision to express ourselves in the life of another does not depend on that individual but based on our selves – what I perceive and conceive. Love then is not based upon who someone else is or has done but based upon who I am as an individual. Consequently, the mere fact that it is a matter of personal choice and more so because I can choose to make this particular choice at any time during the relationship, should warn us 'there is no guarantee that anyone will grow to love us'. Thus, I can choose never to be anything in another person's life and no amount of good or bad they do, can cause me to alter my course. In this position, they become a lighthouse to us on the sea of life and we are the ones that will have to alter our course if we do not want to destroy ourselves on the rocks of a broken life.

Let us accept it. Feelings are fickle. They could very well remain unchanged. Even though in most instances, I thought it was changing and changing for the better when it was not. I am not excluding the fact that an individual could very well start out having only a feeling of disdain for us but later change to liking us or open up their protected heart to us, as this is what feelings do, to love us. The converse is also true, for an individual could in fact started out with a feeling of love for us but later resort to hating the very ground we walk on. In either instance, a definite choice has been made to, a) act in a supportive or b) a vengeful manner towards us.

The fact remains, however that whether an individual started out neutral, not knowing whether they loved or hated us, a spiritual choice has to be made if they are going to remain in our lives. By spiritual choice, I mean, a definite position must be taken to bond with us even when we are not getting it right. If feelings do not change to a definite decision to be something specific in our life, all we could be left with, after they are through stringing us along is a definite decision that they are never going to be anything in our lives but a 'hurtful part of our past'.

In which case, we in return will have to make a definite decision as to what we will do for ourselves. Either we will continue to act according to our ideals that of telling ourselves that we love them and hope that they will change their mind and love us in return. I must tell you though that this will hurt very badly, for nothing hurts more than to desire someone who has gone deep down into your soul and you cannot have him or her. Alternatively, we could go against the established principle of what love is and go find someone else. In either case, we will continue to either love them or hate them. We cannot do both and the longer we live without the object of love is the more, if allowed, a state of bitterness sinks in and eventually we become hateful towards them.

Oh, how this takes great effort!

If, however, we chose to love them, it might be a decision in futility, for then we could be allowing ourselves to entertain emotions and desires that the next individual will never reciprocate. They do not feel the same way and can never bring their self to have any of the feelings or desires for us as we have for them. This is what I call 'prolonged pain'. It is truly a difficult task to want to express our decision to act and be in a particular way to someone, who does not have the slightest regard for it.

On the other hand, if I chose to hate them, it will take equally countervailing decision to break the one I had made before.

This explains why hate is so destructive when it turns from love.

Hate becomes so because it has to override the most powerful human decision that was there before. For just as we need to give ourselves a reason to love, so we have to give ourselves a reason to hate. Additionally, love is not dependent upon the object of love, neither is hate dependent upon the object of love. It does need some level of acceptance or reciprocity but it does not depend upon them. As such, I can never stop loving or hating someone unless I make a definite decision to do so. This is where grace and mercy comes in, for only grace and mercy can replace love without it turning into hate.

I know that in many relationships, 'spirit tek' or 'attraction', partial commitment and longer tolerance level on some individual's part is often misinterpreted for love. Or in an age where 'Until death do us part' means until you lose your physical appeal, your money, your fame or some other personal status in life; it is easy to move on and it appears as though no real hurt occurred. However, some of us do love and we love with our whole heart. We have made a decision that we were in it for the long haul and as such, we cannot live without the one we chose to love or undo a definite action of our soul; merely upon the basis that they have moved out or are living with someone else. Certainly, we can let them go but our decision to 'be' something specific in their life, no matter what, does not change because they are gone. This is why loving another person is a risk and often times a risk with deadly consequences.

To know that someone we love is still alive and moving around us and we cannot express ourselves to him or her; in the way we would like to is tantamount to imprisonment and death. True love leaves no room for sharing and partial visitation, as it is a decision to give of one's self and the accepting of another wholeheartedly, no matter what. To do otherwise is a compromise and a 'watering down' of what it truly means to love. Hence, separation becomes, 'if I am going to live and you are going to live, we cannot stomach each other and I will have to find someone or something to replace you or fill the hole you caused'.

Take it from me; there is a thin line between love and obsession and few are they that know the difference. Perhaps this is why a man or woman kills the other person when they feel like they are losing them. Death to some of us is a way of holding on for dear life, not an act of insanity or barbarity.

Therefore, I believe that we have to spend the time, at the outset, to ensure that the one we are about to give ourselves to actually wants to 'be' something definite in our lives. We have to take the time to ensure that what they are offering us in return for what we are giving them is not a touch and feel, emotional or sentimental expression but a purposeful, honest, open and definite decision of the soul. If they fall short of this, our expression of what we call love will never grow, for love does not exist in a heart that is subconsciously closed to its own desires.

I know that all of us, if we patiently and diligently search, will find someone who is determined in their heart to work along with us, through the thick and the thin of life. However, I am not very sure if it is in this desperate search to identify if this kind of desire exist in the heart of the individual, we are trying to woo that makes it look as though they appear to fulfil some of and maybe all of, the fantasies we have in our minds, why we turn into idiots. Could it be the reason we fly off into a state of hysteria and begin to invent our own reality, are we afraid that we will never find such a person? Whatever the real cause is, when we do so, we ignore reality; facts, sound reasoning and we abandon the ability to be critical in our judgement. In doing so we become fools for love and we lose ourselves in the process.

It is at this decisive juncture that we forget one salient truth, we forget that any promise made, stated or implied, at the commencement of the relationship is expected. The other individual will require us to keep each promise or offering, especially during times of crisis. They do so because it has become a part of the terms of the agreement. They now want it even when it was not required, wanted or needed by them in the first place, as it as becomes the only reason they would stay with us. To some degree, they know we would never be able to meet these elaborate promises and as such it become the reason things fall apart. Let me say this, after the surety is given and if the individual we are pursuing gives in to our chase, come hell or high water, they require it and they do not want a resemblance of it either. They want the real thing. Why would any of us settle for something that we did not want in the first place? Every promise has to live up to every bit of expectation and justify our reason for settling for it in the first place.

Therefore, we must never think for a minute that they gave up what they originally wanted, because they did not! What they have done instead is bring their thoughts into alignment with the new offer, which then becomes what they now expect from us. They will not say that this is what they have done. Albeit, held together by bonds of unwritten terms and unuttered conditions, it will not appear to us that we are been held to a contract but we are. In fact, they will not even tell us the timeline in which they want to start seeing these promises begin to materialise before they switch back to their agenda. Based on my experience, my advice is that we pray that they resign from the list of items completely, because if they do not, they will revert to their original plan and we will be made to feel as though we had never done anything for them, if our plan takes too long to come into maturity. We all have a timeline in our head as to when we want to see specific things manifesting in our lives. We want the promised items and if we see the timeline been exceeded or ignored, even when it was not communicated to the other person, we go on the offensive and fight for it.

I know this for a fact, it is one of the main reasons my wife rejected me. I was moving too slow on making good my promises. She could not wait. I promised a dream and I could not fulfil it within the time frame she had in her head. I was taking too long to excavate and build a solid foundation. Buildings are what we crave. A foundation looks good in nobody's eyes and we cannot live in it. We want an occupied space. My going to school, working long hours and 'not spending much time at home' – as she put it – had nothing to do with her. However, when someone starts out with nothing and has no one giving them aid, what else are they to do to get to the top? You tell me!

I still remember telling her before we got married, 'Babes, I am a dreamer and I am going to go places. It might take a while but I am going somewhere.

So, if you stay with me, you are investing in a dream and you will never regret it if you do!' Ah, the problem with dreams. The do not always play out the way we saw them and in the period, we set for them. In addition, we have no tangible way to bring them into visibility except for consistency, continuous work and at times blind dedication. Back then and even now, I knew of no better or other way to pull one's self out of the status of the 'have-nots'. Yet, she saw none of the sacrifices I made as a path to fulfilling the promises I had made to her. She saw all that I did as something that served my cause and had nothing to do with her. In addition, my ability to communicate how I felt, at that time, did not do any justice in allaying her fears. Although I tried to explain, this only resulted in a justification or a cementing of her concept as to what I was doing. Thus all things, between us, became adversarial in nature, even the simplest things became a pain to her. In the end, her dreams were more important than her forbearance with me or my happiness; as a result, staying with me was like sucking the air out of her and she left.

Was I wrong to promise a dream? Perhaps yes. However, when we have nothing else to give or from which to make our appeal, a dream becomes the only treasure we can use to make our case. Let us be honest, not all of us have the dowry upfront and if it is required or insisted upon at the beginning, even with our great looks and audacious dreams, we will be passed over by many potential partners along the road of intimacy.

Besides, this is one of the ways classism is reinforced or why individuals with money keep getting married to other individuals with money. 'You do not have, so go look elsewhere!' is the attitude of many. Some of these individuals, who practice this sort of behaviour, have long forgotten that they never had it either, when they made their appeal. They also forget that one of the reasons for been blessed or given a position of stature in life is so we can help others or prevent others from going through what we have been through. Yes, they work themselves up to the top by their 'bootstraps' but now that they are there, everyone else must do it on their own and without their help. Or, because no one helped them or had faith in them, they forget that all we are asking for when we do not have the resources or wealth upfront to make a salient offer to our possible mate is for someone to take a chance on us.

I know that many parasites and opportunists are out there looking for an unsuspecting victim to pounce on but we are not all the same. Some of us are not looking for a handout or a meal ticket; we are just trying to find ourselves and need a little help. Often times, the help we need is the person we are trying to make a part of our lives. They give us the inspiration to dream and become better. Before them, we were just getting along fine, with our boring lives. We had no reason to want to go to any higher level or be anything great, we were just happy to get what we got and move on. Meeting this individual changed it all, they became the medium through which life gives us a swift kick on the butt and says to us, 'You cannot continue to live this way, you have to throw off the bum mentality and reach for greater!' This is why neither a broad-brush approach nor a short-sighted vision should be used to categorise us all. Nor should the slowness with which we are getting off the mark, be used as justification that we are in fact 'failures and a grand mistake'. Not all things start out and end the same way. Can you imagine me being called 'The worst mistake someone has ever made' just because I was a late bloomer? God help!

Sure, it is difficult to identify the sheep from the wolf in this dark, hypocritical, self-seeking and misguided world but when we treat everyone as wolves, all we do is covert sheep into villainous creatures. Hence, when we have nothing else to offer, because we have skipped a stage in our psychological development, all we can bank on is our ambition to sell ourselves to those we would like to want us. It is not much to go by, because it is not tangible, hard to quantify or cannot be measured in specific terms but it is all we have. Having an ambition then becomes the only chip we have at our disposal and the Lord knows that if some of us are given enough time and space we will come through just as we said. Of course, we know that some will not but the ones with deep convictions will and all we will have to do is just find them.

I mentioned recently that a stage in our psychological development might be skipped. I will expand to remove as much misunderstanding as possible, before someone writes me off as crazy. As per Erikson, each of us can sum up our development through five basic stages: infancy, childhood, juvenility, adolescence and adulthood. In these five stages, albeit at different rates, we should reach a certain level of maturity before we move to the next level. He set forth the notion that at each stage, we should learn some specific lessons and develop our technical and critical skills. In order to do so, we should learn how to express certain desires, control particular attitudes and behaviours faced, deal with problems rationally and achieve certain ideals. In essence, we should move from absolute dependency to an acceptable level of independence, for we can never really be void of others. In other words, we should grow both quantitatively and qualitatively. By quantitatively, I mean that we should reach a particular range in height, age, weight, position, possession, etc. By qualitatively, I mean that certain principles should have been learnt and are being practised, personality trait established and certain actions or behaviour cease from our repertoire, etc.

What psychologist Erikson is saying is that it is possible to be six feet tall and still behave like a five-year-old, because one's cognitive skills have not been developed or be 35 years old and still not know how to handle a disagreement, like I was.

Therefore, when I say we have skipped a stage, I am not talking, in most instances, quantitatively but qualitatively. Hence, we could be of the right age, height and appearance for cohabitation but we have skipped developing the traits necessary to be persistent, tolerant, patient, wise, disciplined and self-controlled. We did not know how to manage money effectively or have proper communication techniques, during the earlier stages. Literally, we have grown but those things that will enable us to live peaceable and in harmony with someone else is missing and will take us quite a while to develop. In such an instance, we need help and patience to get there. We do not need someone beating us over the head to 'Get with the program'. We cannot be rushed because someone feel we must hurry up, for doing so only exasperates us and makes the attainment of our ideals much more difficult.

Many of us took years to skip the stage we skipped but others expect us to fix it overnight. However, it does not work like that for anything that took years to destroy, will take a longer time to be rebuild.

What they are forgetting is that in many instances, we were not at fault why a stage was skipped in the first place. We are victims. No one taught us the basics. We did not see or have any grand examples from which to learn. We just made do with what we had. So, the flow of our development was stunted. Yes, we are the product of a broken existence. One where the root lays somewhere else and to annex ourselves from it, we do not know how. Certainly, I am not saying, blame mom and dad, society or even ecology for who and what we express. I am simply saying that expunging it from our psyche, will take more care from a patient heart, not one that is contriving the best way out for its own purpose.

I know that as adults we should never blame the past for anything that had happened to us. I also know that it is not what was done to us that really matters but how we react to it or the power we keep on giving it to rule over us that is the problem. Note that I did not say what happened to us does not define our personality, embolden our resolve or stunt our growth, for enough research is out there to prove that we are both creatures of nature and nurture. We thrive on encouragement and wilt under negativism. Read carefully what I said. What happened to us does not count. By that I meant, things will always happen to us but it is how we chose to response to them that ultimately defines us. Even though we cannot blame the past, we are not totally inextricable from it. Why? Our past is either our continuous struggle or it is our testimony. Therefore, if a man or woman does not know how to do something, he or she just does not know how to do it. If we do not know how to do it now, it is because we were not taught how to do it from our past. Consequently, it becomes the responsibility of the one we are now with or those around us to help us to learn. Take it from me, we cannot fix our present on our own, we need help, patient help.

Look at it this way, someone helped us to damage our past and it ricocheted into our present and we are going to need someone's help to fix our future. It is not that we will never learn how to do it on our own but to us this new level of learning will have to span our present and into our future, because our past is already a messy experience and we cannot do anything with it except learn from it. In fact, if most of us could have fixed the relics and vestiges of our past by ourselves, we would have done so long ago. Our present and future would be bright and shiny. In fact, in some instances we never even saw that we needed changing until you came, so be patient.

Notice here, I am not advocating a nursemaid type mentality. Neither am I giving credence or excuse for anyone who does not know or have certain things to take forever to know it or get it. I am quite aware that time and urgency is of the essence, when we have missed a season of rain. I also know that our crops will not grow the further we go into the season of drought and that we will end up dying before we have any form of nourishment coming to our mouth the longer we delay to get water from elsewhere. This is what I felt happened to me and now I know the truth of the statement, 'There is danger in delay.' I am, however, saying, when we make a judgement call and accept the offer made by another, we should be mindful that they have shortcomings and be patient with them and especially so, when they have bared their heart from the start. It is both unfair and cruel to expect 'blood out of a stone', which is what most of us expect from others in our relationships.

Another thing I noticed as I looked back at the note is this, we generally make the mistake of disregarding the advice we get from those who are not 'tied up' with us in the heart racing, sweat running, sleepless night affairs that we are in. We fail to recognise that other persons will see the pit falls or fault lines that lay in the relationship we are seeking to establish and point them out to us. In most instances, they are not pointing them out because they do not want the relationship to work or because they are evil. They just want us to be careful and ask ourselves the correct questions that must be asked at the beginning of every relationship. Questions we are not able to ask or think about ourselves, because we are so 'in love' or spell bound. However, my grandmother, now long dead and gone, always had a saying, 'You cannot hear, you will feel,' which always ended up being the case. As we never listened, we all ended up feeling. We are so emotionally bedazzled that we cannot see nor hear clearly. As such, we go ahead into the quagmire, like a lamb to the slaughter. We do not see the knife or the bitter and battered life ahead of us.

Hence, we fail to heed the warning upon which this chapter sits. We again justify our position and ridicule the advice given to us by wise counsellors. In our naivety, we take wisdom in our own hands and we ask of them or our cronies, 'What do they know about our love?' Nay, if we had followed the advice given to us by these apparent detractors, we would have seen that in many instances, it is not 'our love' it is 'my love' or 'your love', due to the fact the other individual does not care if we live or die. We would have seen that they may be enthralled by the novelty of our sentiments or be pushed to accept what we are offering but they remain detached in heart. The problem with this type of behaviour is that the novelty and sentimentality of it all will wear off after a while and we will see that they never felt the same way for us, as we did for them. In all cases, when reality hits us and we see things as they really are, we would have made the mistake already and missed a glorious opportunity to be elsewhere. The only way to sum it all up is, 'trapped like rats on a sinking ship'.

We end up this way because we ignore facts and we tell ourselves that the apparent detractors 'Have never experienced or just cannot understand what we have found!' We examine their past and we look for similarities between theirs and ours or for mistakes they made and we use it as our linchpin to validate that we are just like them or wiser – and deserve the right to form our own judgement and make our own mistakes. We tell ourselves that we are in a better position than they were in, when they made their choice. We use our conviction to override their rights to talk to us in the way they did. After all, we are the ones pushing the fire. Hence, we end up seeing the advice given to us by others, as trying to block 'Something that is real and true!' Now that I have been down the road myself, I must ask, 'Real and true to whom?'

Presently, I can boldly say, the facts were ignored, because we were submersed in the pit of bewilderment, infatuation and worst of all lust. We just could not see clearly, even though we truly think we did. Yes, we see stars, how flawless the other person is. We see bright and sunny days ahead but what we do not see is the incompatibilities that must be questioned or the traits that must be patiently learned and assessed to see if we can live with them, hiding like icebergs under the waters of our soon to diminished hope.

To be honest, sometimes there is a subtle and nagging voice on the inside asking us the real questions but when hormones, the ticking of the clock and the possibility of monkhood or nunnery is staring us in the face, we stifle the little voice and verbally batter every critic. Those who oppose what we want, will be ostracised or disrespected, overtly or covertly. They will be branded as 'roadblocks' and be avoided. All because we allow present emotional instability to cloud our judgement and in doing so we abandon reality. Whereas, someone who does not have our 'butterflies' or our 'inerrant beliefs' can see that we are heading into dangerous winds; winds that will destroy the serenity of our voyage and condemn our union on the rocky shores of despair, during some dark dismal nights, when we begin to call each other 'Jancrow and dead meat'.

I know that no one knows the future. I also know there is no one who can tell or determine with any level of true accuracy what an individual's outcome is going to be, as life and times are in God's hand. However, if during the making of our decision of a life partner, we justify infatuation by using emotionalism or visual appeal, instead of sound reasoning, we set ourselves up for self-destruction. For from time immemorial, women and men have always looked appealing but this appeal always changes. Whether by time or by state, we all change physically. Over time also, our sentiments, feelings and emotions towards things and people change. Therefore, it is what we have decided in our hearts, from the beginning that will stand in the end. How we decide to handle the 'lack of', 'more of' or even 'none of' when the initial mushiness fades that will determine if our bond will break or stand. This type of decision, however, can only be made by an individual who has a level head and a heart of commitment. Be it known, however that a level head and heart of commitment are two things that cannot come from any individual who is not willing to sacrifice or one that is selfish.

I also know from many cases, if we follow the critics, we miss a true blessing, as the dissenting voices are not always correct. However, it is our encumbrance to make sure they are correct, for: 'In hell is the worst place to find out that we have made a mistake!'

Therefore, since I know first-hand that marriage can become Hell if we proceed into it without both individuals agreeing on the fundamentals – simple things such as, how do we handle disagreements, how will we handle money issues, how will we handle illness, a baby crying in the middle of the night when both of us are tired? Do we agree that x will not come before achieving y or how will we handle infidelity, etc.? I am warning you, be careful! I know this for a fact; that a child coming too early can throw all the plans you make out the window. Not to mention an injury, a job loss, a reduction in salary, a change in living standard or even an inability to perform intimately.

Although certain circumstances are discussed beforehand, when they arrive, they can make individuals who started out well, end up in a ditch. So take my advice, before you dismiss the critics, ask yourself, 'What do they see that I do not?' Many times, answering this question properly can result in us redefining and sharpening our core values or preventing us from self-destruction.

The fourth thing I saw as I looked back at this note is that we think intimation or verbal mastication means that we have brought out into the open our true feelings regarding the other person's behaviour and habits to them. It does not. Whether these behaviours and habits are directed towards us or not, merely mentioning them without inspiring a need for the individual to change them, does not say to the individual, 'I cannot never live with this and if you want me or want me to be a part of your life, you will have to make adjustments'. It sounds like an ultimatum is it not? Then again, what is wrong with an ultimatum that will prevent us from settling for what we do not want? It is better we draw the line at the start, than start and have to do so when 'the horse has already gone through the gate'. You see, people do not change because we point out their fault or their need for change; they change because they want to and for them to want to, there must be something that motivates them to do so. We all change because we have something to gain from the change. It means then that our advising will not change anything if it is not more than just talk.

In this regards, our talk has to have substance and fervour or the promise of a greater reward if it is to accomplish anything. In our human experience, nothing goes away or changes until we face it and properly deal with it. Talking or acting out alone does nothing but highlight the fact that a problem exists. It does not solve it. Sometimes talking makes it worst. The more we talk without systematic action; whether physical or otherwise, only serve to aggravate the other person's temper, because it feels like nagging.

Let me say it this way, if habits are going to change, we will have to demand that it be done and when done, determine that it remains so. I say this because my experience is that things long dead and buried, in the fickle waters of our desires and wants, have a way of floating back up to the surface. If we do not insist that they stay buried by chaining them down with weights and counterweights of self-discipline and commitment, it does not matter how we distract ourselves from it or how much time elapses between our last fight, they will come up again in the heat of our future temper tantrums.

This is why I say talking without a strong resolve to transform is endless babbling. There is a tendency not to deal with the issues that faces us before we get married, many of the issues that we excused, overlooked or even ignored; have an uncanny way of showing up when we least want or expect them to. Trust me, one of the worst place you want them to show up is during the familiarity of marriage and on a day when frustration, fatigue, inability and insufficiency runs high.

I have learnt that issues that are not resolved before the wedding day, becomes a part of the, 'A so me stay' mentality afterwards. Without the proper handling of the relevant issues before we say, 'I do,' all we are allowing is a smokescreen to cover the hidden groundswells of later grievances. Things will lay dormant until a door is open and that is when the ghost of Madison Elizabeth Frank, what every demand this might be, comes out and shows its true colours. This is so because some individuals will play possum until the chance arises to rule over us.

So, yes we might have shown or voiced that others are not satisfied with our choice but we never faced it from the perspective of our personal conviction. We never faced it as though it was a problem. We 'beat around the bush' as we fed the tiger of our own ruin. Many of us say we did not see this trait before we got married but it is a lie, we saw it but ignored and justified it. We gave ourselves many reasons why it was not a problem. We went as far as self-projection, 'in time he or she will learn to value me when he or she sees how much I will or have made them better than they were before'. Oh, what lies we use to spin the wheel.

Take for example, if I say, 'I do not like you,' but I still allow you to pursue me without making it clear that I do not like you and stick to it. I will see it as you 'playing hard to get' or as a 'let me see if you really want me bad enough' test. None of us sees finicking as an indication that you do not want us. Some of us even believe that 'No' does not always mean 'No'.

This is what we often do, we mention and we act but we still allow the activity. We forget that anything that we allow over time generally becomes the norm, because we eventually warm up to it. This is so even when it is wrong and against our conviction. If we allow it, it grows. However, if we do not want something to grow, we kill the root. Anything that we definitely do not want and we are adamant about it; does not happen but if it does happen, it is usually over our dead body. So, in essence, because we want what we want, neither of us told the other how we truly felt; we kept it to ourselves. When we became truly honest with each other, we were already in too deep. So deep that it becomes the time when we hate each other and want to run from what we hear and see.

My question is always, 'why is it that we can never see the pitfalls or become totally honest with ourselves and the next person before we are in too deep?' Well, the more I ask this question, the more I get the same answer: There is no other relationship where we feel truly honest with each other, like when the ring goes on. This is so, because, at this point we feel that we have already conquered and we have what we want. We now own each other and all restraints are removed to show the real us. We no longer fear losing each other especially now that we have experienced each other and all we see is the 'Hell we are facing'. At this point, we have little or nothing to lose. 'Anywhere is better than this Hell hole…' was her vehement shout. When the ring goes on, we become so familiar with each other that we begin to lose respect for each other. Nothing breeds contempt like sharing too much of a close encounter with another person. It is as if being this close is a recipe for us to say, 'I have experienced you and I do not like it.' Thus, instead of seeing this closeness as a time to really learn about each other and grow, we develop all kinds of maladies towards each other and push each other away.

Having said all that I must now ask myself several questions at this time. Questions I am seeking to answer when it is too late. How did it happen to me?

Was it that I did not take advice? Was it that I could not accept her honesty when she told me, 'Leave me alone!' Why did I continue after hearing this statement? Was it that my persistence was too overwhelming why she accepted me in the end? Why is it that we could not be as serious and adamant with each other as we are now that we have gotten ourselves into this hole? Why does it appear as if we can only accept, 'Stay the hell away from me!' or 'Mind your own damn business!' after a separation? What drives us to see negatives as something we can live with or see emptiness and barrenness as something we can cause to become fruitful? Is it that we are naive or is it that we make these mistakes just because we can and are only expected to learn from our mistakes, for another person's mistakes or 'their' mistakes; not ours?

Certainly, we do not make these mistakes because we are dumb or because we have never seen the product of some of these very same mistakes in others. We make them because we are overcome with awe and our desire to capture and possess the individual who we see as our life partner, strike a nerve in us that alter the very way we think.

Some call the feeling of awe; being 'love struck', while others call it being 'dumbstruck'. Whichever one happened to you or will happen to you, will have the same effect as it did on many others before you. I was not the first and I surely will not be the last to taste of this phenomenon of the heart. We all will see someone and we all will go head over heels for them, even when we see signs that tell us that this particular individual has the power to dismantle our world. It is not as if we did not see their shortcomings, it is just that something inside us told us, 'This is just a barrier, let me see if you want me bad enough,' and we end up misinterpreting the signals. Having seen how it happened, I can now say, not all signals are a testing of our resilience or a barrier for us to climb in order to prove our worth. They are actually warning signs that say, 'Run the other way. Hell cometh!' In this matter I say, a word to the wise is sufficient.

Chapter 2
Is This How It Was Supposed to Be?

'He who findeth a wife findeth a good thing and obtaineth favour from the
LORD.'

The question that springs into the mind of many individuals after they have read the passage above is, 'Which Lord?' and for others it is, 'How can I be sure that such a one was given to me by the Lord? Why would He do this to me?' However, if we honestly examine ourselves, we would see that in many instances the 'lord' that gave us the one we got was self, for the Lord God of Heaven did not give us that one. We were the ones who went out and chose who we wanted. No one comes into our lives without a door of entry opened unto such a one. Someone had to let them in and that individual, unbelievably is us. We may have received a little cheer on by trusted friends or family or even forced together out of necessity. However, ultimately, we were the ones who allowed them to feel that they had a say in our lives and heart. Now we blame God and others. However, we had the ability to choose independently of God and anyone else. This is how He made us. He gave us free will, so we can make our own decisions. He will not alter our choice if that is what we are stuck on or keep going back to after numerous attempt to pull us away.

However, are we too far from his grace to correct our mistakes or do we deserve and should live with all the Hell we are getting, just because we made the wrong decision? For some the answer to this is, 'Hell no. I will never stay in an abusive relationship, with someone who cheated on me or with someone I no longer love!' To others, the response is, 'I will hold strain and bear it until the Lord makes a way. I will not run out on my covenant!' Which of these two responses is the most accurate one is always one of the most difficult questions for counsellors to deal with. For telling a couple to do either one carries with it some form of consequences, be it short or long term, in some instances, deadly consequences. So, how do we tell an individual to stay or to leave?

Another question that came to mind as I reflect on the difficulties of answering the ones above is, 'Is it only individuals who have made the wrong choice that suffer Hell from their partner or is left holding the bag?' To this, I will quickly respond 'No'.

In every relationship, there are individuals who lose their way. Even the best of us, at times, lose that little spark that brought us together, thereby, putting our partners in a deadlock. As I said before, we all make mistakes and we apparently make them because we are human beings. As such, we make them before the wedding and the Lord knows; we make even greater ones after the wedding day. Actually, the ones we make before the wedding day pales in comparison to the ones we make afterwards. To be happily married then is something we all must know and be prepare to work on from the day we say 'I do', until day the dusty rest upon our sinew.

If both the ones who were 'in the will of God' – to be married to each other – and the ones who just got up 'unadvisedly' and got married are in the same peril, who can say to get married and remain does not take the same virtues, whether it was God ordained or not?

Ignoring this fact, to justify the reason for their decision to leave their partner, some individuals behave as if they never saw that they were getting married to the devil before the wedding. They behave as if they suddenly found out a couple of weeks after the euphoria is over that they are in Hell and living with one who has a tail, horns and carries a fork around the house. Others are a little more honest, they saw that they were getting married to the wolf in sheep's clothing but behave as though they could convert him or her after the 'I do!' is said, only to find out that water does not run up stream. In both cases, when the lights come on and the gloves are off, which usually happens even if the marriage was a match made in heaven, someone is going to ask, 'Who are you?' or say, 'If I had known that this is how you are, I would have run the next way!' It is as if before the wedding day we are as blind as bats. We see nothing for which we should be concerned or we see only flaws that we can live with or time will fix. However, as soon as the ring goes on our fingers; it becomes the eye drop that clears up all of our inability to see properly and we can no longer tolerate or live with the discrepancies. As Sidonie Gabrielle Colette puts it, 'The day after that wedding night, I found that a distance of a thousand miles' abyss and discovered and irremediable metamorphosis separated me from the day before.'

Let me be very frank. The day after the wedding is when reality sets in and most often than not is when we realise two things. One, we realise that have done it and we are bond. Whether we read this bondage as a prison or a space to grow depends on the next realisation. Two, we realise that something has changed. The woman or man we marry the day before suddenly became another person. Who that person is, however, depends on whether we sought to have an intimate – sex – partner or a companion, someone we can talk with or make a conversation out of nothing.

It is these two realisations that will determine where we go from there, as it appears that after marriage we become brave enough to throw everything away: the baby, the bath water and the bathtub itself. In the depth of dealing with these two realisations, we often forget that we were the ones who were 'bright' enough to go before God and man; to make a solemn vow that we will love, honour and cherish each other for as long as life shall last. We forgot the 'Oh I so love your: laugher, hugs, kisses, dates and intimate moments' and grab hold of bitterness instead of accepting what is and work from there. A relationship is about replenishment and not to mention marriage for it is the pinnacle of all relationships. Hence, we should always seek to refresh what we have else we will fail to be what we should be, married.

So far, I have had no need to mention the serious and archaic part of the vow which states, '…for richer or poorer, in sickness and in health, until death shall do us part…' However, here it must come up, for in these modern times of prenuptial agreements and the writing of our own vows, we can choose to say all the niceties to each other, without using these internal conscience-riding statements. My ex-wife would gladly tell you, 'Watch back the video and you will see that I did not say 'for richer or poorer or in sickness and in health'. I am not into that…' You know what, she was right! She did not say it. I did. I guess I got what I deserved. Sickness! When we decide to throw everything away, we do not care who gets hurt, as long as we are happy. As long as we plan our escape route, heaping to ourselves our best justification, we are good to go.

Okay, let me not be so extreme and dramatic, because deep down on the inside, we care about some individuals and about some things. For example, if a child or children are involved, we will worry about the impact our decision will have on the child. We will also worry over its impact on our long-term relationship with some pivotal individuals in our lives. I was afraid of how it would affect my position at church. However, these will not be sufficient to stop us from doing what we want to. 'They will just have to understand that this is my decision. They will have to understand that this is for my happiness and peace of mind. Then again, if they do not understand so what, I am not asking anyone of them for anything!'

The interesting part in all of this is that we did not have to get married in the first place; we could have stayed single and moved from pillar to post, having a girlfriend here and a boyfriend there. Nothing is wrong with being single and no one was stopping us but we chose to get married.

Did we give in to social pressures or accepted norms? No. I do not believe so, for what this really shows is that deep down on the inside we know that there is something spiritually wrong with having a partner when we are not married. It also shows that we know there is a higher value to being married than to be single. Moreover, if we see it as such, it means that the institution of marriage was ordained by a higher power than that of the legislature or cultural sycophants of our day. It comes from God. Perhaps that is why one of the major moves of the end time spirit is to change all laws surrounding this God-given ordained institution. On the other hand is it that we see marriage as the only way to truly possess and dominate someone else? If that is how we see it, marriage becomes the true revealer that points us to the fact that we can never rule or dominate the human will and consciousness without a fight. Many of us are not up to this fight, so we rather take flight.

How do we stop these: 'God put us together!'

'Faith brought us together.'

'I love her so much!'

'He's my soul mate!' only to break up later; mistakes declaration? Or, can we avoid making these mistakes at all? My answer to that would be, 'Yes we can.' However, this is only so if we accept the truth that we are human beings and we are not perfect. When we accept this we also allow ourselves to see that we need God's help to find, establish and sustain that which we must have. Herein lays the problem. We are not perfect but we believe we are. We operate as though we can do it on our own and without His help. Somewhere along the line, we see everything through the eyes of our own perfection. I say this because, none of us would see an outright life altering problem and still go headlong into it. Marriage is a serious business and divorce is even worst. Therefore, it does not matter how skilful or crazy we are, we will not know that something is this heart wrenching and still go after it. So what is it?

There must have been something that caused us to see the struggles other couples go through and still yearn for the place that cause them so much pain. A veil must have existed over our eyes that caused us to see something that will consume us, before the wedding day and still run headlong into it. How else could we ignore the obvious or what could have caused us to invest so much time and effort into something, only to throw it away shortly thereafter? How else could we have ignored what the Bible tells us? It says, 'The wise man sees trouble coming and hides himself but the fool continues on and suffers for it.' Note, the prudent man hides himself. Nobody did it for him; he did it for himself. The problem is that too many of us act too simple minded and expect too much from everyone else but ourselves. We forget that life will not protect us from the pitfalls that lay before us and neither will the other individuals who we are allowing to enter into our space. We have to do it for ourselves. We have to count the cost for ourselves. However, because we allow the veil to cover our face and hide the facts from us, many of us suffer when the rigors of marriage begin to unveil us. Then we are in the pressurised process, because the intuition of marriage makes gems not just stones but we cannot be bothered with the process, it is too long and hard, so we tap out and settled for becoming a fancy coloured stone with our integrity damaged forever. Who can really trust someone who made a vow and dishonoured it? How can we be sure that the same fault they found with the other person, they will not find with us? What guarantee do we have that we are not marriage number 2, 3, 4 or even 5, for as individuals we do not have the tendency to look beyond the essence of what we are wearing, the veil.

However, anytime we see things clearly or for what they really are and act accordingly, this is when we have begun to operate outside of our natural range or self. We have moved from sight to faith. This move however, requires that we know that the answers to a working relationship does not live in our present perfection but in our continuous growth. This means growing with someone else, who was ordained to complete us, for we were never perfect before we got married, male or female and it will take time to become a person of worth and real interest.

As men, we are without a rib walking around and the women are just a rib, seeking to be restored to her rightful place. I know there are many who fancy it up and say that men are the prototype and that we are not perfect because God's original intention was to make women and therefore women are the crowning glory. I am not disputing that. What I am saying is, He took a part out of one to fashion the other and as such, neither is whole without the other. I will hasten to say, He created man to be the woman's covering and He fashioned the woman to fit into this covering. Therefore, if as men we are not providing any covering, we are missing our purpose and as women, if you were not providing any fitting, you would have missed your purpose too.

Based on the creative process of God, it is clear that one should not see him or herself separate from the other. This is the design for marriage. It is designed that we would be able to isolate one individual from all the possible others and cover or fit into that one. The two become one. The system of the world wants us to either: live incomplete lives by ourselves, form bonds with things and people we have no right trying to bond with or it wants us to be disjoined; as we continually try to fit another and still yet another into our being. However, we cannot become one or complete, with more than one individual or with an individual who is of the same sex, for only one individual is designed to complete us and that one individual is a male or female, the one we should seek to married. God never took a rib from a male and created a male. He created a female who could bring forth other males as well as other females. However, finding such a one is problematic because many of us know not how to find such a one and so we take anyone who presents themselves, the one who comes closest to our ideals or what we were given as a model. In many cases, 'monkey see monkey do'. We stick to tradition.

Thus, before marriage, none of us is complete, even though some of us behave as though we are, because we have accomplished and amassed some things. I will dare to say, neither are we complete after the wedding day either, as it is the continuous process of 'putting up or tolerating the other person's foolishness' that makes us who we should actually be: a complete man or woman.

In fact, who we are, ultimately is not even within the purview of our wives or husbands; it rests in God's direction and leadership over our affairs. A three-fold cord is not easily broken and when God is the third cord, it is impossible to be broken. If each of us could just understand this and work with each other during the challenges of marriage, it would solve so many of the issues at hand.

If from the beginning, we could accept this simple truth that we are two imperfect beings who are getting together or accept that this individual really does not love me or care for me and go find the one who does, it would place us on a good footing from the start.

This however is not the end all and be all to the problem of separation. Not at all! I am not saying either that it is easy. Sometimes the one who gave us a 'warm time' or in some instances never loved us at the initial stage, eventually end up being the one who sees our worth as well as their ability to contribute to our lives and come in agreement with us. 'These are they' who abandon their initial hopes, dreams and expectations, and help us convert ours from a pipe dream or individualistic approach to a spirit of unity. They convert us from a place of personal selfishness to a place where we serve each other and both benefits. Trust me, marriage is much more difficult when two selfish individuals are in it.

The issues then become, 1) How do we become unselfish or serve each other in a self-centred world? 2) How do we work for the mutual good of each other, in a time when the easiest thing to do is run away? Well, my foremost answer to this question is, do the necessary research – a search that takes discipline and wisdom. After the research is done get to know the critical truths and devise ways and means as to how we are going to avoid the pit falls that are inherent in the process of two individuals coming together. We must also learn to interpret all the signals or give credence to every advice given to us. It would be inadvisable to do this without God's divine help, as He is the linchpin that holds a good marriage together. As the linchpin, we must constantly allow Him room to help us navigate the uncharted waters of this world. We must not just solicit His help for the wedding day, in order that the day goes according to plan but we must ask Him to be a very present part of the marriage; for all along the road from the 'I do' until the 'death do us part' are pitfalls along the way.

Many times these pitfalls are offshoots of our own doing, for whether the Lord made the choice for us or not, our human nature will kick in and things, although meant by God to be perfect, goes berserk. Why? Marriage is a union made in the spirit but it is lived and practised in the realm of humanity i.e. the flesh. Therefore, flesh will always come into play and as such, we are going to have to learn human principles from a spiritual perspective to deal with the humanity of it all. Principles that are difficult to learn in the face of verbal and physical abuse, infidelity, insufficiency, hatred, resentment, loneliness or absence, just to name a few. I know that few of us can deal with pain and I am no masochist myself or far be it from me to tell anyone to stay in an abusive or

51

life threatening relationship. Yet, the principles that underpin a marriage or cause the expression of love for that matter to grow, can only be learnt as we determine in our hearts to deal with each other in the face of a misguided world-a world that tell us to bailout at the slightest infraction.

In addition, the learning of these principles takes a surrendering of one's own self to another, because the learning of these principles lies outside of our human influence and the only way to get out of our own influence is to surrender who we are to a power greater than we are. Doing this however is hard, because, whether we like it or not we want to stick within the boundaries of our socialisation. None of us wants others to look upon us as being weird, because we go against the accepted norm. 'He hits you and you still staying with him, you must be mad!' 'She cheats on you and you still love her, the same way, you soft and foolish bad!' 'He cannot meet your needs, why not find someone else?' or 'She cannot live up to your expectation or satisfy you but you still giving her your all, she must have bewitched you!' In these times, the acceptable norm is simply this, 'This one is not working, go find another.'

Sometimes the pressure is not even within ourselves but with others who call us, 'fools to be putting up with that!' 'If it was me; you see, God see and know what I would do!' In this arena, the voice of those individuals who expect us to go out and find someone else, speak the loudest. Hence, what else to do but follow suite, for that is what we do in a world where there are options. If you do not want tea, you chose Milo or if you do not want regular coffee, you choose decaffeinated. Nobody wants chicken every day, even when it is cooked a million different ways, because the appetite is never satisfied with one thing. Is that not how we think of marriage? If we do not want this partner, we choose another and expect the old one to go find someone else, 'Who will actually love you, for I don't!' Oh, what a nice cop out! In other words, 'I do not care if you love me at all, we are done. Goodbye!' These words play repeatedly in my head to the point where I felt like something was wrong with me.

However, under God's standards it is not that simple, even though it might be simple to us but not to Him. He holds marriage to a higher standard. He sees marriage beyond our three phases of self-expression, ravaged and quit. He sees it as an earthly symbol between him and his bride but we see it as a conditional risk we are taking with someone else. If you are willing to do, become this or act this way, then I will marry you but if not, goodbye. In our self-expressive nature, we see individuals, as we would like them to be and we try to capture them as is or convert them into an image that suits us but in doing so, we forget that no one is as they appear. We all change overtime. Each of us reinvents ourselves every five to ten years. These changes in and of themselves are not meant to be bad. We need them, if we are not to find life dull and boring and by extension; our partner down right stifling. When these changes are taking place however, we do not understand them and the best person to blame for all the 'Hell' that is happening in our lives is the person closest to us. At these moments in time, it appears that we always forget that seasonal pressures generally cause each of us to do and say things we would never normally say under other given conditions and so we tell each other how we feel without care or consideration for how they feel.

Is it not funny or amazing that during this self-expressive period, even when someone does not want us, we want him or her? We take every opportunity we get to yell, 'Baby I'll do anything for you!' We pursue them with abated breath, not counting how many things we are losing along the way, only to throw it away in the end. We never consider that cost during this time but there is a cost, as there is always a cost to get into someone else's life or to allow someone else into ours. In many instances, this cost is our own genuineness but because there is nothing there to tell us that this is selfish aggrandisement on both individual's part, we continue. Thus, in our bid to convince them of our deepest desire, we tell them how many mountains we will climb, seas we will swim and fiery darts we will face just to have them. In doing so we let them believe a lie and at the same time we either undervalue ourselves or over compensate for their inability to see us for who we really are.

This happens because we do not know our own worth. However, anyone who does not value us at the start will seldom grow to value us at all. It takes a special kind of person to stick around until the worthlessness in an individual becomes valuable. Notwithstanding, we hope that saying and doing all of these endless diatribes, will raise our value in their eyes and so we go all out to impress to the individual in am your knight in shining armour.

We take every care not to drive them away and even if we actually do not love them – something we will never admit to ourselves or anyone else – we take every possible step to secure the mask we wear. We do so because in truth and in fact, there is some merit to the madness or spoils to be gained from the psychodrama. Sometimes unconsciously, we are not even aware that we are doing this. It is as if an undetectable force is driving us. This is why we need others around us during the process but as I said before, we blacklist them if they appear not to support our expeditious exploit. Hence, this becomes a time of, 'Yes, this just might work and I will do nothing to jeopardise it,' but it never does.

Certainly, we write and sign the prenuptial agreements but we still go and buy the dress and rent the tuxedo. We still plan the big flamboyant day and we still subject our family and friends to the ordeal of been there for us on our 'day of pledging and expressing our love to each other.' Why do we do such things? Waste other people's time and resources. We do it because we want the experience and we want to express to others that we can do it too. Oh, how we forget that this is not the 'Punchinello little fellow…' ring game we are playing. This is real. We are missing with people's lives, people who have feeling! We seem to forget that a big sprawling wedding is just the doorway to the life that must be lived after the 'Big Day' and we end up living like 'puss and dog'.

A wedding day is easy to plan and execute given the right conditions. In fact, anyone with money and time on their hands can pull off a spectacular wedding day but it takes two individuals with a serious level of maturity and commitment to pull off, even the slightest resemblance of a good marriage, a life of giving and taking; one with the other.

You see, marriage is a life of helping each other to grow from one stage to another. It is much like owning a vehicle. And I say vehicle because, a vehicle gets us from point A to point B and sometimes back to A or even if it is a collector's item, it serves the purpose of been shown off to our friends or acting as a status symbol of our wealth. We do not own a car simply for the sake of owning one. It serves a purpose. Marriage serves a purpose. Outside of the fact that it symbolises God's union with his Church, it is the only true symbol of a stable society. Show me a nation where institution of marriage is not protected and the principles and virtues thereof are not maintained and I will show you a nation with much shame and disgrace.

However, just like owing a vehicle, most of us want to get married but do not know what goes into it or what keeps it fresh and fluent. We see it as something nice to have and because others have it and it appears to do wonders for them, whether this is true or not, we want to have one as well. Purchasing a car is one thing. Licensing, insuring, maintaining and servicing, purchasing gas, paying the toll or paying parking fees and not to mention preventing others from stealing or destroying it is another. Some gladly purchase one only to find out that it becomes a burden to them after a while. Ultimately, they let it go, because anything that annoys us for too long leads to stress and negative reactions. In the same manner, having a wife or a husband that is miserable, takes nerves of steel, patience, forbearance and sometimes long-suffering to stave off wars or quitting.

Sometimes the issue with owning a vehicle has to do with the fact that we had no need or reason to own one in the first place. What is so wrong with walking, taking public transportation or even a bicycle? What is so wrong with been single is it a crime? Even the Bible tells us that been single, we please God more. Not that this goes for all, for it does not, as some will wax wanting and they will end up burning in lust. Do not get me wrong now. This analogy is not the same as 'not owning a cow but still drinking milk.' I am not saying that we can have the benefits of marriage without been married, especially having sex. Anyone who does that sins against his or her own body and against God. What I am saying is that we were living and can live without others doing particular things for us. Besides, 'He who gets married because he or she needs a maid, a financial scratching post, sex, shelter or any other humanely condiments, have condemn themselves to an endless chasm and their union will not last, as marriage goes further and deeper than emotion and mere things. It is a partnering for each other's glorification. Two individuals who are in sync with each other shine like the sun in its brilliance or it will take an army to defeat them or squelch their fire.'

Despite the fact that we did not need to own one, we decide that we had to have one and take out on expensive loan. Push by the desires in our hearts and the expectation of others, we saunter on to the dealer and make the decision to purchase one and fail to recognise, even during the process of purchasing it that it is out of our league in every sense of the word. We knew that owning one would be an insurmountable problem, because, it just did not fit into our budget or into our profile but still we push on. We ignore that we have sufficient money to purchase the one that suite our level, because something inside of us or some unrealistic ideal cause us to want ours to be like so and so and then we work feverishly to make it happen. We purchase one at another level and often times one way above our won. In doing this we lose sight of the fact that it just will not work, as it was either too old or too new. It was too fast or too slow, of the wrong colour, wrong make and model or it just did not suit our location and vocation. Our choice was just bad.

In making our choice, we allowed our interpretation and perspective of how others appear or how they are handling theirs to cause us to think that we can do it as well. 'Oh look at them, they are not as educated, wealthy or informed as I am and they are not doing too badly at it, so why not me?' We forget that the reason many have failed at it is that they misjudge it or that some have failed at it before and have learnt enough from that experience to derive a better conclusion the next time around. It is never because they are so good or perfect for each other, they have issues but it is not 'washed in the machine of public opinion and view'. Every couple has issues. Multiply that for married couples. Therefore, we often fail to understand that married life when viewed from the outside is deceptive, as it gives the appearance that there are no problems occurring in the marriage. However, there is always some friction going on in a marriage. That is how we grow.

I do not want to belabour this point but I know that some individuals are more private than others are and some are just better pretenders. Therefore, we will not see the tears that fall or the blows received behind the walls of what looks like a match made in Heaven, if these partners do not show it. Then again, every day we have more of the negative aspects of relationships thrown at us, than the positive ones that will actually nurture us. Who talks about the couples that made it through marital storms but are still together after forty-odd years, like my parents? We do not see these people because they are not readily highlighted or setup as the pinnacle of example for other to follow. Then again, thinking about it, they do not talk about their struggles either. Therefore, we cannot just look at others and use their appearance to say that ours will work because theirs' are working, because one formula does not fit all.

We can come from the same family, graduate from the same college, have the same profession and live in the same community and still have different results in our marriage. Marriage is one of those things in life, where one can have all the education, money and right connections, in the world and it does not ensure that he or she will get any part of it correct. For, unlike many other things, marriage is not based solely on facts or even truth but on moods, perspective, expectations, ability to cope and a willingness to tolerate another person's mistakes; which are unending in marriage. I would also like to add that sometimes it also has nothing to do with love, because we can love an individual but we cannot live with him or her. Call it emotional attachment if you wish but if we are with them for too long, they suffocate us. So, whether we are some monarch, inclined academically, culturally, medically or fall into the industrial, transport or science and technology sectors, public services or sporting arena, it takes God and a diligent search in order to have a glimmer of hope in finding another individual who will respond, meet or can cope with all of our idiosyncrasies.

In this regards, certainly, marriage is really a challenge and an endeavour for both the wise and the novice. Neither the wise nor novice hold sway over it, as both will face some form of ordeal that will make them ask, 'What a fool I have been, to take this vow. Why did someone not warn me?' What this means is that each individual who comes and takes up the gauntlet of marriage, will have to prepare him or herself, beforehand, to learn as they go along. This is so, even while looking at what works for others, as none of us is the same. The fact that my parents have been married for forty-four years and I have seen their example and had been coached by them in many sound principles, yet here I stand separated is a testimony of this fact.

To illustrate another point, let me go back to using the analogy of owning a car. Often times in owning a car, we forget our own basic needs, because we become overwhelmed with those things that rob us of the pleasure of owing it. Anyone who has ever gotten a traffic ticket, had an accident, had their car stolen, broken into, towed away, messed up by a mechanic, had to wait in traffic, drive around in a crowed city looking for a parking spot or drive behind some slowpoke or garbage truck on a narrow street; knows what I am talking about. These nuances cause us not to enjoy the journey or pleasure of owning the vehicle. In fact, some of them make us curse. When we bought the vehicle, we did it so that we would never have to deal with certain things ever again but they kept showing up. Here in lays an essential truth. We generally do not factor in some of these things that are inherent in owning a car. It is not like they were never there, we just did not have to deal with them and so we think that they do not exist. However, every honest car owner or driver will tell you that 'car problem' exist and when you own a one, these problems just keep showing up. If we however keep our eyes focused on them, they will cause us to fail, as we will not be able to recognise our purpose and destiny. They will constantly mess up our moods and cause us to become bogged down by the mere pressure they cause.

Another thing, if we fail to recognise that the main purpose of a vehicle is transportation, we will convert it into something that it is not, an idol. Yes, to the rich and affluent it becomes a status symbol but even to then it still comes with the cost of upkeep. In a similar manner, if we miss the purpose of marriage, all we will end up with is a wife or a husband who is around but eats away our health, wealth, vision and dreams. He or she becomes costly to maintain and gives little or no benefits to have around.

I know to some, money is not an issue, as they can always purchase and maintain a good one and it does not faze them but to others, it is. Unlike a vehicle, however, money is not the only issue of concern in marriage. Marriage comes with greater fires than that. Marriage concerns can be as small as 'What do I cook for dinner each evening?' to as humongous as 'How often should we have sex?' However, unlike a vehicle, who can fix a partner who does not love us anymore? What is the price tag to keep such a one smiling or can I oil, gas and buff such a one, then park them in a garage somewhere until I am ready to show them off to others? I dare say no, for they are not an inanimate object, despite the fact that the longer they are in our lives, like on antique car, the more their value as well as ours should rise or fall; they are individuals with a heart than can be crushed.

Hence, unlike a vehicle which comes standard and we know what we are getting for our money, people are not like that. Standard wives and husbands are not available. They do not come customised either. We all have to work on our own from the get-go, for unlike a vehicle that says and does nothing unless we push, turn and press some gadgets; a partner without prompting can say and do so many things to us that it feels like a dagger through our hearts. My wife used to return home upset and cross, in my opinion, over nothing but id eared not tell her that. When our partners act, it is worse than being in an accident. It leaves us with bruises, lacerations and scars that not even surgery can fix.

When a car meets in an accident a mechanic, auto technicians and auto electrician can get it back on the road but who can fix a discarded and battered heart? Sometime the hurt is so deep that it disfigures our interaction with others and overtime, we begin to wilt away or becoming just a figment of ourselves. I became a little caustic and callus. Thus, we lose our spark and take on a victim's approach to life. We become untrusting or timid in much the same way a person who was in a major accident would react when faced with a similar situation.

Look at it this way, when a partner does not love us, it is like meeting in an accident. We just never planned for such a thing and sometimes we never saw it coming, we just end up swirling asking, 'How comes'. However, when it happens, we have to sacrifice too much of ourselves to make them happy or recover when they leave. In some instances, like a car that is too badly damaged and can no longer be covered by insurance, it is better that they leave. If they stay, they become a drain on our emotional health. One of the trade-offs for them staying is that they do not allow us to be ourselves but demand that we allow them to be theirs. Thus, we just keep on giving and giving our all until it hurts and even then, it is still counted to them as giving nothing at all. Let me be frank, nothing can survive like this. Even if there is an intelligent and well-crafted plan to put up a front, it is bound to fall apart. Marriage needs to breathe unselfish air if it is to survive.

This type of air though, only comes when a man and woman recognises that God made them separately but when they come together in marriage, they lose their individuality for the sake of oneness. This losing of oneself, to become one with another is what love really is. This is why selfish individuals do not make good partners. Then again, neither does anyone who is immature to the point of always giving into the whims and fancies of someone else. There must always be a balance, knowing that things are not as they seem, sometimes they are just only bad and sometimes they are worst.

Therefore, in a marriage where a man and a woman love each other, there is no issue of self, because the self of one becomes the self of the other and both sees the next person as an extension of his or her own self and would give anything to make that extension better. Simply put, the two become one, as they offset each other's shortcomings. In this type of atmosphere, love makes us stronger even in our weakest of areas.

The reality is that by patience, we complement each other's strengths, even when we do not fully understand each other's views or reasons and we cover each other's inabilities and lack, because by doing so, we are securing our character. In doing so, we avoid questions which questions our own sense of judgement. 'How can you stand such an impatient woman?' or 'What have you done to deserve such an ignorant man in your life?' Hence, covering each other takes time and effort. To me, this is what finding the right partner is to do for us. However, ending up with a wife or husband that is not willing to give up self is a barricade to the one who would be willing to do so. It also kills our ability to be true to our own self.

Therefore, choosing the correct one or answering the question of, 'Do we really need a husband or wife?' is always the big issue. How do we really make the right choice in such a life altering decision?

I believe this is where the Bible seeks to give us guidance. In short, it tells us where to start and after starting how to continue. For the man, it says; 'start with finding a virtuous woman, for her price is far above ruby' and for the woman it says;' start with a man who has the heart of God, because he will be self-sacrificing and give himself' for her. In essence, start by finding a partner whose' purpose is higher than they are in their own eyes. Find a partner who is self-sufficient but God dependent. One who says I can do so much for and by myself but I need you.

This takes me to the main aim of this chapter, answering the question, 'What exactly is marriage or exactly what is found when a man finds a wife?' Not that a wife is lost somewhere and needs to be found by a man, for not all women wants to become wives. For that matter, not all men want to find a wife to change or mess up their flow either. So, what exactly are we up against when we say finds a wife?

Well, the Bible tells us, 'He that findeth a wife, findeth a good thing...' Note, it did not say, he that findeth a good wife findeth a good thing. What exactly is the 'good thing' that is found when a man finds a wife? Is it the wife that he has found that is good or is it saying that all women are good since they all have the potential to be wives? Personally, I do not think it is saying any of the two. I will speak plainly here, for just as all men are not good and are not fit to be husbands; even so, not all women are good or should be made into wives.

Acceptance is the key; we have to look for the good ones. This is why my focus is not on finding the wife. Pardon my expression. Women are s dime a dozen. It is finding the good thing that I am after and the blessing for doing so.

Notice that it is after finding the wife, the man receives the blessing from the Lord. It is not before. Hence, in my eyes, finding a wife is only a precursor to being a blessing. To a man, a wife ushers in a spiritual change, one that is both destiny and purpose in nature. In receiving her, he learns why he was created and he gains an understanding of what he is to be doing with his life. A good wife makes a man sees himself in a light he had never seen himself in. He sees hope, prospects and a future even in desert places. He feels like a conqueror and she appreciates and affirms him. His vision takes wings.

This is why; I hope he does not get an antagonistic wife who does not help him with what he has received. For, it is in her submission and he in the obedience of his commission, he becomes a real man. The reality is that at no other time does a man's life have as much meaning as when he is married and have the responsibility of a family. I know that if allowed, family life can become a dull and boring grind. Nevertheless, this explains why when we cannot find fulfilment in our homes or family, we are so miserable and take it out on the passively or aggressively. A sense of fulfilment is something we yearn for and when it is not at home we are forces to look for it elsewhere.

Simply put, a stable home makes us stable and gives us worth. Hence, marriage makes a man become a benefit to others. Hence, the aim of marriage, for me is to receive favour from God in a unique way, which will result in the betterment of others. All good marriages benefit others.

So, since as men our destiny and purpose is clear to us when we get married, how can we interpret this passage correctly? Especially, if we do not want to say later on when things start to go wrong, 'The Lord made a mistake by giving me this one' or run off to find that 'special one' after we have anchored down with the one we had declared before as the only and true one.

Honestly, I do not know which is worst, whether to feel ashamed at the outset or to be humiliated after the big day? Well that is not exactly true. I know now walking away or even dumped at the start is much easier. We hurt yes but we have far less pain. Well, this is if we were not living like husband and wife, having children and tangling up our assets and hearts. Trust me the humbling experience after the big day, kills you on the inside and makes you wish you were actually in the grave. For months all I wanted to do was hide and cry.

In answering the question though, I heard someone say it like this, 'The blessing is having a woman answering 'Yes' to our proposal for marriage, for she did not have to respond in kind. Even up to the last minute, she could have still said no. Look how many brides have run away from before the altar, leaving the man standing there!' In thinking about that response, I realise that to have someone accepting the offer we made him or she to become a part of our lives is truly a blessing. I also think that it is really a shame for a man to work so hard to get a woman to say yes, only for her to spit on her own graciousness and trample on his efforts. However, the more I think on the issue of receiving a blessing when a wife 'was found' is the more I realise that this answer could not result from such a simple response. There had to be something more. The answer to 'something more' came to me one day while I was musing over it on my way to work. I heard in my head, 'The good thing that has been found when a man finds a wife is the ability to recreate and expand himself and the blessing that will be received is the favour of the Lord to do so, as all good gifts and precious gifts comes from Him!'

Thus, marriage is a creative and re-inventive process, one which starts with a man looking for the best mate with which to chart his greatest accomplishment, self-creation.

Sir Winston Churchill said it this way, 'My most brilliant achievement was my ability to be able to persuade my wife to marry me.' I know that saying it this way flies in the face of modernity, because in today's society, a woman can go looking for a man just as much as a man can go looking for a woman. However, in God's order, the man should look, because he has the seed of future generation in him.

I am not saying that women should sit down with their hands folded and say, 'Mr. Right will come my way without my effort.' He will not. 'He who has raw meat must seek fire.' And, 'He that will have much must be he that sews much.' The virtuous woman then is not a lazy woman but a capable woman and capable woman is whom every sensible man wants. The truth is, no woman should sit idly by and expect a man to do anything and everything for her.

Besides, every woman has the ability to attract a mate and to attract a man takes doing something, even if that something is 'putting herself together' properly or walking with flair. Again, pardon my expression. They saw men are like dogs, they pant after everything thing with breast and a swing hip, thinking with their little head more than with their wits. Notwithstanding, it takes wisdom to keep him after she has attracted him. It is not the responsibility of the woman to vindicate herself as to how good she is by going to look for him, this is the man's responsibility to her but she must show herself worthy. What do I mean by this? Simple, it is the man's responsibility to see to it that no fair maiden pines away waiting for a suitor, because her desire to be married is unmet. However, it is the woman's responsibility to herself to be independent enough to stand on her own if none comes.

As I look at the text again, the easiest thing to do is imply that the man should be doing the seeking and the woman waits until found. However, this is not the case; both are to be carrying out their task as individual human beings. Both should be active learners and preparers. The woman should be exercising her capability to be a nurturer by learning the principles of what it will take to be a wife, mother and steward of whatever power is placed in her hands. The man also has a responsibility to show forth his prowess in been a progenitor, a protector, a supplier and a provider, by learning what it means to be a caring, supportive and helpful husband. This can only happen though when one generation takes seriously the responsibility to teach the next generation.

This is why one of the main principles in the scripture is that of the older women teaching the younger women, how to be a diligent woman and the older men to treat the younger men like sons, in imparting wisdom to them. I cannot totally blame the older women or the older men for the total degeneration of everything, because the younger generation do not take advice graciously. I was one, so I know. Nevertheless, we need the senior married couples to teach us that it is while both individuals, in the union is learning how to be one aspect of the creative process that each one becomes one with his or her own self and with their partner. Or that will each individual is truly developing a sense of what type of person he or she is, he or she learns what he or she would like 'to be' to another individual. Without another person in the mix we do not really get to prove our theory. Yes, we know we are Mr Nice guy or Miss Sexy girl but can we still be nice and sexy when we have someone else in our hair all the time or when we have to practice submission and self-sacrifice at our most moody point.

This is why I believe, in all honesty, that none of us should seek to become one with another before we become one with our own self. I said this because, if we are not one with our own self, we are going to be constantly looking for our own selves in the midst of our relationship and this will in turn, suffocate the other person. I also believe that before marriage, it is OK to look for ourselves but after marriage, we should become, with each passing year, a better self. This would be because we would have already found our self in the things we have become passionate about, things the other person accepts and share to some degree in.

The concept of finding ourselves is not a concept I relish. However, it is the reality I have come to accept, for all of us mature at different levels and so it is possible that what we thought we wanted at one stage is not want we want at stage two. So, should this concept of becoming more decisive, as we mature, be applied to every area of our lives? Most certainly not. I am not saying that we cannot get something at an immature stage and maintain it until we are mature enough to handle it. However is there nothing that we can choose that says, this is the only one we will get, take care of it or 'Give it your life!', like I was told by dad among a set of men on the eve of my wedding? To this question, I will say yes. We can get things from our immature stage and still have them when we are mature but it will take a great deal of effort on our part. This is much like giving a vehicle to a teenager or a new driver. It will have a couple of dents and scrapes after a while but if they are going to keep it for any length of time, it will only be possible with much help from others. No wonder the disciples of Jesus said after hearing his comments on marriage, 'If that is the way of a man with his wife, it is better not to be married.'

Marriage is a heavy responsibility to take on, who can bear it! He that will do so will purchase to himself a great weight and whoever resists the authorities opposes what God has established. So, just as how individuals seek to take up the weight believing that they can manage equally there are forces out there that seeks to discredit marriage. Call them humanistic belief or the devil, they are there. They do not believe that marriage can work and because so many are not working, it gives them greater ammunition to say, 'See it, single individuals in a relationship enjoy happier and more fulfilled lives over those who are married.' This may appear true in many instances but God established marriage, so it can work and will work when we work.

Then again, we are not vehicles; we are individuals of flesh and blood. None of us likes when others rub us incorrectly, much less cause us pain. Therefore, to make us comparable to a vehicle may be simplistic, for none of us is prepared to stick around until someone else comes to their senses or have a good understanding of what they really want. No one can park us in a garage somewhere, to gather dust, until him or her feel like returning with the key. We go where we want to go, when we want to go. God made us to have autonomy. In fact, if we are not willing to wait on a meal to be prepared, who is foolhardy to think that we are going to wait on a partner to become organise? No, sir, we have better things to do with our time. Such is the mentality of this modern generation, especially those persons who do not examine how their present action will influence their future or scoff at the virtues of the past.

In our contemporary era, where almost everything is based up on perception and legal correctness, when it comes to matters of the heart, seldom any level-headed planning takes place among the young. Most, if not everything, depends on feelings and emotions. Thus, since our feelings and emotions is what it because it came from the art of instability and popular view, what we see around us, we keep yelling, 'That is of the pass. Hardly anyone thinks like that anymore.' Now I can laugh at what my wife had said, as it was too painful to do then. 'In a time where anything is likely to happen, it is best to be self-direct. I will live the way I please. You can go on fooling yourself'. Self-direct. Yeah right! If I never determined in my heart to be a good father, our son would suffer pain of not having anyone drop or pick him up from school, staying home with him, giving him dinner, etc many a time, as this self-directed woman was too busy to do so. She never looked at the future and saw how it would have affected him. Kids in a single-parent situation pay the price in many ways but it is worst when they are split between two homes. It is in such an atmosphere as this, we become fickle in our approach to even life's most serious decisions. We fail to ask, 'How will this impact everyone around me not just me?' We simply say, 'If I feel it's right, based on my mood on the day, it is right or if it does not directly affect me, I do not do business with it.'

However, if there is any place where stability or the need for honesty, maturity, sound reasoning or a level head is needed, it is at the beginning of a relationship, the point where the foundation is laid for future growth. I can assure you that a foundation improperly laid cannot hold up a structure, which exudes so much pressure on an individual such as marriage. This is why the way in which we seek our mate is of such importance. Mate selection is something we cannot afford to be light-headed about, for a poor method leads to a poor result, which is perhaps why we are always ending up in problems. When we fail to evaluate our method or even from whom or where we learned it, we will fail to see what works or see that what satisfies Tom, Dick or Harry does not hold true for us. When we check our method, we will also see that if we accept major principles of the time, we will always be looking for and choosing the incorrect partners for ourselves instead of the one who should be an extension of us.

Hence, the word 'find' as is used in the passage, could appear to imply that we have searched high and low, looked at the myriad of possibilities and selected the best one. It also suggests that we have examined which woman deserves to be a wife and we have selected the most suitable one to be a part of our life. We have done so because not all women should be wives; in fact, some of them are knives who cut men off from their purpose. This truth also holds the same potency for men, as it is for women, because not all men deserve to be husbands; some of us are 'house-bands' who place women in chains of heartache and pain. So, find as is used in the text, does not mean to find something willy-nilly or without a strategic plan but a diligent selection of one woman out of the many variety of women or the selection of one who is most compatible with us in the fulfilment of destiny. Most compatible as I used it, does not mean perfect. It simply means the one who is most willing to work with us or the one who will avail himself or herself to the lengthy process in order to become one with us.

The process of connecting is never an easy one, for if it is so difficult to connect with our own selves, how much more is it an ordeal to connect with another individual? Even in instances where the partner is the most suitable person for us, joining to us does not happen overnight. It takes some level of storming, norming and then performing, before we can have a sense of normality. In short, it takes years for us to know someone.

A point to note here is that even among the members of the world's most successful teams, there are disputes. What makes them the best, however, is that they have learned how to handle their disagreements through proper communication, which in turn cancel out individuality and allows them to perform at their optimum, they win. They find a way to work across differences and individualism and they keep winning. Some members earn more than other does, play more than other do or are more famous than others but they are a time. Anytime they forget that the team dies. In the same matter, just as how there are no teams without individual differences, there are no marriages without personality differences and other disparities either. However, what makes them work is an individual's willingness to understand and compromise. When we are able to take 'self' out of the picture, even a match made in Hell can come over as flawless.

It will, however, never look flawless if we are yoked together with an unbeliever and by unbeliever I mean, an individual who does not share our vision or destiny. This is why marriage is comparable to dancing. This is, however, not a dance with one's self or a dance to show how rhythmic one can be alone but it is a dance with someone else who knows the moves of what we are trying to accomplish in our short existence. For such a dance to go well, however, we cannot take onto us a partner who is a novice. Note however, I am not saying that an experience dancer or experts do not make mistakes, for I know that many do. I also acknowledge that even if the individual is an expert, we will still have to take the time to know them well enough to be in harmony with them or for them to be coordinated with us. Hence, what I am saying is that when an individual is an unbeliever, they sap our creativity and make us look inept, simply because, they do not know our moves or want to force us to conform to theirs; they keep stepping on our toes.

I know that not everyone will share our dreams or aspiration and certainly, we cannot expect someone who is not an extension of ourselves to share in where we are going or even fight for it with us. However, the partner we choose should be able to support our endeavours, even when they do not understand them. This type of support system is what separates a partner from everyone else in our lives. Everyone else can afford to say, 'This is foolish! And then leave,' but a partner should never have anywhere else going, because they are one with us. Our dreams become theirs. It is never about, 'This is your idea, not mine.' Who cares who thought about it first! What is important is that someone thought about it and it will be for the betterment of the relationship.

Hear me and hear me well, in a marriage it does not matter who was or is the conceptualiser, what is important is the execution. The execution of any project in marriage will always take the two individuals who are involved and rightfully so, because unless one party is a conniving scoundrel, the benefits accrue to both individuals. When two persons share the benefits, one person should never be the 'pack horse'. Or, since the benefits are shared, may not be equally, regardless of who came up with the idea or dream both must be willing to hear the other person's perspective before jumping to conclusion. Marriage is about sharing and doing things with and for each other. The greatest sharing in marriage, outside of sharing our most private parts is the sharing of our minds, our dreams. There is no other way to share a dream except talking about it or constantly executing it to others. In addition, a dream shared with a partner, whether its manifestation is apparent or not, becomes a dream expanded. This means that our partner must be receptive and have enough confidence in us to know that we are going places. This confidence must be in us as a person and not just in the thing; we are trying to achieve. You see, if our partners do not believe in us as a person, they will not believe in our dreams either and by extension, they will unknowingly or in some cases, deliberately stall or derail our progress. In doing so, they will see love only as an expression of selfish pursuit. 'If you love me you would...!'

In writing this just now, it came to me that one of the worst opposition we can ever encounter, as it relates to our dreams is an individual fighting us from the inside. I hate Trojan horses just as much as I hate friends or lovers who sell us out to our enemies. Thus, during the period of looking for a compatible mate, we have to look at who is most appropriate to be an extension of ourselves, for we cannot become one with everyone. This is why the saying, 'Every hoe has its stick a bush' is true. Some partners are square pegs in round holes. They just do not fit!

In this, the word 'find' means to select the best extension of ourselves in another. However, to select the best, we will have to see our own self as the best. We are the criterion by which we judge others. We have to know where we are going and to possess an idea of what will be required to get us there. Marriage to us then, cannot be about the selection of a partner for the purpose of sex, meeting security, gaining favour or building of networks. It has to be about something everlasting: the strengthening and expansion of two spirits.

I want to be a bit controversial here. I will say that except for one special case, i.e. Adam and Eve, the Lord gave no man a wife or a woman a husband. Even if it is in the will of God for us to marry a particular individual, we all have to go and look. We all have to work and sometimes die for such a one. That choice and decision is ours to make. What God does for us during the selection process is guide our choice. He does not select for us. Then after we have selected, He acts again, by giving us His blessing for wanting to walk in the correctness of His word: the two become one flesh.

In short, He simply blesses us for endeavouring to be like Him, in not walking in the natural desires of our flesh. It is in our human nature and will to try and have all the familiarities of marriage fulfilled in a non-marital situation. According to us, we can have a meaningful relationship between ourselves and another individual without been married. We can have sex, children, get our laundry done, our house cleaned and meals prepared, all without getting married. We simply 'drink milk, we do not own the cow'. So, just for the mere fact that we will seek to go against the basic nature of our humanness, to be like him – making another person a part of ourselves – He blessed us with the favour to do so.

Only marriage makes another individual a part of us, no other relational practice can do that. That is why we should not hop, skip and jump in and out of it. Then again that is if we want someone to be a part of us, in the first place.

Therefore, the man who finds a wife finds a helpmeet, one who will help him in all of his toil to become a well-rounded and complete individual. One who will ensure that progress occurs at each turn in his life.

I know men, including myself, have a tendency to get side tracked and when we do, it takes a great woman to steer us back on track. That is why 'Behind every great or successful man, there is an even greater or forceful woman.' Or,

'Behind the fall of every great man, there was a passive unwise woman, a woman who wield power wrongly.'

I can boldly say that based on my knowledge, men do not fall when they have stability or bedrock on which to stand. We do not do rubbish, when our backing comes from the skilful hands of a shrewd wife and an even more present God. When we have such a woman in our lives, often times we are more meticulous and sound in our judgement and this occurs because we learn how to listen to them. The words of a caring wife are likening to a rope extended to an individual sinking in quicksand. The second wisest man who has ever lived – Solomon – said it this way, 'Every wise woman buildeth her house: but the foolish plucketh it down with her hands.'

These words were what I heard plainly one evening, as my wife rants and raged. The problem with hearing them that evening was tell her to which she responded, 'OK Mr Righteous, there is nothing here to tear down in the first place.' She was probably right, for look at us today, in two separate house.

This is why I feel that with all the chips, men carry on our shoulders; women are the true builders of societies. Their advice and counsel goes further than our brains and brawn. Thus, the hand that rocks the cradle, really rocks the world.

Hence, a man who finds a wife actually finds the medium to be complete and whole in all of his endeavours. Oliver Goldsmith in the Vicar of Wakefield writes, 'I . . . chose my wife, as she did her wedding gown, not for a fine glossy surface but such qualities as would wear well.' A good wife is the crowning glory of every man who loves himself to the highest level.

Thus, the good thing that a man has found when he selects a wife is the opportunity to have someone sharing in his self-replication. When this term is used, I mean, the creation of another individual who is not him in outer features but him in personification. A wife to a man then is someone who affirms his ideal and champions his virtues as if they were hers. She wants to see and help raise another him. Hence, this person is another individual who wants to intimately share with him in the expansion of his core values and principles. Not everyone can do this for him. It takes someone who is the reciprocal of him. Often times this individual is almost the total opposite of him but has a stable head to steer a 'pig-headed' man into an unlikely future. Only a wife can do this, no girlfriend, no fiancée, mother, sister or you name it.

Everyone outside of a wife or husband can share with us but this is only up to a particular point. They cannot share with us intimately and this is so even if they are having or have had sex with us. Intimacy is the sharing of our souls. Please note that emotions, although an expression of the soul is not the soul. Our soul is the part of us that will be receiving or experiencing our ultimate blessing and reward from its Creator. It's a pity, some will not be receiving a blessing or a righteous reward, as they replicated 'yes' but they did it outside of His ordinance and plan for our continuation upon the Earth and ultimately eternity. In other words, God did not give them the blessing to function in the realm of replication the way they did; they usurped it, they made their own way.

God's design for replication is righteousness. He is righteous and that is who He expects us to be. Moreover, since all His works require righteousness, He expects ours to be so as well. Therefore, what He wants; is for a righteous seed to be upon the earth or continue upon the earth, not for us to do things the way we feel, because the blessing of freedom of expression was granted unto us. We have been given free will yes but anytime we replicate outside of marriage; we perpetuate sin upon the Earth. This is why the blessing of replication is only given to the one who has become one with us through the keeping of God's word: 'Let a man have his own wife...' his own help meet.

I know in our modern era, we can try to circumvent this truth; by having what we assumed to be an intimate relationship with a whole host of people and things but this will only cause us to be a stagnant human being, a person groping in the dark, looking for eternal truth but finding none. On the other hand, having a sex partner or an individual who shares our emotional space, yes but still are unable to come to the understanding of what it means to be righteously whole is just as unbearable as living in Hell.

In our generation, we think that wholeness is to achieve wellness and that wellness means; to eat right, get adequate exercise, rest and relaxation or do some form of meditation to feel good about ourselves. However, to be whole is determined by God's standard, not ours. In fact, we are never whole until we are one with him or he makes is whole. His standards are holy and righteous and that is what He expects from us. In many instances, some of us fail to comprehend that righteousness is not determined by popular opinion or by the legislative prowess of a few learned men or women. Anytime righteousness is determined by men or by popular opining, we end up with a state of Sodom and Gomorrah, a state where men ask, 'Who made you a judge to us?' They ask this because, they begin to interpret things based on laws decreed by individuals with darkened motives. Thus, righteousness can only come from Jesus because that is who He is, righteous. Hence, when two individuals get married, what they are doing is fulfilling God's righteous requirement for their existence, an existence that goes beyond this life. Therefore, if we do not place a ring on their finger, we will live and die alone. Something we were never destined to do, either on Earth or for eternity: 'It is not good for man to be alone,' and so He made a woman for him. This means that when a man and a woman are in harmony, neither is ever alone and both stand a greater chance of going to Heaven. Thus, when compared to Heaven, Hell is a lonely place.

In this regards, every man who selects a wife must know that he is doing something of monumental proportion. He must know that he is doing something that finds its genesis and termination in eternity. 'Marriages are made in Heaven and consummated on Earth,' writes John Lyly in his book *Euphues: The Anatomy of Wyt*.

Let me say it this way, the selection of a wife replicates what God is doing with the human race, which He calls His bride. God is replicating himself in us: 'Beloved now are we the sons of God and it does not yet appear what we shall be but we know that when He shall appear we shall be like Him, for we shall see Him as He is.' However, in order to replicate Himself, He does not force a choice on us, he allows us to make that decision for ourselves. Let me repeat myself, He will never force the human race to choose Him. He will make the way possible for us to do so. This was what Calvary was about. He will also show us the benefits but He will not twist anyone's arm. The acceptance must be a personal choice, just as it is the woman's right to say 'I accept you as my lawful wedded husband' free from coercion.

To ensure that the duplication of Himself occurs just as He intends, He went to the cross. He was not, nor is He ever afraid, to go to the lowest Hell or the highest Heaven to make it possible. This He showed us, with the action of providing salvation for His bride. He gave up Heaven, suffered humiliation and lack, sacrificed Himself in death and rose to life through the power of the resurrection; in order to share His power with us. His action lifted us out of sin, therefore, giving us the power never to return to it. This is what a man is supposed to do for a woman, give himself as a sacrifice in order to raise her up, making her happy that she chose him.

Thus, any man who is not willing to sacrifice himself to make the way possible for his own expansion, should never be married, as such a one is violating the principles upon which his own expansion hangs. Also, any woman who accepts a man's request to expand himself and does not submit herself or live up to her decision, violates the spirit of unity and becomes a blot upon her own dignity. In that case, both are evil and selfish beings and do not deserve to be blessed. However, God is merciful!

No wonder so many marriages are in constant turmoil or ending in failure in our societies. It appears that in the age of 'get out of jail free cards', neither party is doing enough to sustain or ensure that the union lasts. Is it that unlike Adam and Eve, we no longer want to be like God is it that we think we can become gods some other way or are we now God ourselves so we no longer have to follow his guide? Why, what is happening? The answer, when I have options, 'God and others will forgive me and I will have another chance at it, if I so desire.' Thus, each party, though married, seeks his or her own good and does so because, he or she thinks they have many chances of getting it right down the road. Given the values of society, it reinforced these thoughts and practices as the acceptable norm.

However, in the hallowed halls of marriage and in the intents of God by His text, there is no room for such childish thinking and expression. Therefore, marriage must be seen as becoming one with one, not one with many. If by some chance we hop out of one and become one with another, while the first one is still alive, we have not become a whole one with another; for 'tis only in death' the connection is broken between us, as it is in death the other person frees us to become one with someone else. I say this within the context of the inner workings of our heart. We do not easily let go off individuals whom we are intertwined emotionally. Something about them stays with us and when we find someone else who we love and have moved on with them and are finding happiness, there is still a feeling deep down on the inside that questions us. It is as if a piece of the previous person lives on in our spirit. In know I am treading in deep waters here, perhaps this is why, when you love someone, death is preferred over leaving them.

Nevertheless or despite this fact, we keep on expanding ourselves into the lives of others. No wonder the values of successive generations are changing and becoming less and less meaningful, to those coming after. 'If this happen to mommy and daddy, it can happen to me and I do not want it to happen to me. So I rather stay single.'

What does a child do under these circumstances, he or she chooses a single life; not knowing that 'Marriage has many pains but celibacy has no pleasures,' as Samuel Johnson puts it. Following these trends, we are losing our souls and the essence of who we are. We are becoming nothing greater than that of animals. There is no centre or point of reference. In almost every marriage in our decade, one individual is always working his or her fingers to the bones and still has no satisfaction from the toil. It always appears that the other, parasitically, sits back and yells, 'You are not doing enough to make this work,' or gives just enough to ensure their own survival. It is as if wholesomeness in marriage is a missing art.

The final thing that came to me as I mused on the meaning of the text; is that God has put no other way in the earth for a child to come into it but through the womb of a woman. I know many scientists are working feverishly to come up with other ways. They have so far tried artificial insemination and cloning, which have both worked to some degree and are the closest to date they have come to having control over bringing a life into this world. Even in this, they need a womb or some form of incubator to do so. Artificial intelligence or otherwise, until they have found a way to make a womb that works, the female is still God's way of continuing the human race.

Here I will be bold enough to say, even if creation occurs another way or based on man's creative ingenuity he is able to create another human being, it would still not be God's design. Yes, he would have used the brain that God gave him and he would have also use what God had already created, for man cannot create anything out of nothing but it would still be man's way of trying to prove that he is God himself. The creature thinking it can improve upon the work of the creator. Acting this way would be another of God's creation, in fact His greatest creation, trying to usurp His position and authority, under the guise of increased knowledge. This would also appear as that mankind has succeeded in an area where Satan has failed, for this was his original intention in the first place. Every devil will seek to elevate it, him or herself, above God by virtue of its own beauty and resplendence. So is it that humankind sure knows a lot or it is the devil working in the background?

Therefore, in my opinion, for a child to come into the world any other way, outside of marriage is in itself a sin against God. If it comes by the way of scientific experimentation, I do not know if such a one would be considered a person, have a soul or is worthy of salvation. Is it human although human DNA is used? The answers to these questions fall under the heading of a theological debate, which is not one for this book.

I am not sure if I should call such a child – if considered a child – an abomination or an aberration. Within the context of God's intention for human birth, I can say this is a deviation from His intended purpose, so by extension, I can definitely say that the act to get them here is a sin. Or, if such a one has a soul and in fact can be save, how would it be done. Well, I guess, if we followed the fact that 'Jesus who knew no sin, became sin for us' then the child is both the product of sin and sin itself, which is what all of us were and needs salvation, just like the rest of us. No wonder the scripture says, 'We were all born in sin and shaped in inequity,' and therefore, were fit for nothing but damnation.

This is a hard truth to speak and swallow but if we, the human race, were holding to the truth of scriptures, children born out of wedlock would have the label 'Bastards' or a 'Whoreson.' One who is a representation of something that should not have happened in the first place that of having sex outside of marriage union. Such a one would not belong to the people of God or if numbered among the children of God – the regular people – it would not be until their third or fourth generation. However, since the majority of the world's population would fall under this heading, I guess it is best to strike such a term from our collective consciousness, as it would not be politically correct to use it.

Again, I will be bold enough to say, the more we expand the world's population, by having children out of wedlock is the more we will think it is the correct thing to do. Eventually, what will happen in the end is that some reputable body will say, 'Marriage is not needed anymore,' and those who stands for it, will be viewed as 'backward' old fools. In doing so, all manner of evil will proceed out of what has become the acceptable norm. This will in turn lead to chaos and because the man is not being replicated properly, as he is not being replicated in righteousness, he suffers. The Earth itself and everyone around him suffers as well.

Therefore, if I should seek to expand the notion of exactly what is found when a man finds a wife through this thought, I would say, what a man has found when he finds a wife is someone who is willing to enable him to have a righteous generation after him. When he is gone, righteousness lives on in the darkness of this life.

Hence, although a child represents the continuation of the human race, everyone who comes into the world, because of that man's action is that man's generation and his prolong existence. Truly, we live on through our children. Even after death, our genes live on and in many cases, it lives on in the desires, wealth, ailments, deeds and convictions that we had. Therefore, the only thing of real merit we leave behind after we are dead; is our partner and the offspring or springs we had with them. Nothing else, no mighty corporation, no goodwill, no wealth or fame, can fill this position. Not even the friends we had or the lives we have touched can do this, just our partner and our children.

Another question I would love to ask; 'Why do we spend so little time pouring into them?' If they mean so much to our continuation, why not invest in them what we want remembered, as well as what we want to memorialise?

The truth is, many of us were not taught any differently or how to do so and so we see having children as a part of the normal process of life. In some instances, we see them as one of the many by-products of having sex and since society teaches that we should love and care for them when they come, we do so, until we can find a way to send them on their merry way. With society continually having these kinds of attitudes, no wonder proper values and attitudes, which that once held dear, are not passed from one generation to the next. On the other hand, it appears that each successive generation to come to the table with the inalienable right to change the dogmas and creeds of the preceding generations. My son would say when I try to teach him certain things, 'Daddy you are too old'. In this atmosphere, many nations find themselves so far removed from the landmarks that once made them great that they are now failing to know what they believe in. Many of them have amended their constitutions so many times, to allow for so many variant ideas and beliefs that they are unrecognisable. If the men and women who wrote these constitutions were to come alive, they would not recognise their own handy work. That which was written to protect us from falsity and anarchy is now been used to cement and promulgate that which will ensure that we never replicate ourselves correctly or replicate at all. There are no way two things of the same sex can bring forth an offspring. This is the truth whether we like it or not! To try that is nothing but an abomination, for that is not how God designed it.

Then again, there are those who do not believe in God, so I guess anything goes with that set. Yes, the loudest voices in our societies are trying nonstop to tell us, under the guise of tolerance, freedom of expression, human rights or acceptance; that we have no need to replicate ourselves in the natural way. They are saying to us, today's ways are more 'truth' than at any other time in history and hence better, anything that came before it is irrelevant. Again, no wonder there is so much confusion of identity in the world. We no longer know if we are

75

male or female, transgender, lesbians, gay, heterosexual, straight, queer, asexual, pansexual, homosexual, homoromantic, paraphilias, bisexual, aromatic, biromantic, ACE, LBGT or a zoophilic. In addition, we do not know if we should cross-dress or have separate bathrooms for specific gender.

When we ignore the old for the new and especially when the new is far removed from the old or is not built upon the solidness of the old, we end up in a world where every man does what is right in his or her own eyes and vociferously beacon to everyone else to 'Accept me as I am!'. This is why I say, the practice of having children out of wedlock is killing the World. My opinion is upon the grounds of, if we waited until we get married, following the context of scriptures, we would not have the kind of World that we have today. One reason: Fewer children would be born each year, resulting in less drain on the World's resources. Then again, some of us do not mind the 'whole heap of' unplanned or unprepared for babies being born each year; we think it will ensure that we will never go broke. One way or another, the steady stream of customers will always be there to fuel our coffers.

If all of this is going to change, then our values have to be much higher than they are now and our standards and principles would need to be more lasting than a few generations, before they change. We would have to revert to the original plan of God for marriage. This return will have to start with how to select a mate. We have to answer the question properly of why and how we ultimately select a partner, for our straying and perversions have been making it difficult for us to have lasting and fruitful replications in marriage.

Think about it. Who can really blame a child who was born into a world of flux and instability for perpetuating what he or she has seen. Brokenness and emptiness produces a better brokenness and emptiness. We produce a world that suites our liking, for it is human nature to make better or worst whatever was given to us if it suits us. We do not really make anything new. All of our new inventions are just a sophisticated way of using something that already existed. Based on my observation of history, we have developed this uncanny way of changing something that is good into something bad.

If you do not believe me, just look at the many great civilisations that have come to ruin or even in our own modern age, how much junk or derelict buildings we have around us. I know there are those who believe that out of chaos comes good or that a phoenix rises out of the ashes of past destruction but the human race appears to be on a skid roll. Hence, regardless of the fact that we know that righteous replication or perpetuation of the human race is what God wants, something is wrong with what is happening in the hearts of men. We somehow know what is required but somehow we are unable to produce it. I will not blame the devil for transforming the heart of men into what it is. The fact that we have lost our understanding of who we are and the legacy we want to leave behind is not his fault, it is ours. We have choices. WE are the ones who must decide that a good marriage is possible and produces offspring who hold dear to this conviction. As Martin Luther puts it, 'There is no more lovely, friendly and charming relationship, communion or company than a good marriage.'

Chapter 3
It All Went Downhill from There but from Exactly Where?

'From whence came, the beginning of the end, beloved?'

'We cannot fix a problem that does not exist, for if an irresistible force meets and immovable object, all we have is a conundrum!'

I must admit, nothing causes me more pain and sorrow than the shame of a broken marriage, mine. Especially, when it happens between two individuals who are children of God or who should know better. Not that 'human things' do not happen to Christians or that we are totally isolated and insulated from the stuff that is common to man but as Christian we have a 'God written tool' to help us see eye to eye. Common problems face individuals; however, as believers we are not common. Which is why, I am convinced that when we stand in obedience to the word of God, others expect us to function differently from unbelievers. Yes, we all face the same 'common' temptations as human beings but as children of God; our manifestation during the trial must be different. Hence, outcome should be different as well.

I also believe that not only should our outcome be different but also, it should always be in line with what God ordained for His people. God said we shall have 'good success' no matter what trials and test comes, if we remain committed, day and night to know His' Word. This good success should be apparent even when faced with trying times, for if in God's eyes death is gain, then certainly, our living must be Christ. Our success then speaks to victor over, death, Hell and the grave. Hence, although our marriages will continuously face Hell, they should survive every onslaught, in order to show others that Godly marriages work.

In other words, 'What God has joined together let no man put asunder' should be our motto and should be so, even when all the examples around us are negative. Why? The answer to that is; we do not see the World as our standard.

We wholly follow the examples set for us in the Word of God and as such, we uphold a higher standard than what is established by emotionalism and popular opinion.

A point to note is that popular views do not prove anything with God. It can validate or repudiate man's conviction, in his own eyes but in God's eyes 'Vox populi vox Dei' is a false notion, it means nothing. What authority do I have to speak for God on this issue or how can I be so sure popular opinion means nothing to him? He said so when He declared, 'My thoughts are not your thoughts and my ways are not your ways.'

Thus, popular opinion can give a million or more reasons why we should leave our partners when the times get rough but the Lord only indicated two reasons – hardness of heart and sexual unfaithfulness. However, even in these two areas of apparent allowances, He did not say that they are the sure fire ticket or way out of the marriage.

Surely, I could name some of the worst things that can happen to an individual in a marriage: from the myriad types of verbal abuse, marital rape, incest, exploitation, suffocation, abandonment, murder and so on and so forth. The list would still not have given a real or valid reason for breaking our covenant. What the list would show is ignorance and a lack of self-control, which is what leads to hardness of heart or unwillingness to change, in the first place.

Therefore, I have concluded that ignorance and an unwillingness to take power over one's own action is the real enemy of all that is good. Anytime we are ignorant and do not accept our role in the discord, we destroy things that should be save and save things that should have been destroyed. In other words, we call good evil and evil good because we want to suit ourselves. In doing so we lose that most important of human character, our integrity.

Integrity is what stabilises us and cause us not to lose our judgment, by acting childish, unkind, unfaithful, stingy, selfish, overbearing or mean-spirited. It reminds us that our ability to keep our bands is the most important legacy we have in this life. It also reminds us that others should be able to rely on us. In addition to the above, they know that if they lean on us, we are not going to be like a piece of board that breaks and runs through their side. They know that we are dependable and stable and that our ability to be rational is unwavering.

Think about it, if we cannot hold a marriage together, which is the highest level of contract we can ever sign, which other contract are we going to keep?

No wonder the world is falling into a quagmire, for the more marriages fall apart; is the more we see a World going deeper and deeper into dishonesty, disloyalty, perversion, promiscuity, instability and disarray. Let me hasten to ask these questions, 'What value system do we want to pass on to the next generation?' Is it the one that says, 'It is okay to break your word anytime you wish,' or, 'How do we want to be remembered?' Is it the one, 'Who had kids with two, three or four different fathers or mothers but only cared for one or none?' This can never be good for society.

I must say this again. God marriages are the strength or benchmark of stable societies. This why we should always seek to replicate our best values regardless of what stress we are under.

I will get a little personal here. This why although my wife and I argued consistently over who should be doing what for our son, I never walked away. At the time we had him, we were age appropriate but emotionally immature and so we struggled. It is not that I never wanted a child back then but in my eyes at the time, we were not ready for one. I knew that when we are not ready for something and we end up with it, for it to survive and for us to live, we will have to learn fast and while we are learning, we will have to play catch up. To be honest, we were not catching up too well. There was always a reason never to see eye to eye and it became frustrating.

To me, she took that frustration out on me. It is as if she did not care that I was working on entire day and night, then leave and attend a class for three hours or that I just drove two and half hours after working a ship in a mosquito-infested place as rain fell. All I could here was, 'You are a wicked man, you come home and all you want to do is sleep. Your child is crying and you would not even take him up,' or, 'When you leave and do not tell him that you are gone, he becomes miserable and cries incessantly.' In my eyes, I was not a wicked man; I was simply a man trying to hold up my end. Yes, I was not doing it well but I was trying. At the same time, I did not see how she could see herself as doing more than me. After all, 'How could she be stressed; if a nanny takes care of the child all day and all she did was pick him up, take him home and lay on a bed watching television with him?'

'How could she accuse me of skipping out on my responsibility, because, in her eyes she was spending more time with him that I?' Yes, he cried after her and did not want to stay in my arms when I held him. So what? I was coming home and helping with everything else in the house, sometimes cooking my own meal because she was sleeping and too tired to cook. At that time, neither of us could understand that we both had had long days and in my case long nights as well, to contended with and so we shook apart. Yet in our shaking apart, I still did my best to stay in my son's life. Reason, he must replicate me and I want him to have one of the strongest reference point in doing do. The example in our societies is to leave and they will 'somehow make it' however this is never the route to go.

I hope we all recognise somewhere along the line that individuals who are 'unstable as water' have values that are constantly shifting. Hence, we cannot rely on them. They have little or no integrity and their basic convictions is never firmly grounded in anything substantial, like father who stayed even when the mother runs him or a mother who still gives her all even when the father is a bastard. To them it is, 'Whichever way the wind blows, as long as it does not trouble me too much, I am OK with it.' I on the other hand, like having purpose and direction. That is when growth happens. No, I am not a coward and my propensity for risk was not well defined; in many instances in the past but I must admit even now grown; I like to know or have an idea of where I am going, before I run behind anyone or anything.

You see, because I know that not all blue and inviting waters is for swimming, I define growth as, an increase in one's worth or personal value, which occurs within a difficult but predictable environment. To be successful in life does not mean we must have a smooth path through it but we cannot operate in ignorance if we are to go places. I can guarantee you that there is no way anyone of us can be successful in something we cannot plan nor have some level of control over. Success does not result from 'buck up,' but from prodigious planning and executing. We must be able to put our 'two cents' in to determining the outcome not diving off a cliff and hoping that it will be OK below.

This is why I believe God gave to His church the Holy Spirit. The Holy Spirit helps us to have a say in the outcome of our existence: Heaven or Hell. For me, I want to know that neither sharks nor jagged rocks are lying below the surface of that blue and serene sea I am about to dive in. I am sure that Venice, Italy or an oilrig might be a nice place to live but I am also sure that they take some getting used to in order to live there.

The fact of the matter is; uncertainty breeds instability and condemns successive generations to all manner of physical, emotional or psychological, financial and spiritual ills. If you can destabilise the home, by wrecking its marriages, then you would have destroyed the moral, ethical and spiritual fibre of society.

I will also say that instability is the recipe for building deviant and nefarious personalities, personalities who not only perpetuate the same thing but individuals who make things worse as time progresses. Let me say this, marriage is about loyalty and loyalty is about integrity and strength of character. Strong characters build strong societies and I know of no stronger characteristic than the one exhibited in a marriage. Trust me, for the little time I spent in it, I realise that a good marriage uses up all the willpower we can muster up in this world. In short, marriage tests every fibre of our being. It also changes for the better or worst depending on how the couple sees things.

My wife and I kept seeing things from too different places. I saw work, church and school as an essential part of our happiness. She saw a man who was just wrong for her.

Owing to our individuality as human beings, we all see and want things from different vantage points, because of this and in many instances, we tend to want the same thing but not at the same time or for the same reason. This is where knowledge comes in. It teaches us that for us to succeed, we have to develop a 'sameness' mentality. We have to know that we are fighting for the same thing. Our expression and timing may be different but we want the same thing. Without this sameness mentality we will always be like the wave of the sea, tossing to and fro against each other.

If you learn anything from this book, learn this. As much as it lies in your power be of the same mind. Work towards the same thing. Do not marry someone who you can never meet their timing or who is unwilling to at least help you with yours.

Learn this, if we want anything to remain as it is, all we have to do is hide the path to knowledge or shut the gate to wisdom. By doing this, we strip others of their power to grow and retain control over their existence for ourselves. Thus, we determine their destiny. However, this is not what marriage is supposed to do. It is supposed to help us develop together, not close the door in each other's face.

Oh for the many times my wife cuts off the calls in the middle of an explanation or hastily tells me, 'Shut up because you do not know what you are talking about'. It did not make a difference where or when, crowed or a lone, she had to make her point. What I had to say never mattered; my point was inconsequential whether right or wrong. Heaven knows that if I had it to do over again, I would be a little less docile, fearing I would lose her and I would let her know that we cannot hang a phone up on someone and expect him or her to come home and talk with us as though nothing had gone wrong in the first instance. In addition, I would also let her know that even though, in her eyes, I am never properly explaining myself I deserve a listening ear. As well as, if she keeps cutting off the call between us in mid-sentence, I will no longer hear what she has to say, which is what I did eventually. I had stopped talking and after a while to hear her voice made me clam up and this translated to even sex.

Bear in mind though that we can also close the door even by sharing information. Information that reinforces and consummates what we are trying to maintain. Thus, even in giving truth, we can perpetuate a lie. All we need to do is get enough persons who are brainwashed in what we want done, to assist us in spreading the lie and it will become the accepted truth for generations. Hence, we can talk our way into believing that something is real when it is not.

Think about it for a minute or two; for years the popular belief was that the world was flat and I am glad that it is not. However, if people could believe that it proves to me that beliefs might conform to popular convictions, which is a fact but it does not prove truth. The truth is, at one time or another we all acted in ignorance. We all came to hasty conclusions and jumped to rash decisions without having all the information in hand. When we acted, we did so with all good intension but we did so accepting a belief system not based on truth. Through this knowledge, I know that having a belief or conviction is different from having the truth. It is like believing that pigs can fly and we might be able to construct a machine for them to fly in but the truth is; pigs were not created to fly.

In like manner, the world can tell us anything it wants about marriage or give us any excuse it wishes for us to have in order to justify getting out of our marriages. We can choose to accept its 'justifiable reasons' with hands and hearts but that does not change the fact that we are leaving our partners due to ignorance, hardness of heart or the acceptance of misguided truth. In essence, this simply means, we are not willing to change our ways, as we are Hell bent on been who we think we are or perhaps who we really are.

I know that there are research findings that highlight the instances where remaining married is a dangerous thing and I whole-heartedly supports many of them. I support them because they are true and valid. Let me list four of the conditions these researches have found.

One, it is best for couples to go their separate ways when there is constant physical and verbal abuse taking place between them and I do not mean arguments, I mean an 'all out fight'. That is if you can call a man beating his wife all the time or a woman spiting on her husband, a fight.

Two, when the children or child in the relationship is being adversely affected by the constant tug of war – verbally, physically or otherwise – taking place between the partners. Fights affect children. So, if the fights are causing the child(ren) to become withdrawn, disruptive, uncontrollable or lose concentration; which manifests itself as an inability to learn or socialise well, then it is always best that the two separate, in order to prevent the next generation from been tainted.

Three, if the activity of one of the partners, outside of the home is putting the other partner or children at risk, then it is also best that someone go and 'get their act together'. After all, it is not going to take too long before someone brings home a sexually transmitted disease – this could very well be AIDS, a baby or until a loan shark, a police or a hooligan shows up on their doorstep.

Finally and by no means lease, if one of the partners is molesting or abusing the child or children. Truly, there are some disgusting individuals out there with no heart. How could anyone have their own, who they are to protect and shelter, stoop so low! Such a one should never have had a child in the first place. In my opinion, they should be locked away in some hole forever! OK, I am being critical and judgemental here. However, even in these extremes conditions, if there is a change of heart, there is life and ultimately a generational change.

I for one know that we do not readily change and those who should help us to change, are not willing to help us to do so. My wife was not willing to help me change whatever problem she believed I had. A matter of fact, if she had told me to clean up my mess by pointing out what she considered that mess to be, I could understand but to keep arguing over things I could not see was heart rending. Moreover, when I ask others to intervene, those who showed up to split justice she did not want to listen to them. They are 'Always in your corner and never fair...' Yet I was the one blamed for not changing or trying to change. This is why I conclude that with no one to help us change and we being who we have been all our lives and in many instances only get worse because we see nothing to change, even under the best conditions, we stick to our own nature. The question is then, where did we or I fell, given these four facts?

Yes, we argue and there were times we stepped to each other, holding up each other's clothing, breathing heavily and speaking to each other loud and aggressively but it hardly when beyond that. In addition, our son was too young to process mentally what was happening around him. She grabbing him out of my hands a couple of times and yelling, 'Give me my pickney,' saw him crying yes but not to the point where he translated it into aggression. Do not get me wrong, the times when she took him out of my hands I was not abusing him but we all know that a child become a pawn when mothers want to show possession or spite. I really do not have to comment on the last two, as incest or any other sexual misconduct was never in play. It was not happening between us as a couple and I can speak for myself, it was not happening with anyone else. Certainly, we had money troubles but we never ran outside of the law or against the grains to make ends meet, we simply argue over it, 'I will work my money and buy what I want' or do without it.

I hope the preceding paragraphs gave you a hint into how I felt when my marriage was overlooking the precipice of despair and until it eventually collapsed into the waters of shame, disappointment and bewilderment. However, I still ask, where did we go wrong? Again, I know we had not come to any hard blows the couple of times we became physical but were these two or three times of 'grabbings' became second nature to us or were we allowing a constant fighting spirit to intrude upon our dwelling? We also had needs but we lived somewhere, were never hungry and necked. We could go on vacation if we planned it properly. So, why did we separate? I do not know. At the time oh how I prayed for the best. So, exactly where did we go wrong? Did we accept the teaching of society or did we invent our own demise? Again, I do not know!

All I know is that at the time, I had constant headaches. I was never a fat man, yet somewhere in the midst of it all, I lost weight. I barely slept at nights and when I did, I was in torment. I had a bed but like a personal prison, I slept most nights on the ground, because of how low I felt. My desire for food was barely above board and I had an insatiable appetite to be alone.

All of this happened because I just did not understand; 'What is it that just happen between two people who professed their love to one another?' I just could not understand why we made so much investment in a particular thing and then turned around and threw it away. Why could we not work it out! I felt lost. I felt like my heart had been ripped out of my chest and when it happened, I was not in harm's way or in the presence of an enemy, I was with the woman I loved and promised; I would love until death do us part. If I was in the presence of an enemy, I could and would have protected myself. Honestly, I loved my wife but I just could not understand why she did not love me in return. I just could not understand how she could tell me that she did not love me, after having told me she did. Did she lie?

In trying to answer these questions, I fell into despair, as though I did not want to live anymore. If I did not know that killing one's self was a sure fire ticket to Hell, I would not be alive today. I was so low that for days I lived my life in seeing lips moved but heard no sound. 'Did you hear what I said or what I asked?' was a constant question during this time. As it were, life took place around me in slow motion. I thought those things only happened in movies. At that time, I made so many mistakes at work that my boss said, 'I was not using my initiative,' and transferred me to another department. Now looking back, I am somewhat glad that that happened to me, because, out in the container yard on the wharf, where I worked at the time, I got a lot of lone time to think, talk with myself and pray over what was happening but more so; over taking control over my own mind.

During this time, I did not speak or shared my hurt with too many people. One, I was so ashamed and afraid to tell anyone that this was happening to me. After all, I was 'Brother, Pastor Junior'. These things do not happen to men of calibre, especially to faithful praying men, Reverent Junior. Two, you do not want to tell some people, 'Wharf Men' that you are a 'Single burner' with problems. 'You are a fool, look how many women out there and you have one woman giving you problem. Is ship you work you know bass. You are a Boarding Agent. Yes, you are a Pastor but God will not sin you for this.' Oh how the advices were many when it eventually leaked. Things tend to leak when a married person being to look meagre, haggard and their good working habits begin to look like the path of a tornado.

During this time, I felt that I was bearing it alone and regardless of others telling me it had a divine purpose, I just could not see it. How can anyone see divine purpose in disappointment and despair? I sure did not.

In fact, as a Christian, I just could not see it as anything but a deliberate plan of Hell. A plan orchestrated by the devil against me to prevent me from having what was better: a better wife, a better woman, a better marriage, a better friend, a better ministry, a better family and ultimately a better life. 'Let him fall into a snare!' was the decree I heard over my life. Whether this decree was imaginary or literal, I ended up seeing it as nothing but a plan that was set to derail me from the plan of God for my life. I saw it as something that was set to cripple any chance I had of being a real minister of God in my generation. 'One, who has one wife and rule his house well…'

Having come to this conclusion though, nearly ripped me apart on the inside and mainly because, daily I questioned, 'How could I stand to minister to God's people with an estrange wife; or without a wife, for that matter?' Besides, I never wanted to be alone. Ever! I did not think I could function or survive being alone again. I did it before and I never liked it. In truth, I hated it. I could not see it as the way forward for my life. As such, each day became a day of survival against my own thoughts. In the back of my head, daily I wrestled with the question, 'If I cannot live it or enjoy the sanctity of marriage, how can I counsel or give advice to others?'

Unable to answer this question, reinforced in my head that it was indeed an organised plan to bring me to an open shame. I saw it also as a plan to confound my conviction that marriage is God's way for a man and woman to be in unity and harmony. A plan that was designed to push me back into a life of obeying my humanness and return me to my sinful ways of having sexual companions outside of marriage and it almost worked. I found myself attracted to a co-worker and at one point when we were alone, I held her and kissed her and she did not resist. It did not progress beyond that moment as something snapped back into place. However, the plan to make me dishonour my covenant almost worked.

'Why did such a plan almost succeed?' you might ask. Well, it almost succeeded because I felt rejected, lonely and needy. In doing so, I questioned my faith. Sometime is the pit we know that God is real but we ask, 'Is he real to be?'

To me it felt like 'Déjà vu' and I hated it. I hate being lonely or like no one can recognise my worth, in order to cherish me. I believe that no one should have to relive a scaring experience and in my book, I had lived this life emotionally before, only not with a wife. To be honest, I did not expect it to be with her either. I grew up feeling inadequate around people in so many different ways and in getting married, I felt that I was finally over these insufficiencies, as finally someone accepted me for me but only to be rejected again.

Growing up I felt like my mother did not care enough to stick around and in my eyes, my father was just cruel and cared only for himself. As such, I was always looking at what others had and because of my constant needs and wants, I felt like they always had the best or that I always had to compete for even insufficiencies. This type of thinking affected my self-esteem. It also caused me to blame them for many of the lacks in my life, even though I was an adult and played a pivotal role in where I was in my relationship. Not for one minute did I blame my behaviour during my teenage years. I blamed my parents, especially when I looked at my potential as well as my siblings. I felt that we would have accomplished more in life, if they had given proper supervision to us. This constant blaming caused me to be weak. It created a desire in me to want the best for me, my family. I wanted mainly so that I could say that I am better than they in every way are. They were divorcee and I never wanted to be one. They had many kids and never spent the time to take care of them, I only had one and I wanted a safe and secure home, with a wife, in it for him.

Wanting the best however, meant finding someone who knew my limitation but still found me worthy enough to want to spend the rest of their life with me. So when I found that one I said to myself, 'I will make sure what happened to me does not happen to my offspring.' In my mind's eye, this individual is my soul mate, 'I will never be lonely again. Ever!'

Therefore, when she just got up and left, it was not hard for me to fall into the trap of saying, 'I was hurt by one and all, so let me be unfeeling with all others.' Besides, I had promised myself years before, after a horrible experience of living alone that I would never do it again. I had the idea, somewhere in the back of my head that now that I have found my life's partner, it will never happen to me, only to find myself alone again.

The hardest part of this was that my wife was in the same house, where I lived but I was alone. In her heart, she had moved on with her life and by extension stopped sharing her spirit with me. If our partner will not share their spirit with us, the loss of sex is just one of the offshoot, 'You do not hear me say, do not touch me?'

From that experience I have learned that one of the loneliest places an individual can ever find him or herself is in a house where two people stop sharing each other's spirit. We literally became lonely in the presence of each other. I dared to 'speak' and she dared to 'communicate' but for some strange reason, it always ended in a disagreement. It did matter how small the issue was, it was always too large. 'Good evening Love1!' becomes a grunt, 'Yeah.' An, 'I will be late coming home!' becomes a, 'So, you do not think I have a life or I want to go anywhere?' In this type of environment, tempers flare over even good gestures, 'Why you buy me this? I told you I do not want anything from you.' The following is a scenario of a point and counter point letter that took place between us.

Backdrop to letter

I could sum up the backdrop to these two letters in a single Jamaican proverb it would be, 'A nuh same day leaf drop a wata bottom it rotten,' because to understand them is to understand that as human beings we can endure so much and no more. We can live with pain and agony but something will cause us to snap. Putting in another way, as individuals, we can only tolerate or put up with so much and no more before inwardly we begin to plot the other person's demise.

The last straw that breaks the camel's back is always lurking around the corner and it will show itself when least expected.

I came home one night and realised that for two years my wife did not entertain me in any form of sexual overture and so I decided that I would question her about the 'rightness or wrongness' of it all. I wanted to find out if she thought that it was right to withhold from me true benevolence and intimacy – sex. I had arrived at place of decision and it was no longer 'OK' with me for us to be in the same house, as wife and husband and not able to touch, embrace or share each other's arms. I wanted this to change. I was not taking a 'bull by the horn' approach or forcing a change but I wanted to deduce the way forward.

Why did I want a change or raise a discussion over this, after two years of living with making approaches and receiving rejections? Was it that I could not take it anymore or was it because I felt it would change anything between us? Was it because other women were now telling me how sexy I was and spreading the path to their bed to me?

Honestly, I do not know why I decided, after two years, to talk to her about her unresponsiveness towards me. Frankly, I was living with it and since it did not appear to be a problem to her, I just kept on living with it. She said nothing and I did nothing. We slept in the same bed, all be it most times with a child between us but nothing. In my eyes, I was just being the patient and understanding husband, saying, 'This is not smooth between us, I will wait.' I guess we both erred. I also I thought that our love was impervious and would sustain us through whatever trial we were going through. I was so wrong. She had long buried love or decided that there was none to be buried in the first place and so all she saw were exit signs. Signs I could not see.

Truthfully speaking though, I think I asked because I was jealous. Why was I jealous? Well, I overheard a conversation early one morning that set me thinking. It gave me a reason to think, 'This was the only reason why she was not doing anything with me. She has someone else!'

That early morning as I was hanging between sleep and worrying that I had made a grave mistake at work the day before, I heard talking in the dark. At first, I wondered if it was a part of the dream. You know one of those dreams that felt like reality. However, the more I fought to sleep, was the more I realised that it was real, a little above a whisper but real. This telephone conversation occurring in the dark sparked a rage within me that ran like lava down the side of a mountain. I was tempted to jump up and turn on the light and yell, 'What in Hell are you doing?' but something restrained me. I kept lying there and pretending to sleep, using the air from my anger to feign snoring. That morning I acted as though I did not hear a word of the conversation.

Served me right, I was wrong to be eavesdropping. As the Scripture pronounces, 'A king who listens around corners, will hear his servants cursing him.' To me such a king is only courting trouble and I was doing just that. I was also wrong for not turning on the light and asking, 'Who are you talking with so early in the morning and in the dark?' Take it from me; some things are best done right away. Doing it right away prevents us from emotionally swelling up inside or give the person the chance to say we are lying or over exaggerating. Believe me when I say, too much pressure on a valve will cause it to blow. I did not blow that morning but I did eventually.

I want to stress this point of speaking up and never being afraid that you may hurt a feeling. Feelings get hurt all the time. Know this, if some things, in a relationship, are going to change, they will only change because someone was honest enough to call a spade, a spade. You see, if we do not speak up, we beginning to develop jealousy or resentment inside and little by little, we begin to whine, taking on a poor old me demeanour. In addition, we begin to come across to our partners as weak and nagging. I still can hear my wife shouting, 'You are always complaining over something and putting down yourself. I am tired of it. If you think it is about you, you are wrong. Oh how I would love if you would stop taking out your frustration on us.' Believe you me, you will not be aware that you are doing it but now having been there and have the chance to look back, I can say, I did it. This is why I am saying to you now, be decisive and say what you have to say, once and move on. It is always better to be honest and open than hiding and being untrusting or dying on the inside.

So although, hearing the conversation was eating me from the inside, I lay there and pretended to be asleep, because I was a Christian lying there saying no to myself, 'This is not happening to me. She would not be so crazy to be talking to an admirer, a lover or a friend at this hour of the morning with me lying there in the bed. I must be dreaming; she is not that brazen. This is a reality like part of the sleep. I am really dreaming!' Honestly, I thought I was. Therefore, in this matter, I held my tongue and said nothing for weeks. At least this was until I began to see actions that said, 'If she has not played the harlot already, she is about to!' Not that she was guilty of what my mind told me. Yet, nothing sparks irrationality in a man, like when he knows his wife will not iron a shirt for him but he sees her ironing a shirt for another man and knows that he was the one she was conversing with on the phone, weeks before.

Up to this point, I held my tongue because he was overseas. That is where he lived. He was not a threat. A competition yes but not a threat, more so, I know she knew Jesus and she would honour the bands of marriage we have. That was what I told myself. However, he was now in the island and she was ironing a shirt for him. Something she had stopped doing for me.

If I had questioned this action when it occurred that morning, I know she would have justified herself. I knew she would have told me that she had stopped doing it from me because I did not require it and he is just a friend who asked her for help. It was not that I did not want it, she had made me feel like I was treating her like a workhorse and I was tired of the arguments. Hence, in my heart, all I was doing when I ironed my clothes, our son's clothing and sometimes hers, was helping with the responsibilities of the home. Deep down in my heart, I wanted it. I wanted a wife who would do these little things for me. I wanted a wife who would give me the responsibility to earn and bring home the bacon but she would make sure that the home is well, I am well and our child is well. I wanted a wife who did not nag me over simply things or questioned my motives. All I did, I did for us. However, she worked and I worked. Besides, it was not how I was socialised to allow her to do everything in the home. Simple things like; cooking, washing and cleaning was just a part of my responsibility in the home as it is hers. When you are one, the responsibility of everything is one, so

I did my best to help. I guess my supportive and helpful ways was misjudged, taken for weakness or 'I don't need you to do anything for me'.

How did she come to be ironing a shirt for him? I know some might ask. Well, he was an old family friend from her youth and he was the son of my mother's good friend. As a close friend of the family, when he came to the island, my mother extended her hospitality to him and so we were all staying by my parents' house for the weekend.

I did not say anything to my mother about this and she still does not know anything about it. Well, probably she will now from reading this section. That Sunday morning, I did not become loud but I definitely took her on about it. I was upset. Tell me now, what was I supposed to do, wait and continue to play ignorant?

Before you answer, let me say this, up to this point, I had just thought that she was only going through a phase. I know you must be yelling, 'You are mad! Two years, what kind of a phase can last for so long between a man and his wife?' Well, I was ignorant and all the counselling I got at the time said, 'Give her time. She is just going through a phase; she will come around, keep praying. Stay focused.' So, I was prepared to give her as long as she wanted and needed. She was my wife and I loved her. What do you expect?

In my defence, I have never been married before or lived in a common-law relationship and I was not a student of psychology, so how would I know how long a phase in a woman lasts. I was ignorant! I did not realise that we had long moved from a phase, to a depression, to 'I cannot stand being around you or have you touch me!', to the position of emotionally and mentally choosing another person. I trusted her. I was still not accusing her of doing anything wrong. That might have been exaggeration on my part but I just wanted to know. I wanted my fears and concerns to go away. I wanted my wife back and I did not want to feel that there was someone else in the way. Based on what she had said to refute my beliefs and pacify my suspicion when I asked her about the ironing of the shirt, I accepted that she was telling the truth, from a physical level that is.

Some things do not have to happen in the physical for them to be accounted as sin in the spiritual realm.

We learn this truth from the scriptures 'As a man thinks in his heart so is he' and 'Any man who looks upon a woman and lust; have committed the sin in his heart.' Then again, although I can speak from a physical standpoint I cannot speak from a spiritual level. What the mind conceives and we believe; we will find a way to manifest it in the natural, as our thoughts determine our eventual outcome. The long and short of it all is that I confronted her and ended up sleeping in my car and then ultimately on the floor of our rented house. I will move to the point I have been trying to make about sharing each other's spirit, by using these two letters.

To help you understand these letters, I wrote her and she responded by only speaking to the parts that are in bold. Each of her paragraphs speaks to only one aspect of my query. If you want to see exactly how her letter flows, just read the bold section, in my letter and then read the corresponding part in hers.

Chapter 4
The Letters

'When writing becomes your replacement for face to face talk, it is either a peace making effort or a sign of a darker truth. I can no longer speak with you face to face. We are done.'

'I will be sleeping in my car.'

I have often heard individuals talking about they got separated or getting a **divorce because of irreconcilable differences between them and their partner and often wonder what they could mean by that. When I checked, I realise that usually this means, someone is cheating, someone is too abusive, someone is too selfish, someone's ideal does not match the other's or someone is just mean and unkind. Does anyone of these applied to us?**

Then again, we are Christians but are we just like everybody else? I can understand when the world gets a divorce because of these things but I cannot understand them for Christians or does it mean that the same ideals that govern the world also govern us. I thought we went with a higher set of standard. I believe that too often we think like the world. I think we should pray or begin to pray on our marriage again. Well then again, you said you have prayed and is praying but **have you prayed with me?**

I am frustrated! Go ahead and enjoy your life. You want to go out; then go on. You are broke and I am broke but when you do not discuss anything with me or plan anything with me, what do you expect from me. *A house divided against itself cannot stand. A matter of fact, who divided the house is it me? Am I the one who refuse to talk to you or draw lines in the sand? Let me get this out, I am not blaming you but are you allowing the devil to wreck our home? You said you have anger inside, how did it get there or was it I who cut you and placed it there? If your answer to this is, 'Yes.' How comes you said you forgave me for all the wrongs I have done but still make me feel like a weight is on my head?*

94

Yes, I was too foolish and stupid in the past, so I said things and did things that I thought in my better judgment was good at the time. Some of these things were even out of my control, as I was not man enough to stand up to my boss. OK, there I have said it. But, must I be made to suffer because of these, even though I said I am sorry and asked for forgiveness? Now, I see the error of my ways but it seems I will never be allowed to forget those days. I hurt you and I take responsibility and great pain for doing so but honestly have I not tried to make up? I am not harping on the past but since I have not done much to deserve the present treatment I do not know what else to think. If I have done new things that hurt you, I do not mean to. They just happen against the run of play. As I carry out my duty with the little that I have, it's hard for me not to do and say things out of frustration and if there is no understanding and constant misinterpretation it would seems like I am only out to get you or destroy you, which I have no intension of doing. How can I convince you of this that I only have your best interest at heart?

I have not taken you places, for you do not want to go anywhere with me. I have also not done the other things you would want, because, I do not have the means to do it right now but are you patient enough with me? Still yet, I have done certain things; because I do not think it is time to do them or in doing them now will prevent us from building a good foundation on which to build later. I do not want to stop you from enjoying living in the here and now or from enjoying what you have worked for right now but when too many things are being done at one time, the load becomes too much to carry and some things get left in the way. I do not feel comfortable carrying bills I cannot pay off or spending money in hope that I will get money. I know how much I earn. Have you forgotten or is it that you do not know or is it that you do not care to know?

Please note that I have worked hard to be where I am today but where I am now is not my final destination and if it appears that it is, please forgive me; as all it means is that I have not communicated my vision to you properly. But then again, if you wrote me off how can I? You are upset by my actions but if you hit me should I not cry. **I told you that I have changed. Do you not see it? Or is it that you have closed your mind to me, so that you are unable to see it or even believe me. I told you I only want the best for my family. Why is it so hard to see that?**

I will never hurt our son and neither will I allow him to grow up with the brokenness or emptiness that I carried around for years, because of not having a biological father who loved me. Yet still I constantly get the feeling that you think I am going to hurt him. **He is not a pawn between us. Neither is he to be use as a battlefront. Know I can deal with you without involving him being involved in the middle but can you deal with me without him being there?**

I know you went through great pains to get him here so please stop reminding me every time. The way you are behaving is as though I played no role in him being here, I want to let you know that if God did make men to bear children I would have been the one to be pregnant with him, for never a time did I ever want to put you through any struggle or pain. So, since God gave you the burden of bearing children and not me, why do you not see that this was a blessing from the Lord and not a point to beat me down over. Yes, you had struggles and pains but did I ever leave you and go anywhere except for the times I was at work or told you that I had to be at church. I helped bear your pain. By the way, no one has the right to abuse him; neither you, who went through the pain and received the tear to bring him here, nor me who only wants to make sure that he grows up with discipline and self-control, because you are behaving like you do not speak to him hard and slap him sometimes.

I am aware of my limitations and what I perceive as the correct time to do things might not be the best but I am still trying. However, if you think I am moving too slow in getting things done, instead of putting me down in a corner and stop doing anything at all for me, why not show me or help me to move faster. You shutting down and shutting me out is not helping me, it's killing the vibes in me and driving me into a hole. Do you not see this? I know you do not intend to do this but you are doing it!

There are times when one thing comes before another and sometimes even when it was not on the list in the first place. We do not plan to get sick or transferred out of a department but it happens and when it does all we can do is deal with it. What comes before what in your book or is everything just bunched together? Well, if that is so, I still have a bit to get used to, as I am still trying to work on my flexibility and spontaneity. Doing things without thinking long about it or properly planning is a bit hard for me, as to me it takes away the stability I know. When you grow up, most times think about where your next meal is coming from, you are accustomed to being stingy or consistently worried at what price a mistake could come at. You can think foreign, hotel and all the other things you can think about without worry but it is not the same for me. I have been a worrier all my life and I will not let the fact that I had a bitter past place me in a careless position now or think because I did not have it when I was young I have all rights to have it now and so I go at all cost – borrow and trust – to get it. I want you and our son to have the world but if we are going to go into debt to get it, forget it.

Yes, yes, yes, you have not or never asked me for anything but listening to you lamenting now gives me no other feeling than that you have some unexpressed need that you are in a haste to fill. However, you have never been cast out on the street two times in your life because of a lack of planning but I have and it is not easy to forget either times, especially when you are a child and seeing this happening to your mother. It is hard to get a wounded person to move than it is to get a person who had never gone through that level of pain. Also, it is easier to use positive reinforcement when trying to get persons to do something than it is to use negative reinforcement. Some persons especially the ones who originally had low self-esteem, like me, need praise; not a stick over the head. I respect you and love you but I now feel like I am throwing water into a bottomless pit. I am hurting too much now and I do not want to hurt anymore. **You are the love of my life and one of the most delicate persons in the world to me. I value you a whole lot but do you know that?** There has not been one day that has passed by that I do not think, 'How can I really make her know this?' but based on where you are at now, can I make you know this at all? I find it hard that you are not able to see that all I am trying to do is love you.

Also, if you think that the world is against you, it probably is but I am not one of them. I have always been in your corner, even in those times when you have heard that I said things that give person a wrong impression of you. I must admit that I have always tried to use our relationship to teach others about some of the things that can go wrong in a relationship, because I have no better example to use than us. You view me doing so as bad, because you are a very private person but I have never divulged any information that placed you in a bad light. So, when you hear bad things about you, it is not because I did or said anything but you must remember that people will be people and they will talk. They will draw inferences from how they see you acting and they will make judgment based on how they think a Christian should act and they will talk, especially when they do not see you around or when they see you around; you look so crass and detached. We cannot help it but in most individual's mind, Christian do not look like that they support their partner, which many thinks you do not do. So, please do not think that I am saying anything about you to people.

97

I have even stopped mentioning your name from the pulpit all together or to anyone, as you have instructed me to do. Hence, when persons ask for you, I just tell them, you are at work or you have to go to school, whether you are there or not.

I do not know what you are up to and you have made it clear that it is not my concern and so it is not my prerogative to answer any question about how you are doing to anyone. A matter of fact, you said to me once that if you were cheating I would not know as I am never there but I am doing my part to stay faithful. I have no reason to distrust you. I have all confidence that when you leave for work, it is work you are gone to and I would like you to feel the same about me. So, why should I worry?

I am not sure now though if you are allowing the devil to open doors into our relationship by shutting me out. There is an old saying that says, 'If the rooster is not crowing in the hen house, he is crowing in the barn.' I know I am not doing anything in the barn <u>but you have stopped doing anything for me</u>. Doing this means that you are doing it for someone else or would like to do it for someone else.

You are going out without me or you make plans to go out without me and you think that I should not care; as you are your own big woman. You're my wife for heaven sake! Yes, you're your own big woman and I am not giving you anything, as I am boring according to you but is this how a wife acts. However, I hope that God will not suffer because of me and by this I mean, you have to be rejecting Him in order to be doing what you are doing, for none of this is according to His words.

I am boring but I still think we can be godly and enjoy life. I am not more saved than you but I know that when we open up ourselves to the devil he takes advantage of us. Am I jealous? Yes, I am! **Which of my friends can call my house, send me text or have me on phone or the computer talking to them about school work or anything else for that matter until the wee hours of the morning?**

Up to this point, I have not said anything about these behaviours and the telephone conversation I overheard the other day, because I trust you but when you afford all these benefits to others and not me; something is wrong. You never know where I am or what I am doing but you know who else is playing ball all the time. Or, **you never have credit to call me or to send me a text but yet you** shut me off from calling you when I do. You always have an 'I've to call you back' minutes to use up on someone else. What am I supposed to do?

If we break up or end in a divorce, it is not because I closed you out or think that you are less of a Christian than I am or that you do not have a ministry but both of us were tested and instead of pulling to me; you pulled away from me. Do those persons who remains married for years always loved each other or was there something greater than love that held them together? You said you do not love me and neither respects me, so how do you expect me to act? **Would you not try to avoid someone who told you that they do not love, respects you and who keeps telling you when you try to talk to them that they bore you?**

I am not talking to you now because I do not want to bore you anymore and frankly, I am tired of the hostility or feeling like I am talking to a brick wall. I have not closed the door of communication to you but you have done so to me. I have not stopped seeking for simple ways to say or let you know how I feel or what I am thinking but what does this means to you? Nothing! I am no longer singing songs so that you can hear or talking to you by talking to myself. **I am finished and from here on out, I will either be in my car or ..... You fill in the blank.** You want to live with me or without me the choice is yours. I said all of the vows and I meant all of it and I am not backing down until you do.'

Chapter 5
The Letter

'On explanation is an explanation but it is what was meant or hides that is the answer'

Sleeping in the car

Irreconcilable difference, in our case can refer to our ideals not being matched and the fact that there is lost love in the relationship which is difficult to recapture or rekindle. Even as Christians, we are no less human and can be affected too by divorce, just like everyone else. If there was love, hell or high waters could come and we would still make it work. There was none there in the first place.

'I am tired of going down this road in explaining to you. I was angry with you for many things that you did and said and I could not understand how you could and why you did or did not do certain things; having said you loved me and yes for a time I was angry. But I explained to you that that was no longer the case. I do not relate to you now and I explained the reason and it is that there was no longer any love lost where I was concerned.

When there is little or no love then one's behaviour and attitude and everything changes. I told you this, more than once. Why do you keep thinking and saying that I am blaming you or that I am angry with you? Why can't you understand that I am having a problem 'feeling' love? And so, it is better to avoid the whole heap of talking and discussions as many times we just end up with further misunderstanding. We just don't seem to be able to see eye to eye anymore. There is always a misunderstanding or misinterpretation between us! Apparently you don't or won't understand what I am going through and said I am not going down that road with you again I am tired of explaining.

Here again, you go off blaming yourself and comparing with others. You just do not get it that it has passed the stage of your doing stuff, it has to do with how I am now feeling. Even if you did the world of good or change, until something changes within me, I cannot force what I do not feel. Please try to understand and stop blaming yourself! I told you some time ago that I won't allow you to make me feel guilty again. So what you do with your life from now on is up to you.

I guess we both have to try harder to not allow what is happening between us to affect our child, for we are both responsible for his upbringing and should bear in mind always that our actions and words can affect his future. I know I need to take responsibility here and I expect that you feel the same way also.

Yes, my son is a blessing from God. He is everything to me but he also needs a father to play with him and one who will take him out. You don't make time for him. I shoulder, most if not all and on many occasions when you are there, what you do; you go and read or watch television. If I don't take our son out and let him enjoy himself, he won't; because, as you say, you never have enough money to enjoy yourself. Your priority is not us as you say, because your action speaks louder than words. You need to practice what you preach.

Sometimes you behave like our son is a big boy and you take out your frustration on him and it hurts. As I said I will grow my child with or without you. You want me to talk, I will, you don't do anything for him. When I think of what you can do and how you don't, because according to you, you don't have any money. Let me stop.

One of the greatest disappointments for me is that I am not able at the moment to return the sentiments you have expressed that I have highlighted. I really wish you could understand that I did not set out to deliberately turn from you and as a result caused you hurt. I am just not feeling the way you are feeling right now. I have been an outcast just like you and my life was also a mess, so don't behave like you are the only one who had gone through hell. Please stop dwelling in the past and move on. You said you have a low self-esteem and you want praise and not a stick over your head. You are a big man. How long are you going to dwell in self-pity? I can't praise you every day, be a man.

Understand one thing, even though I may not be at the place I ought to be in God, I am still aware of what is right and wrong and it is still my desire to be true to God and not man. Let him be my judge of what I am doing or not doing!

With regard to me not doing anything for you – please remember that I assist with the financials in the house. I also am responsible for helping with Jah-le-el and keeping the house clean as well as prepare food, which for some time now you have not been eating even though it is prepared and left available on the *stove, for whatever time you may wish to eat. You have taken the decision to do the washing of the clothes even though I have taken out my clothes and my son's and put them to soak; you go ahead and wash them. I am quite prepared to do my part of the washing. You do not need to wash for me. The arrangement has always been that you assist with your washing and ironing. Is it really unfair therefore to say I have stopped doing anything for you? I have already told you how I feel, so if it is sex you are talking, I will not go there, so you can hold that against me.*

You and I are not the same person and therefore you should not use your action or reactions to how your friends may or may not treat you to compare with how I allow my friends to speak or treat me. Your reaction and what you do is really your decision. I do not try to dictate to you how you should treat your friends so please don't tell me how to run my life.

Although you may think it strange or untrue, there are times when I DO NOT HAVE ANY CREDIT to make a call and when you send me texts and I do not respond sometimes it is because I do NOT indeed have any credit to call you back. I do not shut you off from calling me! Have you one day put credit on my phone, no, so don't tell me who I call or text.

What you do is up to you and what I do is up to me and God.

I respond to this statement because this particular mention of 'boring' happened once when we had a blow up and I used those words. I don't recall ever using those words to you ever again. A lot was said in that blow up as is usually said when persons are arguing and are angry. I have not complained about you not speaking with me because as I have said to you before, where I am concerned things have turned out the way they are and I am simply tired of all the problems and I feel that keeping things the way they are is better for the both of us. I don't love you as a husband and I said, I have lost respect for you and it is true and at this time I can't change how I feel about you. What will be, will be!

Whatever decision you take regarding the future will be up to you, as I have already apologised for having gone into a relationship with you and realise that I am unable to give back what is expected of me. I told you that I wanted to move out to make things easier for you. Now you are saying you will be living/sleeping in your car or… what and I am to fill in the blank!!!!, I can't fill in the blank. You don't need to sleep/live in your car, as it would be better for me to find somewhere to sleep/live, so you will have some measure of peace and I will not be further blamed for the unhappiness you are experiencing. I cannot force love, it has to come naturally and I have tried, although you may not believe me but I have tried. I am sorry.

Thank God, you are able to say the vows and keep the vows, I am sure you will continue to pray for me who am a sinner.

Chapter 6
The End

'It is never over until the fat lady sings.' Well, someone is song.

As you read the letters above, who would you say was at fault? Well, since I wrote one of the letters, I will take the blame. As I reflect though, I realise that I was not one of the smartest men in the World based on how I handled the past. I allowed work, church, school and most of all the lack of money to get in the way. I allowed these things to take priority over my wife. In retrospect, I could have at least seen things through her eyes. Perhaps if I had done so, we would still be together today. Then again, would this change anything? I still do not see my flaws as the root cause of the problem why we are not together. Hence, perhaps is perhaps. As she said, it was not about me. Therefore, whatever I did, I would still have had a problem.

Problems however do not just drop from the sky; they are always the result of something. Either something we ignored, something we did in haste or something we did without careful planning or diligent execution. In my case, I did too much of one thing and too little of another. I guess I had feared losing my wife so bad I could not decide whether I was a follower, a leader or a partner in the marriage. In my eyes she was the ultimate catch, I was never going to get anyone better than her. I knew her, 'I have been on my own for most of my life, so I can take care of myself' independent personality. I felt that if I could just make her happy I could she could see that she will never have to be on her own again, a man, me, actually love her.

Looking at it now, I realise I was not doing it because she was the best woman out there; I was doing it to cover up my own personal insecurities. I doubted myself. I had never really been in a stable relationship before. I had never been married before. I wanted to protect what I had; losing her was to lose everything. How would I recover? So, if I felt that arguing over sex, food, washing of clothes, ironing, purchasing grocery, taking care of a child, purchasing a car or house or you name it, would make me lose what I had, I would rather not. I could not see how by not arguing over it, it could be viewed, as they are unimportant or worse, I am a 'Weak man'. However, when we do not deal with things right away, we usually stray from the issue at hand and when we stray, we rehash too many old and buried things. Bones stay buried for a reason. In the end, by not saying anything, I lost her. In the process over, I learnt that arguing over some things reinforces the strength of a relationship.

OK I am willing to take the blame but obviously in the process of trying to fix problems and working towards a better life for us, she lost respect for me. Yes, I said I was weak before but how comes; what did I do to deserve that? Did I belittle her in anyway? Was it because I fail to hear what she had to say? Did I disregard her feeling or act emotionally detached? Was I not strong enough or was she not able to count on me? I supported her dreams and so she could not say I rob her of her motivation. I willing took over our house and the care of our son in order that she could go to classes and I did it without complaint. In addition, outside of the one time mentioned earlier, I never showed jealousy or worse cheated on her in anyway. Yes, I was always busy but I never tried to be busy so that I could stay away from home, leaving her with the household chores. In fact, I was never bossy in anyway. As a man, I never even had friends who I went and hang out with, it was always, work, church, school; when there was school and 'I am going home to my family'. In all of these questions and to the best of my knowledge, I never burden her with my work pressures. Besides, she was not interested, 'Here take your child, I had him all evening.' Perhaps my only weakness then was being too simple and not moving at her pace or level. I let her live easy and tried not to pressure her just because I never wanted to lose her.

I guess what we do not want to lose we must be prepared to lose. I lost her.

Also, if no love was ever there, how can we ever recapture what was not there? Love was there. She told me that I meant so much to her. Was she putting on a show for her friends when she told me that? OK, OK, since no love was there, certainly, we could have respected each other to the point where we begin to love each other. That was a good place to start was it not. Even after I had read her response to my letter, I was willing to wait. I was OK with the knowledge that she did not love me and I was willing to stay true to our vow until love came. Knowing what love is, I felt it would have come. All we had to do was stick it out. Certainly, I know that when that feeling of respect goes, even the figment of love, goes as well, for it was not real in the first place. Yet, I was willing to be patient and live through the process. However, instead of showing me that she was trying to change or that she wanted the relationship to work, she read my patience as annoying and became aggressive. What did she want me to do after telling me she did not love me, walk away?

Reminiscing, I think I was only an option in her book, as I was never 'thee option.' She told me, 'There was nothing you could do to change anything,' and she was right for I started jumping through hoops. If the wanted a car, I bought it. If she wanted to go overseas or on a vacation, I facilitate it. Whatever she wanted I tried to let her have. Yet, she was literally thinking about her other options. In doing so, she reverted to thinking of her definite option and she made a choice. I was 'left standing' alone.

Back then, I could not understand her position or how she was feeling and so, I behaved like a lovesick fool. I blamed myself for what was happing, when I had no need to do so. Now I know better. Now I have learnt that when the possible option, becomes the likely option, there must be something that caused the shift. This 'something' is most time unrecognisable from the standpoint of the individual who became the likely option. In most cases, they are so glad to become an option that they do not recognise that they are going into something that might not work. They never ask why the change of heart. 'You never wanted me before, why now?' They just accept the change and enter into a relationship made possible by someone's last chance or convenience.

If I want someone to change or for them to see things through my eyes and they have started to respond, I would give them enough time to complete the process. No matter how long it takes. As long as they have started to come around or begin to see eye to eye with me, I know that they have started to value me and my opinion. However, in a case like this one, one individual took too long to change and the other realised that 'Oh, I never really wanted them to change in the first place, because I never wanted them at all, full stop. I was misled. I did not know what I wanted at the time of marrying him or her. Sorry! Move on with your life and know that I did not deliberately set out to do this to you. Please understand it is not you who has a problem, it is me.'

Yeah, right!

This is a classic case of, 'You will not change, I will but my change is a reverting to my old ideals and desires. I will go back to my old self-independent nature. I was tough enough to make it this far on my own and I will make it even

106

further without you. So, no big deal, just pick up the pieces of your broken heart and move on, for I will not be coming back to you, ever!'

Marriage is not an institution for individuals who think that they can make it on their own. In fact, if you can, you should remain single; for nothing kills a relationship like independence and selfish ambitions. Anytime a relationship falls apart, look and see if you do not see these two things as the underlying cause. Either, one individual felt that they can make it on their own or someone is too selfish to concede for the good of the relationship.

Note, I am not saying that marriage is for weak or needy people, for it is not. As such, it should never be used as an escape pad, a financial sanctum, a get back at you tool or a solace from desperation and depression. In this institution, an individual gain more than just on extension of the dating game, because that is how many individuals see marriage.

When an individual gets married, they should gain the freedom of knowing that they have a support system, whatever their shortcomings are. Although marriage is not a remedy for personal fears, lack, timidity or even abuse, it is supposed to be a sanctuary. In other words, marriage is supposed to bring couples together in the spirit of giving and taking. Surely, there are some fears, distress or habits that we will never get rid of, even after marriage but when we are married, we get someone who should help us clam and lessen them.

In this regard, marriage is about nurturing each other to become what we want in our own lives. Notice, I did not say change each other but nurture each other. There is a difference and that difference has to do with blending. It has to do with how well we blend or balance the other person's qualities to match ours. This is much like baking a fruitcake. We do not make over the individual fruit we are using to make the cake; we blend them together so they complement the other. How nice the cake tastes in the end, depends on how well the fruits were blended. This includes using fruits that mix well and in their correct portion. In like manner, marriage is never about finding someone who is complete to complete us, for even the man or woman that has become one with himself, will have to learn how to become one with another and this takes time and patience, much churning and turning, if you please.

Interdependence and reciprocity build relationships, pushing and pulling for the boat to move forward in the water of life or one hand washing the other patiently for both to be clean. Let me say this again, marriage is not an institution for independent or stubborn people, individuals who wants their hands 'to be washed' first and then seek to control when the other person gets his or her hands washed. Independent people like to 'call the shots', 'You cannot tell me what to do ...' but hastily tell other, 'This is how you must do it...' and gets irate and upset if things are not done their way. Marriage is about both making the shot together. Listen to me. Although in marriage one cannot be selfless, most certainly, one cannot be selfish, for if anyone is, the marriage will fall apart.

I really do not want to be labour the point. However, marriage is one of the most fluid things that exist on the face of the Earth. It requires movement and for it to move positively. If it gets negative, it can fall apart. There has to be a spirit of TEAM and not me, as it requires persons who know when to push and pull with equal force. This involves giving each partner the time and space to grow and connect with his or her own ideals. Albeit, connecting with one's self requires doing things in such a way that is beneficial to both individuals in the team. In marriage, what we do for ourselves must ultimately make the marriage better. I cannot go to school simply for me and neither can my wife just have a spa day just for herself. There must me an aim in mind. I will become more educated and therefore earn more, so we can do a little bit more. Alternatively, when see leaves the spa, she is more relax and rejuvenated to be a better conversationalist. We should never seek to do things for ourselves that result in stressing out our partner.

Therefore, one cannot be seeking success independently of the other. Anytime this starts to happen, it will not end well because the root of self-centeredness begins to kick in. All one will be seeing of the other is how that one is holding them back from achieving success, instead of spurring them on to it. Marriage is for individuals who recognises that although there are some things they could probably do well without their partner, they can only do those things great with them, because they complete them.

Too many of us see our partners as hindrances, instead of an individual who completes us. As such, we jump on the escape pad known as 'Divorce'. Then we classify our partner as just another of the mistakes we made in life. Take it from me; 'I can get this on my own' mentality has no place in marriage. A marriage foundation stone is giving and relenting, in a team preserving way, not a self-preserving one.

Let me now go back to something my wife had said in her letter. She had said she was angry with you for many things that I did and said and that she could not understand how I could or why I did or did not do certain things; having said

I loved her and that said she was angry. I am still pondering what I did that had caused her to be angry in the first place. As I said before, I never cheated on my wife, hit her and I never purposefully set out to do her any harm. Everything thing I did had an 'Us price tag'. All the classes I attended. All the nights I was up working. Even my attendance and participation at church was for us. Being godly stabilised me. This is why I ask her to come with me even to work and school, not only so that I would not feel alone at the office or church but for us to be together.

I am not a perfect man. If I have any faults, it is this, I work too much, I worship too long and hard and I dream too much above my level. All of which only makes me an individual with a desire for greater things beyond my limitations. Hence, all the things of which my wife intimated in her letter that I did and said to her that hurt her, are things over which I had no control. I only want to be a good and decent man and this is why I involved her in everything. There is no bank account, life insurance, are health plan that I have that her name is not on. However, there was always an 'I or me' factor on her side.

For example, she gave birth to our son at a hospital that we discussed and agreed she would. Yet, she still turned around said, I saved my money and allowed her 'to almost die'. Do I have control over a hurricane? Do I have control over the hospital? How was I to know that the main maternal hospital in the country and during a hurricane, would reach full capacity with pregnant women? I had no control over any of these things, yet she did not consider my feelings. All she saw was that I saved my money and she got a tear. I know of couples, who had their doctors in the room while they were giving birth and the mother still got a tear as she gave birth. I have also known couples whose baby died during delivery, even with the child's father in the room and those couples are still together. Yet, I am reminded constantly that I was not there for the birth of our son.

Yes, I should have taken paternity leave for the birth of our son but I was ignorant and being under the leadership of a boss who was less than understanding, did not do anything to strengthen my case. Also, there were so many things happening at once. The hurricane had just passed and the port reopened very quickly and all the vessels we had at anchorage or at safe harbour elsewhere were all arriving one behind the other. What was I to do as the person in charge? How was I supposed to know that there is such a thing called postpartum preeclampsia? Neither of us was educated on the whys and

109

wherefores of having a child. I had never been a father before and she was not a mother either. Those who had children told us nothing about this. We had read books but we must have missed the part that says, 'Blood pressure of new mother could spike without warning.' I have many nieces and nephews but I was never intricately involved in their birth. So, how was I to deal with one of the things that my wife has used to steamroll me?

'You almost let me die!'

I admit that she it, she went close to death's door however, I am extremely thankful for friends who were at our house the morning after she came home from the hospital. I was getting ready for work when they said, 'Let's take her to the doctor, because she does not look too well.' This was something I was mindful to do but even then she said, 'I am fine and we will be OK. Go to work Junior. We will be fine!' She was not aware of what was happening to her and I was not either.

Yet she said, 'You almost let me die!'

Thank be to God I listen to wisdom of friend that morning.

God knows, I would be willing to die first before I let anything happened to that woman. However, if I should sum up all the evils that I have done to my wife, I would say this is the worst. All the others, if you knew the details of them or could examine them for yourself; you would see that her view of them is an exaggeration of the truth. I may have been wrong in the following statements to her but I certainly was not trying to be mean:

'I am not buying you another pair of shoes when you have over fifteen other pairs that you have not worn in a while and are there rotting away in the closet'

'Honey, I cannot have sex tonight, because I am exhausted.' Yes, I said that.

'I am sorry that I cannot take you because I have a meeting at church'

'I have to go to work but I do not want to leave you alone with the baby, come with me.' Oh God, on the one occasion she decided to come, I did not know the path I chose to drive would cause us to be stuck in floodwaters, resulting in a stranger having to take the baby through the car window as the car began to fill with water and we were not able to open the doors.

'Babes, I am not able to leave as expected, I will have to work late. The ship encountered a problem and I do not know when or how long it will take to be rectified. Either you wait for me at the office or take the bus home.'

'I have a class tomorrow morning; can it wait until I get home?'

'I will keep him after school, so that you can go and get your hair done but I cannot keep him today.'

I know from reading the statements above, it might appear as though I always had something more important than her needs but were these unjust request or statements? Alternatively, it might come across as though I was always justifying myself or putting my priorities above hers. However, in none of the circumstances from which these statements derived, was I trying to be selfish or wicked. In meant instances, I was only putting forth the condition under which I would be able to do the thing requested. I was never saying, I will not nor I would never purchase, stay with our child or allow her to do something for herself, I was only saying, 'allow me to do this and I would do whatever is asked or needed' You are the judge, was that so difficult or unfair to ask?

We have this tendency to pressure each other from our own perspective but always remember, we all do not view things from the same viewpoint all the time. In my defence, I was just trying to deal with things in the best way I knew how.

This is why understanding in marriage is such a vital part and by understanding, I mean, having an honest knowledge of our partner. If we know our partner's character, when they act out of it, we know and can make informed a judgement. Instead of taking offence, we can take a caring and understanding position and ask, 'Love, Hun, are you OK? You are taking a position that you have never taken and acting in a matter that is crude, I everything OK with you'. We all face pressures and on any given that something simple can cause our valves to blow. So, it should never be first about us. A loving partner is never attacking us. Something is attacking them and because they cannot handle it effectively and we with our, sometimes selfish ways, are not helping the deeper underlining issue forces them to spill over on them. I can say this was what was happening to me. My wife had never taken the time to ask me, 'Junior, what is happening in your life and how is it affecting you mentally?' It was always about her and our son, never about me.

In life issues arise and we all deal with them based on the information and skill we possess, at the time. I was no different. I handled them within the constraint that my wife knew I had our best interest at heart, not because I was trying to spite her. All I was asking for in all of these instances was an understanding heart and a flexible spirit. Surely, if I knew then what I know now, I would find a way to make things work out right. One way or another I would definitely purchase the extra pair of shoes or skipped the class. Then again, who knows what other crosses would have come up for there was a reason for not purchasing the shoes and most definitely for attending class. Next time, I will simply say, 'Babies, I am broke right now, I will purchase for you two pairs when I get some money,' for I was actually broke and was using the art of deflection to hide the real reason.

Hear me and hear me well. If you are broken, say you are broke. Address the issue. Do not beat around the bush. Going to class for me was my only way of learning. I should have helped her to understand that. Once I attend a class and the lecture or teacher, gives good notes and explain the topic well, it cuts down on my reading and study time, time I never had much off since I had to be working such long hours. Then again, if she was perceptive or caring enough, she would have recognised that I am attending university but hardly even seen with a book. How else did she think I was managing my studies?

Certainly, I am not trying to trivialise the seriousness of these statements or down play, what they meant to her. If I were to accept that I am a wicked person, I would have to accept that my wickedness stems from the fact that I was busy or absent, doing things I thought would better our family in the end. I never did anything with selfishness in my heart, including going to school, working or even going to church but with an end in mind, our end.

Besides, there was never a time I did not seek to include her or have her input in what I was doing. I explained myself and had discussions with her every step of the way. Yes, I believe that success is never the result of seeds planted yesterday but the ones planted years before but I was not busy planting seeds by myself. I always asked, 'Do you think we should do this?' From the making of the decision to the accepting of the position of being a Vessel's Agent, to the starting of university there were many discussions between us. She knew what was involved. She knew that we had to sacrifice and endure some level of discomfort to get what we wanted. I never went out and said to myself, 'You know self; I would want to have some sleepless nights. I would like to miss my son's birth and I also would love to have my wife waiting on me at an hotel or at work for days and hours. So, let hurricane come, baby get sick, car break down and let me lose sixty percent of my income.' She nor I many not have known how much and how long the sacrifice would have lasted for but she knew that it would not have been forever. All of us know that blood and sweat normally comes before joy and peace. Hence, what was the problem, why was I made to feel I did nothing right?

To me, I was busy trying to deal with the normal course of life that we had discussed. I was busy trying to lay a foundation on which I was hoping we would reap the rewards from, together, later but she was she could not wait. I was not moving fast enough so that she could say, 'I have been there. I live here. I owned. I wear' Hence, I was not guilty of anything other than that what is normal to man. Therefore, to brand me as 'wicked' is an unfair verdict meted out to me just because someone was building their case to justify why they walked away.

I am not saying that we planned everything down to the T. None of us with all our capabilities can do that. It does not matter how skilled we are there will always be unplanned factors and abnormalities that shows up. I can tell you without hesitation, we both did not take into consideration many of them. As all other married couples will tell, they did not do it either. However, they patiently work with each other. Something we should have done.

I know it is hard to make the right decision when not all the facts are not in our hands. However, if things go wrong after we have made that decision or during the course of a decision, it is unfair to say one person was more responsible than the other was. Accidents and unplanned events will happen, why kill each other and our marriage over it.

This is why I feel she should have been more patient with me, as I was with her. At no time did I argue with her or judge her wrongfully. She said I did but I did not; it just did not make any sense to judge her for her shortcomings. All of us have them. She came home late without excuses. She purchased things without telling me. If she is honest, she can look back and see that at all points along the way, I supported and even recommended ways of strengthening the choices she made. If she did something I did not like, I never even mentioned it. I would tell myself, 'Don't make a big deal out of it, it is not worth the argument' and move on. I did so because; I realised that she like me, was also dealing with life within the constraint of her limitations. It is only a pity she never saw me that way. I had to give reasons for all my actions and for any decision taken. It got to me; especially when I noticed that everything I did or said was either exaggerated or blown out of proportion, to justify her actions.

Perhaps it was a sign of weakness on my part but I always felt judged, convicted and condemned, for my stance as a man. So of course, I took a safe zone. I avoid the confrontations the best way I knew how, I hide in books and since she was not talking with me but always arguing over something, why not watch television or work until I knew she was gone to bed. These were wrong things to do. Now I know that they only compounded the issue but at the time, it was my only way of keeping calm or not losing my mind.

Again, I go back to something I said earlier. Do not wait until things fester and get out of hand before you try to fix it. If it is to be said, say it. Do not hide from it, it will not go away, it will only make things worse. Here I was trying to avoid confrontation and still ended up with the thing I feared the most in my marriage.

Listen to me; if you do not want it, say that you do not want it. Your partner will not like that you said it and perhaps the both of you will argue over it but they will respect you for saying. A matter of fact, when both partners say what they want or do not want, it reaffirms their individual position in the marriage: Wife, Husband. Marriage comes with roles. I know both partners can play multiply roles but the one who was created best to play it, best plays some rules. Oh how I wish more of us would clearly define our roles and then ask our partners to both ratify and stick to their ratification than having us fighting over it or forcing us to alter it every time.

Take it from me conflicts in marriage is health. I am not talking about constant bickering or arguing over every little thing. What I am talking about is heated discussion over the reason we are deviating from the plan, improve the plan or even resting the plan. Arguments in marriage then must be because we both want the same thing. This is something we should have established from the inception of the relationship. Too many marriages suffer from the 'Let us make it up as we go' syndrome. From the get-go we should know what we want and how we plan to get it.

Therefore, when my wife speaks of the things that I have done to her, she cannot say it was anything except for my busyness.

Another factor played a critical role in her calling me wicked. This I would say was my inadequate way of explaining to others why she was so scarce or why I had begun to look so depressed, as though I was not enjoying the bliss of being a married man. Clearly, it is not my fault that when an individual gets married, there are those who expect their appearance to change or for others to see their partner around them. In my case, neither my appearance nor countenance changed after marriage. Work was stressful, school was stressful, church was also stressful and to come home to a constantly cry child and silent and sometimes cursing wife was even more stressful. To make it worse, my partner took a position to leave me on my own. I went everywhere by myself. To many this was abnormal.

No matter how I tried, I could not explain why my countenance did not change or why my wife did not support me in any of the things I did. Therefore, when others asked me, if I am happy and I responded, 'Yes', some of them would question my response. Some would make statements that forced me to defend her and support my actions. 'If your wife was supportive or submissive, she would be by your side. She would not allow you to dress like how you look. If you were such a 'man of God', she would see God's calling upon your life and support you. Why are you staying back at church, what are you going to eat? Why don't you go home to your wife and child? You look tired, you need rest.'

Can you believe it? I was hiding. I could not stand being so lonely in the presence of the person I loved. When you love someone, you want him or her to talk with you, supports you in your endeavours and allows you to be the best you for them by treating you like somebody. I felt I was just an object of regret and disdain in her eyes. I was just there and in many ways, I did not want to be there. Death called out to me, 'This is a better place than suffering.' Thanks be unto God; I did not answer its call. Perhaps I was too churchy and in my bid to show how much a man of God I was, I develop a habit of praise for being a loner. Even to this day, if I go anywhere to minister I go alone.

More to the point, how was I to know that others are reading into my 'Yes.' People are people and they will read into things, whether we like it or not. They expect to see certain familiar things happening between couples and when they do not see it, it is natural for them to assume things and talk about it. I never gave them things to talk about deliberately but they found them. When they talk, I did my best to make sure that I did not give anyone the impression that something was wrong between us in anyway, yet thing was taken out of context. These out of context assumption always find a way to get to her hearing and when they did, she did not excuse them but chided me over things that I did not say or do. These became our real struggle because everything else could work in my eyes.

Even during times that I felt misunderstood and unfairly treated, I went about doing things with the knowledge that I was part of a team. I had to protect the image and reputation of my wife. I never relented from trying to be consistent at what I did, because I felt it was my duty and to show a good example through everything that happened to me.

We always have others looking on. Hence, life is about being on example.

I do not believe that marriage, promotion or even suffering should be an excuse to fall off the standard we have always upheld. I never reacted in any negative way towards her, until the frustration that she was treating me with disdain kicked in. I began to withdraw a little and sought not to go home even when my church activity ended. Even then, I went about as though nothing was wrong with me or at home. Why are you not going home? Simply became, 'I am on a fast or I just want to pray for a while.' I was really fasting and praying for our situation. However, it was hiding and not facing the bull by the horn. Yes, all that was happening wearied on me but even then, I held my ground and hoped for the best by asking a few trusted individuals to pray for us.

I did not complain that she had her own defence mechanism, which said, 'No man should be able to order me around or tell me what to do, if I don't want to. After all, my father never did anything for me. I do not know him. I have only seen him a couple of times in my life. A partial stranger took me in, as a child and showed me more kindness than my own mother and father ever did. Therefore, when I was of age, I deed poll my name to what it is. I will not give this up for any man. So, no man can tell me what to do. I do what I want to do or because I want to do it!'

When I heard her say these words, I felt as if we were doomed from the start. The first thing that came to mind was, 'God I hope I will never be treated like her father or be seen in anyway like him.'

When she blurted out this inner truth, I was not trying to be bossy; I was only insisting that she change a particular behaviour. I hated when she hangs up the telephone on me; in mid-sentence and when I call her back, she ignores my call. Her excuse what always, 'I said what I wanted already and I do not know what you would be calling me back.' I was not even 'putting down my foot.' I never like that approach. The approached or the example I saw from my adopted parents was one of respect, partnership, team and compromise. I never saw my parents lording it over each other and I never felt I should be 'Lord Junior' over my wife.

I guess I could not escape the stigma, for it was a constant feature of our courtship. In hindsight, I wondered why I thought it would not have resurfaced in our marriage. It did resurface and when it did, it showed up as, 'I never loved you.' Her old independent self-allowed her no chance to submit to anyone or anything that was outside of her desires.

I suffered for it from the get-go. Two weeks after we arrived home from our honeymoon, she misunderstood something I had said and left yelling, 'I do not know why I married you in the first place! It's over!'

Yes, she did return that same evening but only to let me know, she 'does not have to take crap from anyone.' In her eyes, she had to be her own boss. Hence, me acting like a man, who told her things that did not line up with what she wanted or acting like one whom she should submit to, was against everything she believed in. I suspect that telling her to wait and be patient, went against her idea of what was supposed to happen in marriage.

She had a timeline and I did not meet it. Hence, she enacted her termination clause,

'I do not love you. Bye!'

Who can argue with anyone who says they do not love another? We all would say to her, 'It is OK dear. It is OK to leave him.' We would tell her this, because we all know that it is love that makes us surrender our ideals to another or continue in something that challenges us to the core.

I wish she had said, 'If there was love; come hell or high water, we would still make it work.'

I have learnt that when there is a reason to do something we create the tools to get it done, even when there is none.

However or again is it justifiable to disregard your partner because there is 'No love' in the relationship? Is it OK to say, 'no love is in it', because one person said they do not love the other? I do not believe so. In her case, it would have worked because she could have made it work, not because there was no love there.

Love was there. I loved her and I still do. However, I know a one-sided love does not make any relationship work. In fact, it kills the one who loves.

In life anything we want to work, will work, because we want it to. Even when the conditions are not right, if it suits us, we make it work. Why? We value it. I realised that I was of no value to her. I must admit, if it was not for the grace of God who caused me to value myself, I would have taken the whole bottle of pills or drowned myself in the bath, as I was about to do the night God told me, 'I am sovereign!'

If there were such a spirit – lack of value – I would advise that you watch out for it in the life of your relationship, it is the spirit of exaggeration. It will cause molehills to become mountains and grasshoppers to be seen as giants. Anytime you start to hear phrases like, 'You always...', 'You never...' or 'I was the one who always...' your partner is finding gasoline to rev up the engine of showing how burdensome you have been or coming up with ways to justify their next move. Emotionally, they are beginning to leave. They have not left bodily, yet but their minds are working out the clauses and its minor details.

However, if you are the one using these types of sentences begin look out! The spirit of the team is going through the window and a bitter self-serving spirit is slowly replacing it. When such a spirit comes in, we no longer see our mistakes and we begin to see everything through our own eyes. We justify everything to our favour and we begin to forget that anything for which we can find valid pros and cons, tells us that the humanness of us is allowing its own interpretation to determine outcomes and passing judgment on our partners. When this happens, even things that are not definitive become concrete. This makes us behave as though we are greater than scriptures. For, even on those issues that scriptures are specific on, we see them as otherwise. Thus the sanctity of marriage loses its value to one or both and in the climax of it all, we lose our remembrance that how we solve problems is to have enough pros that eliminates or cancelled out the cons.

Oh, how easy it is to forget what brought us together or how easy it is to allow simple misunderstandings to drive a wedge between us. OK, let me ask. 'Did you see anything in our point and counter point that said to us we had to go separate our ways?' Again, I must have been blind but I did not see it either. What I saw was, two misunderstood human beings who needed an intervention form a wise counsellor. For, all that we said to each other in the two letters only echoed the same sentiments spoken by countless couples who are still together.

Many an unfaithful cheating man, still have their wives. Many nagging and dreadful wives still have their husbands. In addition, many abusive and unsuccessful partners are still together. These are a few of the many deviants out there but they are still together.

What made ours so hard? I do not know! I guess I could say this happens when individuals no longer share each other's spirit, as aforementioned and so it becomes easy for letters or words of this nature to pass between them. Why? Misunderstanding and confusion abound when physical things no longer attract us to each other but divide us and spiritual things no longer guide and sustain us but liberate us to march to the drum of a narcissistic world. Thus, it becomes easy to forget simple truths.

One such truth is that in every marriage, couples fall in and out of love all the time. Those who survive and remain married have the common sense to know that quitting is not the answer. That recognition that quitting is not the answer caused them to take the time to be honest with themselves and with their partner. They do not clam up or run off into some dark corner by themselves and expect their partner to understand. They say to their partner, 'Yes, I do not love you or I no longer have the same feelings I had for you as before but I know what I was getting into when I said 'Yes I will marry you' and I want this to work, love or no love.'

They took the time to change as well as gave the other individual the time they need to change as well. Isadora Duncan said it this way, 'Any woman who knows the terms and conditions of a marriage contract and still goes into it; deserve every bit of the consequence.' When we know what we are getting into and we go into it, we should never be quick to run away, when what we knew could have happened starts happening.

The problem with this is, for many of us, it is after the fact we begin to behave as though we did not have a clue what we were getting into. However, by this time, the horse has already gone through the gate and we no longer have any tolerance to deal with it or if we do, all we want to do 'is put it out of its misery'.

Another truth is that those who survive the 'love or lasting' phase of their marriage. There are many phases to endure. These couples were never too busy to fix whatever was wrong. They identified that they wanted their marriage to work and they toiled long and hard to fix it. I must admit, I was busy and my wife was busy. Perhaps this is why we ended up where we are now, separated!

Having been in a loveless situation for a lengthy period, I can now say, the process leading up to an eventual split, can be long and hard. During this time, all we are doing is holding on to straws, like a drowning man, praying, 'God do not let this happen to me' or saying to the other individual, 'Please don't do this!' but to no avail. It is frustrating. It is also a time of, 'Hun, stay with me. Come and talk with me.' Much the same as when an individual is injured and is losing consciousness and we are trying to keep them talking until the paramedic comes but in many instance, the blood runs out before they arrive and we end up holding a corpus in our hands as we cry, 'Why?'

To echo the words of Colley Cibber in The Double Gallant, prologue, 'Oh, how many torments lie in the small circle of a wedding ring' is but a simple summation whispered before we die.

Chapter 7
Resuscitation

'It is better to have loved and lost, than never to have loved at all.'

I do not know who came up with this quote but it is an expression of a painful tragedy, for to never have loved; is to miss the true joy and meaning of life but to have loved and lost is dreadful. This is such a conundrum. On both extremes lies the risk and possibility of a dismal state of being. If I never loved, I would never have enjoyed the bliss of having someone truly care for me but having loved is to run the risk of having it ripped from my heart, leaving me with a feeling of regret much greater than anything I have ever felt. So, why should we love if the pain and regret of loving is such a maleficent reversal of what we felt when we love?

Honestly speaking, some things are worth the risk. In my eyes, though, she was never a risk. She was the one who I loved. Now I know however that there is nothing more painful than having loved but not having it reciprocated. Thus, a separation from the person or object of love, whether by them never loving us or by loving us but having him or her plucked from our bosom by death or some other devious mean is like a hole from which one cannot crawl.

I wrote what you just read, when my wife left. I was searching for a reason and a meaning for getting hurt in the first place. It was not that I honestly believed that on both sides of love lies a dismal state of being. For when two individuals are really in love, birds sing, flowers bloom, the stars come out at night and even a rainy day is an opportunity to dance and prance hand in hand amidst the drops. However, I was so hurt that all I could think was 'Come on, keep it together. Don't die!'

I felt as though all that I knew was irrelevant. I wondered what I had done to deserve this. I also wondered, was she hurting as well and if she were, what would cause her to hurt? Is it her guilt that she never loved me but still strung me along and then condemned me to this lonely place or was it that she felt 'caught between a rock and a hard place'? I just could not grasp who was really at fault or how would each of us explain to any sensible person what happened.

How does one tell the truth, when they do not even know what is happening? Do they lie? Do they speak what is in their heart? Do they become venomous and bitter towards the next person? Do they hide in their secret enclave and peer at the rest of the world from behind emotionally self-constructed walls? How does one answer such questions? I can tell you one thing, one of the hardest things about a separation is how to deal with the wondering of our minds. The millions of questions that loops infinitely around in your head or just how to stop your minds from condemning the next person or ourselves. Answering these questions is generally hard for individuals but they become worse, especially, when we believe in God and see things falling apart. In our despair, it becomes easy to ask, 'Where is God in all of this? Is He not supposed to help us prevent these kinds of things, because to allow them dishonour His name?' When we ask these questions and God does not seem to show up or send help from anywhere, these further plunges us into despair.

Hence, for this and many other reasons, being a Christian in a separation is not as easy as being a non-Christian. The position of a Christian prevents us from acting the way our human nature would have us act. It also prevents our viewpoints and expectations from being the same as others. Yes, both Christians and non-Christians alike are bound by the virtues of honour, commitment and loyalty but the practicing Christian is also bound by the laws of God; not by the popular opinion or the universally accepted practice of finding someone else, when this one is not working out.

Think about it. In the heights of loneliness, we cannot go to a club, have a few drinks to drown our sorrows or have a one-night stand with the next best option that presents itself. Our codes of ethics and conduct have to be different. I know in some cases, many of us resort to our past and behave in ways that are unbecoming of Christ but this is the minority. The majority of us just hurt in silent expectation, as we try to bear the horridness of the experience and we try to do so in a way that is both pleasing to God and man.

In some instances, we cry ourselves to sleep – yes, men do it too. We are not all heartless as some women might think. We hurt too and in many instances more detrimentally than most women – We have constant headaches, stop eating or become unsociable and withdrawn. In my case, I was tired of hearing, 'Boy, you look like John Crow is roasting plantain for you!' I could not help it; I had no appetite. Not eating and staying up late most nights can, 'suck down even an elephant', much less a man who is of no muscularity.

I had insomnia because closing my eyes brought back too many memories and questions: 'Was this all a lie? Was every laugh, every hug, every passionate embrace, every discussion, every plan, every supermarket visit or shopping experience together, every trip and every meeting and sharing with friends a lie? Just how could this all be? Was there never an honest moment? Where did we go wrong? Did I really hurt her? Was I so horrible that she could not just bear with me until we pass the seven years of crosses?'

I fell into an emotional depressive state, one that bordered on hate. It was a place, I knew I could not stay, because Christians 'do not sorrow as those who have no hope' and we do not allow hatred to develop in our hearts. Yet, it was a difficult place from which to move. Truly, it is difficult to move on with our life when we truly and honestly love, because for some of us, the pain is so overwhelming that we choose death.

I know there are those who will say that this is not healthy and that all we are doing is prolonging our own pain. 'Why not let go and pursue our natural created drive?' I know they will say that this kind of behaviour of waiting around and hoping for the best does not help us to come to grips or deal with the issues at hand quickly. They feel that this type of behaviour slows the process of us picking our lives up for the good of ourselves. 'Come on man, how long are you going to grieve, don't you see that she is gone and not coming back? Get back into the grove of things again, man. You owe it to yourself. Look how many attractive women are out there!' However, to say and so is to say we never loved our partners and that as Christians, we should ignore our faith and our conviction. In obeying, what many expect us to do; we reject our standard as Christians, which should never happen.

In every case we have to ask ourselves, what is God's take on this issue? We cannot just run off and do as we please or as the World expects. I am no Bible scholar and so I do not know the specific interpretation of 1 Corinthians 7:27 – 39 but I cannot hastily ignore that it says, 'He that is joined to a wife seek not to be divorced and he that is not married seek not to be.'

Neither do I know the full details of Numbers 30:2-9, Deuteronomy 23:21, Matthew 5:31-32, 14:3, 19:3, Mark 10:2-12, Luke 16:18 and Romans 7:3. All I know is that when I jump and follow my own desires, I am in for trouble, for I have proven that my desires are not always correct. Let me put it this way, when lust is conceived in me, it brings forth sin and sin; when it is finish, it brings forth death. I really do not want to die because I am ignorant of what to do next. Some things are too important to be based on mere gut feeling or a hunch. I am trying to survive and so I will take my time to figure out what God says about the whole issue. I will wait.

Besides, losing someone, we love to either death, divorce, migration or rejection is no better. The place and space that they held in our heart will be left empty and so we grieve. However, when someone we love leaves because they no longer love us, what they leave behind is not an empty space but an empty hope, which later turns to fire that borders on bitterness, oppression and a desire to make them regret it.

Yes, we might love again and in some instances become friendly with the individual after a period but we are never the same. If we really loved them, something has to give, as true love, a decision to live for, with and through some; do not just let go. We have too much invested in it. It hurts and we have to vent. Some individuals express their pain different from others but we all seek an avenue to do so. Our human survival instinct acts to cover certain emotions and save face, because the more we allow ourselves to recall these feelings and emotions is the more we become bitter, hateful and revengeful.

We can never forget the good times. If we survived bad times in the past and built a legacy, we will not forget that we had worked together as a team. Being in this kind of survival mode, makes us appear to have forgiven the individual but deep down we bide our time. We will even appear to have moved on with our lives but if we truly loved someone, we want them back. This is why 'old fire sticks is so easy to catch', even when they have someone else in their lives.

There are different levels that we get to in love and relationships. There is the being tolerant level, the accommodating or survival level and then there is the one I call the selfless level.

At the onset of a relationship, we are usually tolerant of our partners. We do so because we want the relationship to work, as this is someone we want in our lives. At this level, we allow them, as it were, to get away with murder. This is good, because, none of us is perfect and if we do not give each other, the chance to make mistakes and find our proper footing, the relationship will not work. This mean we will have to develop the heart of endurance and patience, for our partner will do things at the beginning that will cut us across the grains. I still hear my wife, 'I do not have to grin and bear nothing.' However, for the relationship to work we will have to grin and bear it. We have to endure real fire that comes after the sweetheart period where all we see is stars.

Enduring is not easy but it is this endurance that leads us to the next level, the accommodating level. This level is the level where love covers a multitude of sin. It is at this level, we accept that we marry a 'Monster' or 'Misguided Princess' and because we love, not necessarily they love, we cover them. We literally make excuses for them. It is a level of survival, because unless we start to accept and stop trying to change our partners, we will never be at peace with them. I will quickly put this in. Many of us try to change our partners because others do not accept them that way. Hence, we argue and fight with them over behaviour we knew they had. However, because we read it somewhere or heard it said that this is not acceptable behaviour, we want it change right way. Note, I am not taking about abusive, lazy or some other outlandish practice, as they have not place in a relationship. What I am talking about is behaviour that is not detrimental to our love for the person. I knew that my wife was not an all the time going out person. I love street she does not. Therefore, when my friends invite me out and she did not come, I covered her. I did not go home to quarrel with her, 'You never go with me anywhere.' We are never in a relationship to meet other people's expectations. We are in it to meet each other's. This may come across to you like madness but when we truly love someone, we accommodate certain actions or behaviours from them. It is literally like tough love; I want you better so I am doing this.

This takes me to the next level. At the selfless lever, however this is where we live in a spirit of enrichment because we have developed a sense of value for our partner. We are no longer putting up with slackness from our partners and we are not making any excuses for them either because, we both have a deep understanding of each other and everyone else knows that 'this' is who we both are. When we are selfless, we serve; we do not wait around to for the other person to serve us. Hence, our partners see us putting out the best of ourselves for them and want to change because they value us. In life, a force change will always face a reverted occurrence but when we are selfless change come easy, as it is happening from a place of harmony and balance.

Therefore, it is necessary that we learn to tolerate or accommodate our partners for no matter how we start out been in love; we will never remain 'in love'. We will get to a stage of 'I made the biggest mistake in my life' and it is after we have learned to tolerate and accommodate our partner that we learn to love them selflessly.

Let us be clear. We all started our relationship in a phase where we like an individual a lot, to the point of even being sexually involved with them. If we are open enough and honest enough we can accept that this is really infatuation or lust. The weeks or months of sex, going out, sending flowers and giving and receiving of gifts will run out and life will call us to commitment. It is this call to commitment that will suddenly force us to question our values as well as the other person's values. It is at this time we will begin to see things that we never really saw before. However, unless we survive the changes and revelations that will come concerning the individual's personality, attitudes, habits and behaviour, we will never see them as our sexual ideal. Hence, no matter how compatible we are, we will have to learn how to survive our partner if we are going to stay together. This 'staying together' means becoming one spirit and to become one spirit we will have to wrestle with the other persons guarded heart. Thus, in enduring, we love.

I also know that some would say the type of love I am speaking of is the possessive love, a love that wants to consume the other person and if it does not get what it wants, it might even arm the other individual. They might be correct in saying that for true love does want to consume the object of love. It is not love if you are not willing to give your all to possess it. 'If you want to be perfect, go and sell all your possessions and give the money to the poor and you will have treasure in heaven. Then come, follow me,' echoed the voice of the wisest one who has ever lived, Jesus. It is not love if it does not hurt to have it. Love cost us all something.

Note, the type of possession I am talking about here is not a demon like activity or an 'I lock you up in a vault to preserve your beauty' for myself. That is obsession. What I am speaking of is a love that works so that others will see what a beauty I possess, a love that serves and works to ensure that the other shines. When someone loves like this, he or she is willing to give their all for it and their heart cannot bear the agony of knowing that someone else has it. I do not care who said, 'If you really love it, you should let it go and if it belongs to you; then it will come back to you.' This is not true.

Naturally, we are not like that. We do not share or let go our 'pretty'. We usually kill every Frodo Baggins and become Gollum on everyone else who tries to take them. After all, we are not talking about some pet here; we are talking about human beings. Individuals with their own feelings and emotions and even if we were talking about pets, if they go out and find someone who treats them equally as good as we do or even better, they never come back. They will wag their tail when they see us again but they are not overjoyed to come back home with us. Even animals know when they find something better. When we truly love, we always feel that we have found the best and nobody let go of the best to get anything else. Love says, 'I have found the one in whom my heart delights and I will work hard to keep it!'

The long and short of it all is that moving on is difficult because we have too many unanswered questions, too many people to face and too many issues and options or possibilities available to us. Uncertainty abounds and where there is uncertainty there is insecurity.

First of all, if we honestly answer the question of, 'Was something wrong with me?' or 'Was I doing something wrong?' and we found out that something was wrong with us, do we honestly make a change and try for reconciliation or do we proceed on our self-destructive way and further isolate ourselves? If we are the antagonist and the other individual was fighting to keep the relationship together but we stuck to our course and let it fall apart, what is the other person to do? Sit and wait is that fair to them? The fact that they were hoping for a change and it is not happening is frustrating enough. Notwithstanding, I know love will always wait and they would take us back no matter how disgraceful the situation had become. This is unless, we have not destroyed them to the point where they can no longer stomach the sight of us or we have taken so long to get our act together that they have moved on with their life with someone else. If we answered these questions and the answers came back negative, then we are led to ask, 'Was something wrong with them?' or 'Why did they do this to me?'

Obviously, something is wrong with them. Why else would they destroy our relationship? They could have misinterpreted what true love is. Individuals perceive and conceive love in different ways, so they could have honestly misunderstood the concept and run ahead with their initial gut feeling of 'been in love'. However, when they realise that they have done so, the only way they see is out. If they do not get out, they become like the beautiful plant covered in a glass dome used to protect it from all ills but all the dome served to do was suck the life out of it. We will have to make the choice of whether to set them free that they might live or keep them in our arms and watch them die there.

Life is all about choices and making the right one is always difficult, because we do not know the future. If we choose to hold them in our arms, can we live with or stomach the sight of a zombie, for that is what they will become. If, however, we choose to let them go, can we keep ministering or living with a broken heart? 'It was you who choose to let them go, because you do not want a dead person around. So you should not feel hurt that they have left' some might comment. I wanted her to be happy, even if that happiness is not with me but it still hurts.

If, however, we find out that it was unfaithfulness, what do we do? Try for reconciliation or leave them up to their reprobate mind? In many instances, there are multiple sides to this issue. It could be we were at fault and they have tried to communicate this to us but we did not budge and so they sought consolation in another's arms. They only fell into it, because we were too busy or we ignored their needs and desires. In which case, they still want us, if we would forgive them and mend our ways. Another case could be they are tired of us and never loved us in the first place and so the only way out is to push us out of their life, not out of their heart, for we were never there in the first place. If the latter case is so, then their unfaithfulness may only be physical.

I used to think that the only reason a partner leaves another is that they have been unfaithful sexually or have seen someone else they desire. However, now I know that an individual can be so self-oriented and self-consumed that they do not have to see anyone else to pack up and run. Having spent so much time by themselves in the past, they have become, mentally wired to be by themselves. Therefore, I conclude that having another person around them makes them feel trapped. Marriage does not take away or change certain specific trait about us. Sometimes it pressures us to long for those traits more. This level of 'I am used to being by myself or having my own things and space' can reach to the extent where they see every delay as something that strengthens the severity of the bondage. Every argument as a means to say, 'If I was by myself, this would not be happening to me' or 'If I was on my own, I would have gotten this for myself already!' In cases like this, the individual honestly and truly believes that they can make it on their own – and they just might – they see their partner as on obstacle.

Hence, the answers we get for the question of 'What is wrong with them?' can be many. Do we forgive them and seek reconciliation or do we keep them out of our lives forever? I do not have the answer to all these questions that keep popping up in my mind. For frankly, how does one let go of love? What do we replace the object of love with when it is no longer there? Do we replace it with work, service or worship? A matter of fact, can we keep on living when it is no longer there? Do we replace it with hatred, bitterness and unforgiveness? Can we live with those fruits? When we hate we do everything to assassinate and malign their character. If we cannot hurt them physically, we make sure we hurt them emotionally, economically and otherwise.

The second thing that prevents us from moving on is 'should I remain single'? 'For an unmarried man or woman, seeks to please the Lord more.' This is a topic I am not sure if I want to speak on in this book. Not just because I do not want to 'put my foot in my mouth' or close the door on my future options by locking myself into a definite position but mainly because I do not want to display my level of ignorance on the topic. I was never interested in the topic before I got married, because in my head I was saying to myself, 'When I get married, it will be forever. Until death do us part!' I guess I was ignorant in my thinking. When we are ignorant, we do not properly prepare ourselves.

Nevertheless, a good marriage is not a thing of chance. It takes commitment and work, from both individuals. Thus, what we get in marriage is somewhat, what we decided before. Now I know why my mother said to me before I got married, 'Son, love with your head as well as your heart.' During this time, our hearts do not allow us to see anything. She must have seen something I did not see. From the beginning, we have to decide what we want. Preparation precedes blessing is one of my mantras but one I apparently lost because I became love struck.

I really am not looking for anyone else just yet, although the loneliness and the constant badgering of others is getting to me. Sometimes life knocks the wind out of us and we need to recuperate. This is how I feel, breathless. I know that four years' worth of emotional, physical and spiritual obstinacy, plus two years' worth of actual separation is a long time to some persons but I want to take the time to understand what happened, without the added pressure.

Besides, who would be so foolish to run back into another relationship? Rebound relationships do not fare any better than one-night stands. In fact, the divorce rate for second marriages was 66% based on an article I read. Not only that how can I think of getting married again? This one told me that she loved me, then turned around and said that she never told me that in the first place. So, how can I trust another with the prospect of marriage? How can I rest assured that she will not do the same thing or even worst? I am scared to death!

However, some people might not share my mindset. So let us just say you are in my position and have decided that you are going to find someone else; how will you chose the next one? What will you do differently this time? Bear in mind that all women or men are not the same but we usually are. Therefore, since we do not change easily, as old dogs do not learn new tricks; our perspective and motives are generally set for life. How are we going to ensure that the same thing does not happen with our new partner? One of the main reasons second marriages fall apart is that we are the same old individuals with the same old bad habits trying to start over with someone else and expecting it to work.

Marriage works when we change. In most instances, we change to look like our partners. Have you ever noticed that couples who have been together for a while start to resemble each other or behave like each other in many ways? Therefore, unless we are willing to change, what new can we bring to the table? If we are not willing to change, we will end up finding the perfect individual in the world for us and still end up ruining that relationship. This happens because, we will project our old ideals on them and they will reject them. We chose badly, we end up badly. Simply put, if we maintain unwise thinking going in, unwise thinking will push us out.

Most times when we are making these mistakes, we behave as though we are more in love than everyone else is and we do not listen or 'tek telling'. We come across with such arrogance that others just leave us to suffer the consequences of our own 'bed of nails.' The only problem with this is that we never face the consequences alone. Often times we have had children, built houses, involved family and friends by splitting them down the middle and we end up having memories that haunts us forever.

When we have something to prove or cannot wait, we do things without sound reasoning. We act in much the same way a drunken man does, forgetting that 'When the wine is in, the wit is out.' Thus, we court disaster and stumble to the point of self-demise. When disaster is 'covered over' with a cloak of love or emotional entanglement, it is one of the hardest things to spot. In life, we generally do not see the seeds of our own demise spring roots below our flippancy. Thus, we ignore the fact that marriage is a lasting commitment and that like everything that must last, it requires the right foundation. Masterpieces

129

do not last for hundreds of years if the master painter ignores the details or no one takes care of the painting.

In the heat of the moment, we see the future as but a distant place and 'we will deal with it when it comes!' No wonder our marriages are not lasting.

We must never forget that an opportunity for the side-tracking of our destiny and purpose will always be more powerful than our ability to see reason. It will cause us to see sheep as wolves and wolves as sheep. Ultimately, in our ignorance, we do not consider the curveballs that life will throw at us and since curve balls comes, to every marriage whether we like them or not, those who got married for the show will not survive, because they will quit under pressure.

I remember saying these very words, 'We will be fine!' when I was asked, 'How will you deal with a lack of money in the future?' Oh, how naive I was. I never knew that I would work long hours consistently and so much to the point where the woman that I loved would leave me. I also did not see that the constant need to get stuff done and the lack of money to get them done was one of the chasms I would have to build a bridge to get over. At the time of the question, I was not working too hard or too long, because I had little or no responsibility in the world. I thought I would be able to deal with it.

Someone should have edified me on the fact that marriage comes with endless responsibilities and that some of these responsibilities have no consideration at all for our plans or budget. Neither of us planned for a pregnancy that occurred outside of our projected time. We wanted children and we discussed when we would be ready for them but somewhere along the road of enjoying each either's cup of love, we bent the rules and a baby came. We cannot throw them back into oblivion like a fish that does not meet the weight regulation. We have to turn our hands and heart to taking care of and supporting them.

Neither do we plan: job losses, sickness, rent increase, utility hikes, food and clothing price escalation or for the vehicle to breakdown or meet in an accident and many more. We expect them in many instances and sometimes they are the result of us not thinking wisely or varying from the plan but we just do not plan them. We cannot predict, guard or insure against them all; we just have to deal with things when they come along. The best way to deal with eventualities or anomalies is to have 'Plan, Act, Revise and Repeat' scheduled into our marriages. We plan because we do not know the future. We act because things need upkeep or fixing. The only thing that remains the same all the time is inanimate things. We revise, because people and things change for better or worse and we have to know how to deal with them. Finally, we repeat because this schedule is never a one-off procedure but a constant management tool to maintaining our relationship.

Hence, we constantly question and answering the 'what if'. Each time one of the 'what ifs' comes up, we deal with it according to our plan. The problem with this is; we do not ask what if questions during marriage. Marriage is the place where we are going to face them and act upon the general agreement and principle of, 'this is how we are going to handle all: disagreements, disappointments, distractions, disrespects, disregards, dissensions, misunderstandings and frustrations.'

If we never agree on how we will handle certain things or situation before marriage, it is always difficult to know how to deal with them without getting our personality and temperament involved afterwards. Therefore, since we cannot predict the future or every kind of issue that will come from out of nowhere, from the beginning, we should have a 'This is how we will handle issues' checklist. However, there must be space for outside help and intervention. For, when tempers flare, rationality and reasoning go out the window. Hence, the 'what if' questions must be asked and must be properly dealt with before the 'I do' is said. Individuals, who asked the 'what if...?' questions and have properly dealt with them, place themselves in a better position and are able to survive the turmoil of life when they come. 'As night follows day' and when they come they are like the experience Paul had in Acts chapter 27, where they were locked in a storm for days; after starting out on a smooth journey.

They also should have told me that we become responsible for someone else, not just for ourselves when we get married and that just like holding a baby, we cannot drop them. Whether we like it or not, our partner becomes our responsibility after the wedding day. However, they are not a baggage or extra weight we have to carry around but individuals who deserve the best out of us. We have a right to treat them with respect, honour and preference. Respect me because I would rather have your respect than your 'love'. If you respect me, you can learn to live with me and eventually you will learn to love me. Love is what we learn to do with and for each other over time. Honour me because I have your best interests at heart. Does it mean that no honour should be given to me if I am 'going nowhere fast' or if I appear not to value you? To this wisdom says, 'Lower

131

not your standards but in all points seek to elevate another above their own standards.'

So, to the best of your ability, seek to point him or her away from the error of their ways. Remember however, 'he who corrects a fool; stands in the position of been hated but reprove a wise person and he will love you for it'. Know as well that we do not waste what is holy on people who are unholy, nor do we throw our pearls to pigs! They will trample the pearls, then turn and attack us. Individuals without value often devalue others but our partners deserve honour, because we value them.

It might feel like I am not worthy of love, honour and respect a few months after the novelty of been married has worn off or because of how I might be behaving. It might also appear that some other individuals – mother in law, father in law, friend, boss, church, etc – might not recognise or acknowledge it but I am yours. It is not because I am good or the feeling of love that makes me yours. It is the covenant we made, with each other before God and man that does. Whether we used or actually said the 'for better or worst' part of the vow, we belong to each other. God, the witnesses who were there at the wedding, as well as our constitution said so. Therefore, none of us has the right to say, I will not value you because you are not as good as so and so. We all have a tendency to want what the Jones have when we look at their plate but our order was what we wanted when we made the order and should still be; regardless of what we see others with.

Stop changing your mind because you see what others have or telling me that you can afford to change your mind or that your taste has changed over time. Marriage is not about taste; it is about constant practice. When we talk this way about 'change over time' or 'growing apart,' it proves to me that we treat everything the same. We become like one of the seven things that has no satisfaction. However, marriage is not the same as anything else. It is sacred and unique union between two individuals who are serious about making it work. No matter what storms come and they will come, they say, 'We are in this together and when we bond tight, no wind can blow us apart.

The third thing that prevents us from moving on after a separation is an uncertainty of whether our partner wants us back or if we will later realise that we have made the biggest mistake of our lives and want them back. We are never certain about a separation. I do not care who said they were or is certain of it; we are never, because the present moment does not dictate certainty for the future.

132

The present moment only gives us a good glimpse into what is likely to happen in the future but it is never a certainty, unless we work purposefully to keep all conditions constant or going in the direction, we envisioned it. Conditions change and yes, people do change. I have known many drunkards who have become pastors and prostitutes who have become great wives. I have known cheaters, beaters and thieves who have become bedrocks and paragons of society. I always say, unless God says 'it is so', it is never 'so' in any area of our lives. Hence, we should never write off anyone.

I am not saying accommodate all kinds of slackness or treat every bum as though they have the possibility of changing from a frog into a prince, because wisdom dictates that we do not. Therefore, we should always seek to find out if our prospective partner has or have a 'pretentious ambition.' This is where they behave as if they are going places but are in fact going nowhere. I will also hasten to say, even if they are successful, we should still be weary. Fat lion, in a time of scarcity, should tell us that he or she is eating its neighbours or its own young. However, no evil or wicked man ever speaks a good word unless it is one meant for deceit.

Thank God, for my family, especially my mother and sister who showed me they cared. If it were not for these two women, I would have forgotten that I had a son and ended up in the sanatorium, when my wife left me. Due to their constant attention, I was able to hold it together for my son's sake. Sometimes we will not get it together until someone steps up and shows us that they will not behave like everyone else before them, before we get back to normal. Some of us would give everything just to know we have a partner who is investing in our dream. I am not saying that some of us are not obstinate liars who echo these types of sentiments, while our only objective is to deceive, conquer and move on. However, in echoing the sentiments we hope that the individual we are saying them to, will see us as genuine and know that we are not the same as others. They will see that we did not come to destroy their life but to make it better.

Many of us can only see the worth of the individual we gave up when we see the 'stench' of the one we pick up. Life is always about giving and receiving or trade-offs. Sometimes we give little and get much and vice versa. There is never an instance where there is a split down the middle. It is always an exchange. Therefore, give up a partner, increase loneliness or some other conditions or take on a partner, technically increase everything else. This is what many fail to see. They cannot see that giving up a good partner or a bad one for that matter does not mean getting a better or worst one in the final analysis. We will never escape the double-edged sword in a separation.

If we give up our partner and we cannot pay our bills, we are either going to do one of two things. We are either going to work longer hours or we find someone who will pick up the slack. Anytime we have to work harder and longer hours, something else is going to suffer and anytime we have to take someone else to pick up the slack, we are going to have to malign the other partner to do it. Well then again, in such a world as this, we accept broken individuals into our lives without asking, 'Why are you broken?' I guess we do so, because in many cases we are broken ourselves. Broken individuals are not fussy individuals. Some of us are just so glad that someone picked us or accepted us. This is why I say, 'that some of us broke up before we came together.'

We were broken in two aspects. One, we were broken as I said before and two, because we were broken, we came together with someone who was not a repairer of the breech in us. They just do not know how to handle us. Some things require specialist. Oh, let me quickly say this. Broken here, does not mean only the experience of bad things in our lives, as there are many individuals who have had a 'gold spoon' in their mouth but are just as problematic as someone who has suffered misgivings. They are selfish, spoilt, proud, cocky and not to mention arrogant. Hence, we were never one, we just came together under an institution meant to make us one, only to find out that we are oil and water, we cannot mix.

When two components cannot mix or are unsafe to mix, it is useless to try putting them together. If two creatures can only cohabit for a short time or work well together under specific conditions, it is destructive to lengthen the time or change the controlled environment in which they dwell and leave them unsupervised. It is so in the state of marriage. It does not fit well for all individuals. Some persons can only come together for a short time. However, it is not for friends with benefits. It is for individuals who play well and fair together for long hours, for it requires constant rubbing and bumping into one another. Those who come to it for only the pleasure and fun will find it a graveyard of despair.

Once more, we cannot wait until after we have gotten married to find out if our partner 'hugs the sand.' We have to look intently at how they played in the past. Many trees drop leaves and we can tell from seeing, hearing and listening if it is going to mess up our yard and destroy what we are working to build.

The problem many of us face is that someone before us have raked the leaves and so what we see is a glorious yard because the tree in it does not create a mess and we become so in love with what we see that we do not worry to ask, 'Where are the leaves. Why is this place so clean? What makes this tree so special?' We jump right in. We do this because not many of us want to deal with the past. We simply say, 'An individual's past is their past' and move on. All we see is the present, the future and its possibilities. All we know is he or she makes us feel good. We are so in love.

We misjudge their personality and ignore the character flaws that could come back to bite us in the future. We fail to see if the individual we are trying to connect with is one who is just setting us up for the three phases I call: self-expression, ravage and quite. Three stages which finds their backdrop in the spirit of uncertainty.

The first of the three stages is self-expression. Self-expression is the part of the phase where an individual sees qualities or things in us that they desire and they give us just enough to possess it. They express what we want to hear and see but they never really give their all. A part of them is reserved, for deep down on their inside they know that they will never ever be able to fully connect with us. It is a phase of manoeuvring and conniving. They know they will never be able to be satisfied with just us. Their appetite is much bigger but they are the cat and we are the mouse. They are up for the challenge and they will even fool their own self that this is what they want. Their lie will be so convincing that we are 'suckered' into it.

During the self-expression stage, impression is everything. They guard their inadequacies, over value their strengths and run wild with their optimism. If anyone asks them, 'How long do you think this will last?' 'Forever!' they will quickly respond in the heat and passion of this stage.

Oh, such an idiot I was for not asking her to prove herself instead of me proving myself. To them, we are always required to prove our worth. 'Show me and tell me how much you love,' is always their sweet song. In trying to prove ourselves, we jump through fiery hoops to please them. Owing to the guile of this stage, the angel of light we see might be an insensitive individual who wants to please him or herself. However, when this self-pleasing stage carries over into marriage, we treat the other individual as though their sole purpose in life is to please us.

Hear me roar, I am man. Yeah right!

When it appears that we have nothing more to give, not that we do not have anything further to give, because all marriages go through a low and all of us have periods of stained enthusiasm – we lose our prowess as it were – they leave us. They leave because they have a valid reason: 'He just did not...' or 'She will not...' They fail to see the devastation of a broken home. Other people's experience means little to them, because they have the answer. My situation will be different and no advice to look at other individuals who have done what they are about to do means anything to them. 'I am finished. This is a prison!' They yell as they leave. However, every place becomes a prison whenever we have no desire to be there.

Therefore, this stage is where we get the justification for the statement, 'I did not know that this is how he or she was,' which comes in after marriage. However, all of us know exactly how we are. Yes, some of us might not fully know who we are going to become but we know exactly how we are now. We cannot hide the real us from ourselves. Hence, when we pretend to be someone who is in love with another and then change our minds, this is wickedness. This is deception at its highest and devilish in its expression, if I may say so myself.

This takes me to the second stage: Ravage stage. The ravaged stage is where the pretence was believed and the bait taken; both hook, line and sinker. It is the stage where we trust that the other individual will live up to their end of the bargain and give as much as they take. In most instances, they started out doing what they said they would do but as pressure mounts, as it always does in a marriage, the true self reveals. A self that says, 'This is not what I had bargained for and if you cannot provide me with an incentive to stay, I am gone.'

It is the stage where we are most vulnerable. We are vulnerable because we really want it to work and we are willing to do anything to make sure it does. Anytime we are willing to do anything for something to work, it means we are desperate. We must work assiduously to make our marriages work but there must be a point where we draw the line and say, 'I will not degrade me for you, because I am worth more. If you want me; respect me and never ask me to do this or that again.' You trust that our partner will not leave because we stood up to them. To them, however, our desperation is like a drop of blood in water to a hungry shark. They go into a frenzy, for they thrive on it. In their recognition of our vulnerability, life becomes a 'you want me, you have to show me how much' kind of affair. They begin to require things from us that they originally never asked for. They want us to tolerate behaviours, attitudes and actions that if we were the ones doing them, they would have blown up and out long ago. They quarrel over things we do and say but when they did it or said it, there was not a problem. However, we are expected when they do something wrong to ignore it or sweep it under the carpet and leave it alone. When they are wrong, they easily forget but when we did it, all hell broke loose. In addition to that we must never mention that they behaved badly. No wonder jackass said, 'The world is not level.'

Their demands are normally fraught with the sting of a threat and once again leave us feeling as though we have no worth. Due to these demands, we have to keep fighting with ourselves each day to remain encouraged. We know our worth or if we can give more to our relationship but their constant requirements and 'if you don't …' pulls us to pieces as we work to make sure that we are not on the wrong side of the expressed desires.

This drive to keep the marriage alive causes us to overwork; to the point where we begin to make blunders. I remember the time my wife said to me, 'This one car situation is not working out for me, because you picking me up late or not coming for me at all and I have to take the bus. It is driving me up the wall!'

I also remember how I responded to it. I did so by accepting more ship duties at the office, which meant working longer hours, day and night, weekends, public holidays, any overtime I could get. For three years, I worked without taking vacation or a full day away from work. We did end up with a second car. At what price?

'I never asked you to do it!' In truth, she did not ask me.

I was the one who wanted her to be happy. Nevertheless, 'the thing I feared the most has come up on me.' I was so afraid of losing her or her leaving because she was unhappy that I became successful at ensuring that she left.

At this state, we usually take the bait because this 'Ravage Stage' is really the stage in marriage where couples generally adjust to each other's personality and preferences. This is a necessary stage in the life of every marriage. For some it may take a week, for some months, for others years. After the wedding day, each individual needs a period of adjustment to their standards and expectations in order to stay together and this remains the truth, even if they were living together before.

In actuality, before marriage, all of us hold back certain things and I do not think or believe that we purposely or consciously do it. I think that many of us do not really know ourselves and so marriage brings out who we are and forces us to accept or be honest with who we truly are. As such, marriage has an uncanny way of changing our mentality, perception and behaviour.

I wish someone gave me a better reason for why this happens; rather than, 'It is because in marriage we are more open and honest with each other!' The more I examined this conclusion though, the more I realise that it is a fact. Familiarity does breeds contempt! Nowhere else do we feel more familiar than in marriage, because there is something about marriage, which makes us feel as though we have arrived, hence we can do and say anything to each other and get away with it. We expect our partners to know and accept us just as we are and so little by little, we unmask ourselves and let down our guards.

Let us not fool ourselves; every one of us has guards and reservations before we get married. These guards and reservations kept us back from answering in a particular way or acting in a negative manner before we got married. In other words, they helped us to get the person we now have in our lives, for if they had seen the real us before they married us, they would have long 'Gone with the Wind'. Thus, we really use masks to make sure that we do not lose our prospective partner.

In taking off the mask, we believe that our partner's expression of commitment and love towards us will cause them to accept us for who we really are. When we get married, we have the feeling that 'This is my partner. Bone of my bone and flesh of my flesh' so we take off our armour and clean up our sword and hang it up and begin to be carefree. We do not recognise that these are dangerous times to do anything of this carefree nature and so we become brutally honest and blunt in expressing our feelings and emotions.

However, whenever we are honest with our partner and ourselves we are going to act in the area of our honesty. We are going to act in the direction of how we felt when we just met our partner. I guess then, when my wife told me that she never loved me and packed her things and left, she was correct. My issue with this, however is why is it that we are never completely honest with others and ourselves until we condemn them to the pit of despair?

The Ravage Stage is really the period where we seek to prove if the other person is as genuine as they claim to be. We do not purposefully set out to do it but indirectly both life's difficulties and we test them. Owing to it being a period of test, we generally make excuses for what they do, because we 'expect' them to snap out of it. We expect them to prove themselves true and genuine knights in shining armour or worthy damsels. We hope that when the test is finished, we

138

would not find someone who looks better because they wear a spell of deception but one who is perfect for us. With the discolouration and corrosion removed, we want to see the true colour shining brightly.

After all, it is only a test and test is to reveal the best of us but herein lays our mistake; they do not read it that way. They see it as us not giving to them, attacking them or not cooperating or working along with them.

Perhaps in our pre-wedding counselling sessions we were exposed to the information that told us we were going to have some disagreements at the start. Yet, we took every strange outburst and temper tantrums to be a storm that will pass, only to find out that they never do. They move from been a whispering wind to a perfect storm. Not knowing how long the adjustment period will last, we took their change in approach, response, presence and attitude towards people and things to mean a phase. We took it to mean, things will change, for we are only facing our 'seven years of bad luck.'

Now I know that phase does not last for years and the proverbial seven years of bad luck is a lie. It cannot be seven years of bad luck, if extraneous things are not happening to us and even if they are happening, it still cannot be seven years of bad luck, if we are seeing progress and even if it is how we bond together during the times of crisis, it is still progress. Crosses do not build progress. We recognise this as the make or break stage, for it is the stage where we decide whether we are going to live or leave. In my case, I decided, regardless of the struggle I am not leaving, we are going to live with our choices, even if he or she was not the right one, until death do us part. However, to them, it is the stage where they make up their mind or confirm to themselves that this 'Was the worst mistake I have ever made in my life!' and they are so convincing about it that ultimately we also believe that we have made a mistake and give up.

The final stage is the Leave Stage. This is the stage of temptation and justification. It is the stage where they have decided that they have had enough and want to leave but need a reason to do so. Simply put, it is the place of believing that everyone else got a better hand than them, so they have to go and get equal share or better than us. They honestly believe that better is out there. They have forgotten that God is not partial. He gives to everyone, him or her, according to his or her own heart's desire and although God is constant in His giving, our heart's desires keep changing. We are the ones who fail to recognise what we truly want and so we go after what is in our sight and coloured by our experiences.

If we had a good experience with something like it in the past, we are good with it now but if we had a bad experience, real or perceived, in the past, we avoid it. Thus, we fail to recognise that 'pretty today', does not mean 'pretty tomorrow'. Alternatively, having the prettiest one today, means a prettier one will come tomorrow.

In reality, this is the stage of testing loyalty and satisfaction. No of us like it but it is at this stage that we all have to find something positive about the individual we are dealing which will cause us to prefer them above, all who was, all who is and all who is to come. It is the point where we declare to ourselves I could have Tom, Dick and Harry or Mary, Sue and Jane but I chose you out of the lot and I am satisfied with you.

This stage asks the question, 'Yes, in your eyes and heart; you might think that you have made a mistake but is there any way that you can turn this mistake into something positive?' To answer this question however, if our loyalty and satisfaction have become indifferent and dissatisfaction, we do not have anything to keep us together. Therefore, our response would be, 'No!' We would have no other answer, because faithfulness, which is one of the pillars of marriage, would not have loyalty and satisfaction, which are two of the other pillars, to hold it so the union will fail.

It also asks, 'Do you know what's worth fighting for and will you fight for it at the peril of your life?' It is simple. Some things are worth fighting for and some things are not. Marriage is at the top of the list of 'things worth fighting for'. In my opinion, there are six things we fight for: 1) our marriage, 2) our relationship with God, 3) our character and reputation, 4) our kids, 5) our friends and family-who had our backs when we were down and 6) our purpose in life. Everything else is a matter of 'play by the ear' for me. These are the only things that will give real meaning to our lives and count when we die. A wreath from the office will never do.

When we are free, single and disengaged, we tend to fight for what is fun and relaxing. We go after things that 'do not hurt our heads too much', things that do not require us to think of anyone else or force us to have restrains. At that time, we are free to be who we want, when we want, where we want and how we want, which is a mind-set we tend to want to carry over into marriage. 'Who are you to be telling me this or asking me why I am doing that...?' However, although life consists of comfortable or feel good situations, not all comfortable situations are good for us. In fact, not all good situations, as sweet as they may

140

be is meant to last forever. Partying or 'lazing back' have its place but draw them out for too long and we will all see that the fruit they bear will poison our lives. Easy comes, easy goes and we will be shrivelled up and broke before we know it. The challenge is to balance the unimportant with the important. There is no more important thing than a marriage; for it forms the bedrock of every good thing pertained to a stable society.

This stage generally does not take long to occur, because all major decisions concerning what to do have been adjudicated already. In these individual's mind, they already know what they want and or going to do but they are just waiting for the right time to leave. However, it can still feel like eternity, especially to the one who has let down his or her guard to the point where their heart is dangling on their sleeve.

To us, even when we are certain they are going to leave; there is never a right for them to leave. We just do not want them to leave and them leaving has nothing to do with reputation, possession or position, we love them and this is so even when we know they do not love us. This is why we are the ones who keep begging, 'Please don't do this. We can fix it. I will change, just give me time'. 'Things will change, just bear with me!' I know this type of pleading because I was there. However, this crying and pleading is to no avail, as they have already made up their mind, they are leaving. And many, because they are not tied to us or have any investment in us or the things we own, anytime they feel like they want to cut the string, they can and will. The statement, 'Let us do everything to try and make it work' has no meaning to them. In their mind, they have tried and they are finished!

If they do not cut the string however, they remain in our lives as the puppet master, constantly reminding us of how inept we are. We in turn take it as a challenge to prove that we are not inept but as we do, frustration builds. In our frustration, we begin to act in ways that are outside of our natural character, which they in turn point to as our failure and faults or use as their justification for why they have or had to leave.

In their eyes, they have no fault. After all, they have been working at the relationship and we are the ones who are not budging. They however fail to see or refuse to acknowledge that they had long crossed over the line which divides 'I am working at it' from 'I just do not care anymore. Anything wants to happen; just happen. I did my part and I do not know what else you or anyone else expects from me. I am done. Bye!' However, one of the biggest lies we can ever tell ourselves is that we have tried, when the only thing that we have tried is to throw gasoline on an already large inferno. We did our best to make sure that our selfishness was preserved, which is what many of us call trying.

Knowing all these truths, why do we linger waiting on someone who has walked out the door? Why do we not just say, 'Bad individuals always leave when the good one is about to come in' and move on. Why do we not just say, 'There are some individuals who are just meant to bring us to a particular stage of development or acknowledgement and then leave? If we keep them around they will only kill our dreams' and move on. Honestly, we cannot and there are two reasons for this.

First and foremost, we linger because we love and would give everything to see our partners walking back through the doors into our lives. Even after it is dead, we want to make sure we did everything to prevent it from dying and we will not accept that it is dead until we hear, 'Ashes to ashes and dust to dust…' or see the last slab covering over the grave mouth. When we truly love our partner, we give them room to chase their own dreams, even when that chasing is really a chasing away from us. Many times our heart will not believe what our eyes and everyone else is seeing and so even when they leave, to us their leaving does not mean forever. We simply go into the prodigal father's mode. We sit and wait, as our heart constantly hopes for better, their return. This prodigal father's mode, as I call it, worsens the longer the break up period takes. In our heart, we feel that the break up period, took long because they too want it to work. We fail to see that the only reason it took so long is that they wanted to make sure that they feel comfortable in what they were about to do.

To an individual who did not or does not genuinely love us, self-comfort trumps love any day, for they walk away and leave love standing in the cold. However, the longer the period before the break up takes, for the individual who loves is the more commitment and resolve appears to take route in their heart and when the break up eventually takes place they will have to find somewhere or something to do with these built up emotions. If they do not find someone or something quickly, they die inside or hurt someone else. This is why it is so easy to fall into a rebound.

I can remember during that period, while my wife was driving me away with her stinging words and biting attitude, I would sit up nights, thinking of ways to win her back. The colder she became, the more my heart yearned and filled with warmth and sunshine towards her. When it appeared, she was getting colder with me and with everything, I tried, I would sit and wondered what was wrong with me and every time she told me, 'It is not about you!' The more I asked, 'What is it then?' and the more I listened to her response was the more it did not make sense to me. I remember getting so frustrated one night that I yelled at her, 'Do you think I would have gone through the embarrassing ways of how you treated me before we got married, if I did not truly love you. Before we got married, I put up with your rubbish and told you I love you. After we got married, again, I put up with your rubbish and still told you that I love you. If I did not love you, do you think I would still be around? Honestly look at how you are treating me, if you were in my position, would you stick around?'

To my outburst, her only response was, 'Do anything you want for I am going to do what I want and I do not want anyone to let me lose my sanity!'

This period for me was crazy but when it eventually ended, was when the real craziness started. I felt I was going to die. It was a blessing, however, having people around me who knew how to put up with mood swings. I become silent at times, loud at others, teary eyed in the midst of singing in church. I become disruptive in choir practice, noisy and demanding at work and aggressive in simple conversations, not to mention dealing with my sexual urges. These were the worst of all and rightly, so, because I was sexually active before I became a Christian. When I became a Christian, I built up such a wall to protect my integrity. A simple hug from the opposite sex met with hesitation; so when I finally got married I felt that I could tear down the wall; only to build it back up again. Something in me did not want to rebuild the wall and resisted. It was the first time I ever considered being unfaithful to God and to her. God only knows the long nights and lustful days.

Second, we linger around; waiting, because we do not know whom we should move on with. For those who actually loved their partner, it is a time of vacillation and mainly because we know, it is an awful thing to 'get a six for a nine'. For when we get such a swop, generally, we do not know what to with what we got. A partner who knows how to handle a situation in a particular way is always remembered when such a situation comes around. We know how our previous partner would have treated us and handled the issues faced; we just do not know how the new one will work. We just do not bargain for them.

Such is the case here. We want to ensure that we are not about to repeat the same mistake or get someone else who is worse than the last. To ensure that this does not happen, greatly depends on whom we move on with after the break up.

However, after a break up has occurred, most of us do not know if we should move on with ourselves, with someone else or stay put and wait on the other individual to return, which is one of the most difficult decisions to make.

Notwithstanding its difficulty, I know for some that it is an easy decision but for others, the root of the problem lies in the fact that they do not know who is most important to them. This happens, because, somewhere along the line, we lose perspective. We no longer have a sense of order for individuals in our lives. We treat 'all man as equal' or in my cause, I was taught to place others before myself and therefore, views a man or woman who sees him or herself more important than others as being self-centred, arrogant, proud and selfish. This type of teaching causes us to lose perspective that we should love another 'even as we love ourselves' or that we should 'do unto others as we would have them do unto us.' This 'As yourself' means measure others based on you, what you would like and how you would like to be treated. Doormats can never become dish-towels but dish-towels can become doormat. We have to choose which ones we are.

However, if eagles have to renew themselves every now and then, by hiding away and getting rid of old feathers, beating off the beak, which begins to curve or gather built up food, in order to regain a youthful vigour and perspective, so must we. We all need to be reminded of where in the line of importance each individual in our lives fall. Let us not fool ourselves; not everyone carries the same level of importance to us. There are some we will die for, others we will let die and still yet, some we would kill ourselves for and even within each category mentioned, there are still levels. We all need to have our people priorities in order, for if we do not; even men of ill repute will rule over us and like many who have earned great wealth but died in poverty so we will die and are not able to be buried because someone else owns the rights to our life's work.

This is why I say, learn to identify who is in charge, because in times of difficulty, you will know whom to hold onto and in times of war; you will know whom to kill first. 'Kill the shepherd and the sheep will scatter.' Therefore, never move until you identify such a one, for him who 'calls the shots', has the power. As such, he or she that is most important to us is the one who generally is in charge in our lives.

If, however that individual is not our own self, this is after the leadership of the Lord Jesus Christ; we are in for some serious problems, because we stand a greater chance of moving on with the wrong individual. To be honest, I did not know who the most important persons in my life were before and after the break up. I know that the Lord is eternally important and so I did not try to jump out of His hands when it got to me but when it came down to my wife and I; I just did not know who was WHAT? Perhaps this is why I was literally pining away when the rough road started. Food had no taste to me and that is why I had stopped eating, as she complained earlier. Now I know differently.

Now I know that the general rule of thumb, primarily we move on with our self; before we move on with anyone else, because we are that important. Saying that does not mean we are conniving, self-centred or bashful. It only means, we know who is number one, number two and so an. In this respect, we must always seek to become one with number one, before we seek to become one with an extension. When we are one with God and one with ourselves, Eve or Adam who comes to us, must always be an extension who came and saw 'us,' and so if they leave, there must remain an 'us' to take care of. This simple principle took me awhile to learn but I will not say I fully gasp it, for I am still grappling with it after six years.

However, if we move on with someone else before we move on with ourselves, we have done so on the grounds of a rebound and rebounds seldom last. We tend to classify a rebound as relationship that got started shortly after a break up or before what we consider as the end of the grieving period. However, a rebound is a relationship, which starts before we have assessed and corrected any shortcomings on our part. This means it does not matter how far away we are from the break up, if we have not spent the time to diligently look at ourselves, we should never get involved with anyone else. This is so because if we do not identify, learn and correct what lies beneath, we are going to repeat the same mistakes again.

This is why my advice is, rather than moving on with the wrong individual, it is always best to wait and everyone knows that a little waiting never kills anyone. We might get some teasing for it or we might have to grin and bear advice from those individuals who we have kept our break up from – some people are too inquisitive and do not know how to keep their mouth shut – but we will not die.

This wait to us, however, must not be dead-weight but a patient and purposeful one, where we decide that 'Lord, I do not know what to do but I will wait and trust you Lord.' Who said trusting God was easy.

During my time of ordeal, I did not know all of this that I have shared with you and although I struggled, I have learned much. During this time, I read so

145

many books, listened to so many counsellors that after a while I just did not want to hear from anyone else. Most of them said almost the same things. 'Give her time.' 'Minister to your wife', 'Serve her' or 'Fix it by following these steps – talk with her, find out what she wants to do or have you do and do it, spend time with her – take her out, share in what she loves doing, take the child and give her time for herself, etc, etc,' and the list went on. All of them told me, I could fix it by 'being and doing without her involvement.' Some of them even intimated that I was the problem and she will come around when I fix me. Every day I got up trying to fix me. Something was wrong with my yes but it was nothing that time and discipline would not fix.

During this time, I had changed my personality, attitude and behaviour, so many times; that I lost me. I just did not recognise myself after a while and the more I did not recognise me, the more she became indifferent and despised me. Consequently, another piece of my advice to you is this, never change who you are because someone else says you are not good enough; for if you do, you will not recognise yourself after a while. However, if there are any changes that must be made and there are always adjustments to be made, do not do it before you have done the research. Take the time to do an inward and an outward perspective review. Ask yourself questions and seek for confirmation. Look at you past and see if what you are being accused of is true. Also, ask others, as getting feedback from only one source is never the best thing to do. Get all the facts before you move. I say this because people, partner of not, lie and they often do not know the real you. They only want us to fit into a mould and come out looking like their ideal, not ours.

Nobody's ideal suites us, unless it is an ideal we were meant to be. Hence, before you change, look at what you stand to gain from losing who you are at present and if you are not about to gain anything, do not change.

In saying this, I know that taking this position might cause you to lose someone important. Certainly, you would have lost someone who meant the world to you when they leave but you must mean more than the world to yourself at all times and especially if you are going to live beyond the break up. I say this as one who returned from the brink and as one who now knows that there is something to gain from where you have been.

No, I am not encouraging anyone to become cold or callous but in a time when the bands of marriage no longer keep anyone committed to feelings that were not true from the beginning, we have to recognise that individuals will leave us holding the bag. However, when they leave, we cannot keep standing in a mourning state and pine away, we must have the courage to move on with our lives. I am not saying that this is easy, for after six years, I still do not know if I should keep a candle burning in the window, to ensure that 'the light can be spotted' from miles away. We have to answer the question of 'Is this waiting around necessary and if it is, who is it pleasing?' On the other hand, admit to ourselves that we have loved and lost and although it is not better at all, we move on.

Chapter 8
Live on After the Storm

'It's over!' Now what?

To be in a relationship is a glorious experience but those of us who look forward to it; we do not want to be in just any and any old fling. We want to have something with life. We always want to have one that is hot and steamy, filled with passion and excitement. Like cats playing with a mouse until it is dead, so are we with the 'good feelings' of a relationship, anytime it is finish, we are done. So, we define our relationships in terms of feelings and since we do so, when we are thinking of a partner, most of us strive to be in a relationship that meets those needs. Often times a feeling need instead of an accomplishment one. Can I tell you, most, if not all of us, will have that exhilarating factor at the start but what will make the difference in whether we remain in the relationship is not good feelings, it is our depth of 'tolerable' sacrifice.

Unless we do not have warped thinking such as, 'Bang every made that works for you.', 'Do not get married to the first person you sleep with. In life, you want to go through a couple of them first before you make your decision. I can assure you, when you find the right one you will know.' and my favourite, 'You are not looking for a wife. Have friends who come with benefits, for the only way to live free is never to have anything that anyone would want to lock you up for.', we want to have relationships that are full of love and intimacy. We want these types of relationships because we are relational beings – that is how God made us.

I know there are some who have no desire to be in a relationship, intimately or otherwise. I am not speaking of someone who is asexual. Then again, even such an individual want to be in a relationship with others, even though they do not want or desire to have sex with them. However, for the rest of us, as soon as we become of age, we want someone in our lives. We will only relinquish that desire, when we feel all hope is lost or when we have resigned and accepted the state that we find ourselves.

Many of us will do anything or almost anything, to have such an individual in our lives that will bring us worthy and comfort. We will move Heaven and Earth or circumvent all rules just to find such an individual. When we find them, we want to spend the rest of our lives with them. This is why we will spare no effort in letting them know, 'I want you forever.'

However, there is only one way to communicate this message of 'I want you forever' and it is through offering them a lifelong commitment by asking them, 'Will you marry me?' We ask them to marry us because marriage is the universal way of indicating to another individual that we want to spend the rest of your life with them. It signals to them that we have made a definite choice; there is no ambiguity in it. We are saying to them, 'It is me and you for here onwards,' Forever! Even the habitual liar among us knows that marriage is to be forever. Well that is until we breathe our final breath.

Everything else says, I love you, I will give to you, I support you, I want to have sex with you, I will have children with you but I do not really want to do it with you forever. I like the freedom of being able to do it with someone else as well. Marriage on the other hand, says all of this and then takes one-step further, 'You will have me doing so, forever, because all I am and all I have belong to you.' However, when persons have been living together for a while without being married, they are saying to each other in the spirit a whole lot of things. They are saying, 'I retain my right and freedom to do as I please for my individuality or identity is more important to me', 'I do not trust you so let us keep things separate', 'I respect and honour you but I am not mature enough to be in something that bonds us together spiritually. In fact, I really do not want your spirit' or 'God and proper order may say this is how it goes but we are out gods so we make our own way of doing it. It is our human right and freedom to do things how we feel comfortable. Ignore God and man; after all, we love each other.' Marriage does not speak like this, it says, 'This is the highest order of love. God created us to be one in intimacy, trust, faithfulness and many more such virtues.' Thus, nothing else says I want to be with you forever than a marriage proposal.

Asking an individual to marry us is a big step because it signals a lifelong union that is God ordained. However, even with this knowledge, sometimes

149

things go sideways. People just remain people and split, shattering the silence of something that is to last forever.

It was a text message from my wife that signalled to me that she was finished and not even God could convince her otherwise. As I read the text again it still leaves me feeling nauseous and asking, 'What did I do or did not do to deserve being expunged or classified as boring?' When I read the text then I knew it was officially over but what really made me knew she meant it was when I asked for clarification to the text and got an answer much like the one Pilot gave to the Jewish leaders at Jesus' crucifixion. 'Haven't you read what I wrote? I am done!'

I know some would say the title for this chapter is a wrong title because I have not received divorce papers but I was assurance by her that they are on their way; so, in my mind it is official. We are finish!

Many have asked, 'Why don't you get a divorce and marry someone else?' One, elderly lady said to me, 'You are a young man. You are not like me who am so old and can do without a husband. I know the church does not believe in divorce or remarry but you are young. Pastor, the ministers and the saints will understand. You cannot go on living this way. It is not right. I am really praying for you! I hope you will not allow this backward belief to stop you from finding someone else.' I must admit, some days I have these self-talk as well, yet I hold my ground and hoped for a change. However, although I have a gut feeling that it is over, because of my strong belief in commitment, I myself will not issue her a divorce request. I believe the wedding vow is sacred. Nevertheless, whenever the petition arrives for dissolving of our union, I will sign it 'daylight' and return it on the spot, because I will not allow anyone to feel imprisoned by me or say that I trapped them. After all, I did not leave her. She left me.

My wife gave clear signals that she no longer wanted to be with me. From the renting and purchasing of another home, to choosing another man to wash her car, drive it around, plant her flowers and being constantly around her. The signals are clear as crystal. She has replaced me in her life. She has shown me that she does not need me. I was a mistake she made. Sorry to say, I am just the father of another of her mistakes, 'For the worst thing I could have ever done, outside of marrying you, was to have a child with you.'

I have included the following conversation, which clearly communicated 'it is official.'

Me: 'Good afternoon, I want to talk with you, for I want to share my life and soul with you but I don't know how to do it, all that I can think about is the fear of losing you. Nothing hurts me more than to think that I will.'

Her: 'Leave me alone, please and thank you!'

Me: 'I find that difficult to do. As in doing so, I would abandon the covenant I made to you before God and discredit what I really think of you.'

Her: 'This marriage is over, so move on with your life!'

Me: 'So, God finally answered you and told you it was not Him who answered you before and so you can declare it done.'

Her: 'I called it a day and I have moved on with my life and I have asked God for forgiveness so leave me be!'

Me: 'We have had bad times and that I must admit but if that means breaking a covenant for you then what can I say but that it will take me a while to get you out of me.'

Her: 'I guess He answered you and not me!'

Me: 'The answer God gave me was, 'Remember your covenant and live like I do!' He told me, 'I love a woman, the church that does not love me but I love her nonetheless!'

Her: 'Well, I have gotten over you. I have only one regret and it is the fact that I have spoiled my life and my son's life. Good for you that He told you that!'

Me: 'Only a pity that you have gotten over me and I am sorry that marrying me meant that you spoilt your life.'

Her: 'I did not love or was in love with you, so there was nothing to do!'

Me: 'Go ahead and tell yourself that I do not believe that and I will never believe that because you told me differently and I am positive when you told me, you did not lie.'

Her: 'I never told you that I love or was in love with you!'

Me: 'If you keep listening to what the negative voices are saying to you, you will destroy what God gave to you and though I might look bad, I am a blessing to you, if you will see me in a different light.'

Her: 'Give it up and leave me alone, you are boring me now!'

Me: You are so upset with me and with life that you are unable to remember what you have said or where God want you to go. I am just the one He placed to help you but you refuse.

Her: 'You think you are a gift to me but you are not. From the day I met you, my life has been a living HELL! You cause me pain. You should have stayed with that other woman. Always blaming the devil when you are worse than the devil. The only devil in all of this is you!'

Me: Now you are hitting below the belt, 'that other woman? That is really hot.' OK, I will leave you alone. I deserve that. Hell! Do what you want; I cannot change a heart that is turned to stone.'

With that 'the fat lady sang' and the curtain came down. I was left alone pondering, 'What a wicked wretch I have been' How naïve one must be to fail to recognise that they were not loved, they were not needed or they were just a mistake someone made? She left me with a broken and resentful heart. I did not want to see, speak or hear from her at all, ever. If we did not share a son, I would never have spoken to her ever again.

Her actions left me alone with questions, a broken heart, restless days and sleepless nights, how could I forgive her for that? How will I survive? How would I answer the many questions from others as to why she had left, as if I could answer them for myself? Was she cheating? Did she get a better offer? Was I a barrier to her dreams? Was I so dreadful and wicked? Did I not give her my support, my attention? Was I not there for our son? Did I allow her to live in a secular or a demeaning place? Was I so nasty, dirty and messy? Was I inept in my sexual prowess? Did I fall short in the department of sexual pleasure and excitement? Did I cause her to feel insecure? Did I know what need she had and ignored it? Did I show her too many of my flaws?

Yes, I have been busy but I took it that she knew it was for our future. How could I have caused her pain from the day she met me until the day it was final? Did I overshadow her? Was I bossy, demanding and aggressive? Did I hit her or did I cheat on her? Did I allow some other woman to cause her to feel as though she was playing second fiddle, without knowing it?

Yes, there was someone else before her. Someone who would have given me her all but I chose her and did not look back and for what, a desire, a voice, a feeling, a word, a what? Sex! What? What caused me to choose her over all the other women I could have had at the time? Women that worshipped the ground I walked on. What, did I hurt her that much? How? When? Where did I do it? If I did, was there no forgiveness? Was it a perpetual habit I have that drove her away? What happen to simple, 'I give up my right for the sake of this thing working?'

Yes, there were those who felt that she stole me from the 'other woman' and that I was making a mistake in marrying her. So some overtly let her see and know of their disapproval. Her reaction towards their contempt was to drive me away but I held my position of loving her. I showed everyone that I loved her and wanted to spend the rest of my life with her and persons backed off.

My mother had cautioned, 'Love with your head as well as your heart!'

She asked, 'Why do you love this girl?'

I told her, 'Mom, my heart loves her. If I have a reason for loving her and she is no longer that reason or have that reason for me to love her, will I not leave when it is not there anymore? However, because my heart loves her and I do not have a reason, I will love her forever. Just understand that. I am my own big man.'

I was so certain that she loved me as well. Based on how she transformed from being one who was aggressive toward me, to one who held my hand, walked and talked with and prayed with me. In addition, when we went and spoke to our pastor, at the time and she asked us, 'Do you both love each other?' we both responded 'Yes.'

What was that? Was that not admitting that she loved me? Did she lie to the Pastor? Did she fool me? So, how could she say she never told me that she loved me? What other reason would she have given me in order for me to marry her? Yes, I loved her but that would not have been enough for me, because I was also looking for love. So what was it? How could she have sex with me, lived with me and planned life with me? Should I have asked for her expression of love in writing? What else should I have done? Why is this happening to us, to me? Was this a plan of the devil? Is this God's way of testing my faithfulness to Him? Will we ever be reconciled? How long will this last?

There were so many questions. After all this time, I do not have the answers to all these questions; only with the help of God, did my sanity remain intact. I had to release all those questions and rely on His grace and mercy to carry me through. If I had followed all the questions that came through my head during this time, I would have been out of my mind. Grace and mercy kept me, for those questions tortured me 'night after night, day in and day out', caused me to develop migraine headaches. I would spend all night twisting and turning in bed. I was so depressed. I thought that I would die. There were days when my head hurt without ceasing. There were some days as well, when my heart raced and I hyperventilated. I felt nausea. I would feel dizzy and unbalanced. My fingers twitched as though I was about to have a nervous breakdown. I felt I was about to die and all I could assure myself with is, 'Thank God that I am a Christian, so if I die I am OK with God!' Many of us are not prepared to die but I felt that I was. I was suicidal. If I did not know that killing one's self is a first-class ticket to Hell and that there would be no forgiveness with God, I would have done it. Oh, the things we consider when we feel despair.

During this time as well, I hated being around people and I hated being alone. When I was around others, it felt, as though they were always talking about relationships and being married they wanted my perspective. I did not want to tell everyone what had happen to me, so I lied and pretended that all was well. It ate me up inside. Depression was on my back like an eight-hundred-pound gorilla. Yet, I laughed and agreed to things I was not experiencing. If anything killed my self-worth, it was this. Hearing of other people's bliss, actual or otherwise, can force us to embellish ours. We know we are not experience it but who wants to feel left out? When all the conversation about sex, meals, 'Who dressed me' and how we pray together as Christians was all said and done, I was the one who had to face my conscience, my living reality.

I can remember; I spent many hours in the restroom washing away the tears. I have learned that when you are crying, it is always good to go and wash your face, as others will see the water on your face, hear the sniffles and think you are catching a cold. I hated being alone because when I was alone, I cried and felt sorry for myself. The more I did, the worse the headaches got and the more self-destructive I felt.

I asked my friend, who is a lawyer, to write a will for me. I also prepared a letter that stated where everything was, account numbers, passwords, cremation procedures should in case I died suddenly. I cut keys for my house and gave to persons; just in case I go missing, they could open my house before I started decomposing. I told persons to call me every day just to make sure I did not do anything stupid and if they do not get me, search and then hurry to my house. This was the first time in my life I felt that I had a reason to hide away from the world. However, I could not, I was too visible at church and they do not give sick leave from the office for a broken heart. Although I felt like my world crashed around me, I kept existing and breathing.

I had to purpose in my mind that while being lonely and miserable, I would not hurt myself. I would not deliberately try to do anything that would offend her or my son. In a flash of motivation one day I told myself that I will never be worse off because she left. This was when I learnt that life does not stop because bad things happen and neither does the sun stop shining because it is hailing, snowing or stormy winds are blowing. Life is going to continue and even after death, it will. We will only change from mortal to immortality and spend it in Heaven or in Hell. The sun is also always going to be there, we just have to change levels to see it on the days when stormy winds are howling and dark clouds obscure it. This was what I decide to do but the question was how?

Coming to the how conclusion for me was the biggest challenge. It was a challenge because somewhere along the line I had giving up my, 'I can make it no matter what' spirit. I gave it up hoping that we would be one. However, during the break up, I learned that we could always plan and have the best intentions in the World but life sometimes derail our plans. I concluded that 'fair winds' or not, I will make it. It decided that it was this time of mentality that caused me to survive being on my own for most of my life and so I had to regain it. I would not allow a woman, the World or a demon to cause me to forget that I am a fighter. I never give up on me.

We must have the stick-to-itiveness to maintain our course when storms blow our way. We must not allow the sulking to last forever. Yes, let the tears flow and wash your face, as many times as it will take to get it out of your system but you must move on! Besides, if hurt stays for too long, it leaves from being a natural hurt to become a self-inflicted prison. It becomes a product of our mind – a mental state – and thus it becomes a crutch and a medium to garner sympathy. Hence, hurt is no longer real, if we have not allowed ourselves to experience it, learn from it and then move on. We must never allow ourselves to become dead and adrift in waters of life. Wind or no wind we must paddle until we reach someone. This experience asked me, 'Junior, where are your oars? Too often, we leave the paddles of our principles and mental toughness because 'it all looks well.'

I know that it is hard to do but we must move on. Not moving forward means passing up many other valuable experiences. Note I never said, 'Passing up many other valuable partners.' Even though we have suffered and separated, from our present partner, they could still be the one who actually complete us, unwilling though they might be now. I do not know about you but I am not a convict. I refuse to live in a prison, especially one I built for myself because someone did not cherish me or discarded me by the wayside. I value myself too much now and so I am prepared to move on emotionally, mentally, spiritually and physically.

I know I have said much in the previous chapters but I have not really dealt with the issue of separation just yet, so let me now put my spin on it. The topic of separation or perhaps I should say the experience of separation is one of the most challenging an individual could ever encounter in their entire life. Simply because, when we love someone and that person leaves, it is worse than death. At least with death, we grieve for a while but we eventually accept that the individual is gone. If we have faith in God, we know that we will see them again in eternity and move on. However, when a partner leaves, there is no acceptance that they are gone. All that remains is a sense of betrayal and the question of 'What did I do to deserve this?'

It feels like a hole in our chest and the pain just does not go away; especially if we decide to wait for their return. The voices, reasoning and emotions are nothing short of being brutal. It sometimes leaves hysteria. Hence, in the heat of dealing with this heart wrenching experience, many have lost their minds, killed their spouse or tuned out of life. Still, some find their wings and become stars. They find an outlet and transform their hurt into something meaningful. They become great lovers of themselves and others. They change. Hence, the outcome for all might not be the same. Notwithstanding, we must seek to determine our own outcome.

I will say it again. I know that when our emotions, desires and feelings are tied around someone else, living without them is not easy. Many have chosen death over life. I almost did. Therefore, my advice in this chapter is simple; give yourself a reason to live beyond today, tomorrow and the next day after that. Give yourself a reason to live even when the memories come flooding into your mind and cloud your vision of what is wonderful about life. I know that our memories do not come to us and ask us, 'Do I have your permission to remind you of all the good times you used to have with your partner?' and then leave if we say no. They simply show up whenever they please and loop repeatedly until we draw depression from what was once precious and endearing to us.

Of course building memories is important in courtship and in marriage, as they are the foundation upon which we establish strong bonds. Thus, our ability to capture and cherish the memory of what we did together will determine how great our relationships are. Nowhere is this truer than in the holy institution of marriage, for marriage is about doing things together. Whether the things we do are permanent such as in purchasing a house or as memorable as going on a trip, captured in a photo, they give us things to talk about and look back over. What we do together proves we have a good thing going on.

We just do not marry someone that we did nothing with, before the wedding day and neither do we stay together with someone if we are not doing anything together. Therefore, all along the way we have memories to look back on which torment us during times of crisis. I sometimes can still feel her skin against mine. If only we could wipe them out of our heads. Our mind and memories are a blessing but sometimes it can become our undoing. Every time there is a trigger, they show up and so does the pain.

This is why I say to you, you need to prepare for the emotional days, these emotional days or days when you just become so sad that you sit and cry for no reason at all. Those days when you remember what you used to do together. Days, when your child asks, 'Why is it that you and mommy are not together?' or when friends and relative press you for the real reason behind the split. Of course, you will fumble when trying to answer but squeeze out an answer anyway. Try to hold back the tears and request their prayers and understanding. Some will not understand and some will be downright judgemental but live.

We also have to prepare for those days when we go home to an empty house or have to look at the empty space in the closet or on the dresser where their things used to be. Days when they turn up to collect their remaining belongings, from the house and you have to look at how the house has becoming empty without them. Also, remember to include those days when they show up at the gate, to drop off or pick up the kids. Of course, you pretend as though you do not see them but your eyes follow them until they are out of sight; each time, you relive the pain and distress of their leaving.

Now, I know why some persons remove the pictures or rearrange the furniture in their house; even relocate all together. It is just that seeing or hearing them, reminds you of too much. It hurts. It is commendable, if you can remain civil towards each other. However, regardless of personal maturity and civility, I recommend a change. This will allow you to get the junk out of your spirit. I know at first it will feel like you are trying to erase this individual out of your life but if you do not want to go home crying every night, you best do it.

Do not behave as if you are a mountain or act as if you are tough through it all. It affected me. I did not begin to feel better about myself, my life, my son, my family, my friends or my wife, until I decided to get it all out of my spirit. I changed my persona. I became someone else, someone who accepted that she was never coming back. I still harboured hope of her changing her mind and yes, it still hurts but I began to concentrate on my son's and my needs a whole lot more.

In many instances, what hurts is not even the fact that they have left; it is to see how they thrive without us. They never appear to suffer, as we do or have a bad day; meanwhile we agitate in pain daily. Whether it is genuine or not, they just look happier. It is as though their life is a testimony that says, 'You should have left that old bag a long time ago.'

When we suffer pain, sometimes we pray that the other individual will suffers greatly as well. We pray that they will shrivel up and die, if they do not change from their errant ways. However, this never seems to happen, they only get stronger and stronger. After all, why should they die or become worse off? They are human beings and are entitled to make mistakes just like everyone else. Why should they die for it? They deserve to live and flourish, even though they have hurt us.

Think about it, where would we be if God treated us the way we want Him to treat them because they hurt us? How many times have we hurt Him? In our irrationality, we can become so judgemental and exacting that only God can save us from our vileness towards others. In truth, none of us really wants to see a strand of hair on our beloved's head get hurt, because we love them deeply. Albeit that this love is clouded with a mixture of hurt, resentment, regret and confusion.

Sometimes we use the perceived notion of success we see on their part to condone how we feel about ourselves: that we were the bad egg in the first place. This we do, especially if others compliment their good looks and well-being after they have left us. Oh, how I felt bad when others say, 'Look how you look meagre and puny and look how your wife looks fat and rosy. You have to do something better for yourself!' God I hated it! Nevertheless, I nod, smile and say, 'I am still working on being fat!'

By doing so, they make it appear that the one who looked the worst, was the guilty party and since I was the one who looked washed up and beat out, I felt like I was really the mistake she said I was. However, take it from me, in this matter, who looks better is not a justification of their correctness or wrongness, as stress and anxiety can cause some individuals to look well; on the other hand, it makes others reduce to skin and bone. It turned most of my hair white. Another side to it as well is that some individuals find refuge in food and they gorge themselves when they stressed and so they will look fuller but are they healthier and more contented. Some people also play dress up and become friends with individuals they would have never spoken to before. Some go all out to show how better off they are for leaving their partner by spending everything they have saved. Yes, in some instances, they might actually end up in a situation where they are financially or economically better off but I must ask, 'At what price?' Such is the game of handling depression and who actually looks better dealing with it.

Still yet, leaving our partner may still come with a price. Remember the analogy of 'the grass is greener on the other side of the fence'; well, the person who left sometimes will have to put up with a whole heap of stuff to maintain that patch of greenery they now have. Thus, the 'jumping out of the frying pan and land in the fire' analogy is applicable, as sometimes they even have to put up with more than they had to put up with before. This massive cover up, often leaves many feeling even more alienated, dejected and alone or forcing them to develop a hatred for the partner, they left.

In some cases, as well, many of them wish they could return to their partner. However, impeded by the new load they have picked up, pride, regrets and self-condemnation or even the acceptance that they were wrong in the first place, they remain where they are. It is really a shame when we allow a phase to grow into a reason for leaving our partners and worst, when we give ourselves reasons to justify that phase. Everyone goes through phases but we often complicate it by doing something stupid; like saying, 'I tried and it did not work,' while we erect walls to prevent any possibility of atonement.

I would not be so hasty to say they do not hurt or wish that things were different. Whatever the case, we cannot sit around waiting on them or measure our life and well-being on how they appear or what they have achieved after us or even what they will do to us. We just have to move on. We have to remind ourselves that marriage is a state of being, although it is with a person; it is not a person. It is a state of continuously become one and as I said before, becoming one with one's own self. If they had remained, they would have been an extension of ourselves, our heart but since they disconnect them self and no longer sees us as an extension of them self, we move on. Hence, a person can leave but God is able to restore us to that state of being, even if it is not with that same person and only with ourselves.

We have to also prepare for and survive what other individuals will say or do to affect us. I have often heard it said that 'kids say the dandiest things' and they do but adults are equally bad. Sometimes, they say things out of honestly trying to help but while so doing however, they hurt us even more out of ignorance. Thus, in many instances in trying to cheer us up they might make us even more depressed. For example, they say, 'I love you very much and I can tell you, you are a good man or woman, any woman or man would want you, he or she doesn't deserve you.' In the heat of the time, I shouted on the inside, 'Why the Hell are you saying these things to me? I do not want all the women in the world, I just want this one!' In this time of change and exchange not many persons will understand or accept that we just want the one that rejected us.

To this end though, I advise be very careful, as out of this well intended desire to cheer us up and get us back on our feet many have fallen into extra-marital relationships even before the courts have decided and thus; blocking off every avenue that leads to reconciliation. Many did not mean to go down the road of infidelity but out of self-pity and the need for belonging, they fell prey to the, 'I would never had done you this', trap of an available arm, without first rediscovering their own self. In doing this they simply, repeat the cycle, one broken heart after another.

The pressure of what to do or not do with yourself after a spilt can range from becoming a couch potato, to a drunkard, to a prolific manipulator and still the list goes on. Therefore, unless you find something meaningful to do other than delighting in self-pity or reparative justice, you will not make it out with that same spirit you had before the break up. Or, if you do not find it, you will become resentful, untrusting and self-destructive. We do not always hurt the one we set out, we hurt ourselves. This hurt then becomes a branded mark on your heart, one that causes you not to see greater possibilities in the life that lies ahead you. It will also become disfigurement that shuts you down from ever honestly loving someone else.

One love leaving does not mean that other people and opportunities will not come into your life. There will be new hope, new dreams and new memories. That is how life is, it will either place the people and the things we need right there before we need them or it will bring them in just as we need them. So, please accept that sometimes life is a mess and that even with doing all we can, we end up stepping in things we had hoped we would never have stepped in. This is because life will have it that each of us at some point or another becomes like a cow's hind leg; we will either step in filth or have it splashed and catches us. Whichever case, we must know that we are never alone. No cow has one hind leg. Therefore, if you still have your five senses, your physical abilities and appeal, others who honestly love you and do not tell me that there is none, the God of your life loves you, even if you are broken or broke, you can still give yourself a chance to live and live well above the present circumstances.

A matter of fact, in life there is a relative truth to everything and because this is so, there is an apparent justifiable reason for every action. If I steal, I can say I was hungry. Who would kill me for been hungry and steal? On the side of a relationship, if I am being beaten and abused and I leave, who can fault me for leaving. If I need to feel good about myself or need a greater level of fulfilment in life and I am not getting it from my partner or where I am, who will take me to task about going after it. Or, if I am not in love with the individual I am with and there is a chance out there for me to find love and be loved, which god or covenant would dear keep me bound to someone I don't love, even if they love me. 'Don't I need to cater to myself as an individual or preserve my own right and happiness?' There are so many different sceneries with which to contend that life just seems to thrive on them. So then, in a world such as this where valid excuses abound, it is easy to say, 'We grew apart and I left' or tender a divorce document which states, 'Irreconcilable differences'. Certainly, I also know that truths, rights and ethics, are being trounced in the cauldron of personal freedom and rights, yet my advice to you is still 'live on!'

I want to say live on, even when they have sought in every way possible to sabotage the relationship, in order to give themselves, in their own eyes, a justifiable reason for leaving. Take it from me; no one breaks up something good. OK, let me be fair, no one breaks up a good relationship for no apparent reason or unless there is a perceived better one to gain. Sometimes the perceived better one is a subtle one but it is a reason, nonetheless. A reason that started out as a mood grew into a desire and ultimately leads to a dream been pursued vigorously. In this frame of mind, we sometimes forget that not all moods are to be acted upon or feelings expressed. However, as the saying goes, 'It takes a grain of sugar to do to a fly what a jar full of vinegar could not do.' Just give some of us a little incentive to leave during a time of crisis and even the best of us will see the crisis as something that will last forever and abandon ship. Sometimes we literally give up our 'dish of herbs eaten with peace and contentment for a large spread eaten in hardship and turmoil.' I have seen both men and women do this repeatedly that I have to ask myself, 'What has bewitched them?' Struggling but will not admit it.

I am not one sided on the issue concerning why individuals leave each other. I have seen women who have left their partner without there being one visible reason. Equally, I have seen women who are to die for left behind by men who could not honestly say she was either this or that. I have met one man who said, 'My wife was perfect!' He left me baffled, asking so, 'So why did you leave then?' I have also noticed that when this happens, it is because she has become 'fed up' with him or she was the preverbal old nag, why he broke her heart. An undercurrent had always existed but neither ever acted on it; it just stayed there and festered. After a while, it became a case of just bidding time. In some instances, hoping for the best or silently saying, 'Give me a reason for which you or I should stay with each other in this relationship. Just show me and tell me that you love me and I will fight on with you' but eventually they give in, if there is nothing forthcoming.

In the case of women though, she does not just get up and leave like that. In her heart, she decided to leave first and even after she has made up her mind to leave, she still will not leave. She waits until in her mind, the coast is clear. In this, I have found out that women are bears. They will bear long and hard. They will store it all up and how you will not that she has let go is in the staying out later, silent treatment, subtle or overt disrespect and the worst, stop being intimate on even the basic of levels.

In fact, I now know that a woman does not have to have someone else or a man on the side for her to leave, even while she is in the same house with her partner, she has already left. She left mentally and then gradually emotionally. Thus, she can leave and go live on her own for a long time but in many cases, if someone else starts to show her attention or appears to have none of the breaches which exist in her partner; he becomes her next mate. Thus, a woman can store up emotions and frustration for a long time and when she eventually releases it, it is like an avalanche, sweeping away all rationality in its path and when this happens, she will not listen to anyone – God or man – as her 'cup' is just full. 'I cannot take it anymore' becomes her vehement cry.

In many cases, when she leaves under these conditions, although she will seek to cover her partner or make it appear as though he was not responsible for the break up, someone will know that he was the culprit, for in one way or another, she will make it known. After all, no sensible woman gets up and leaves a good man; it just does not work that way. 'What is wrong with you girl?' is always the question to such a woman.

On the part of the man however, a man will never leave a woman unless he fancies his chances elsewhere or he is certain that he has nothing more to gain from her. Something definite has to entice him: work, friends, the freedom to explore, another woman, etc. The man leaving from where he is for the sake of 'peace of mind' is not an option for him. Men value stability, security and certainty, all things that gives him a sense of control or the right to feel in charge. Yes, we do love having a peace of mind but we would rather come home to a definite miserable woman and a clean house than to be alone saying, 'I have peace.' Alternatively, even if we leave and bury ourselves in our work, work will not be our only motivation. We harbour a thought of a better future elsewhere. Men do not get a 'cup full'; hence, he will not leave all when his patience is running over. A man is not a bearer but he is calculating. He does what is in his heart and do not need time to think about it. Hence, when he moves, he totally removes himself or he spends less and less time with the individual. He has no desire to be where such a one is. Unlike the woman who will leave mentally and emotionally but still remain in the same space, the man has no desire to be there; when he leaves, he is gone. Outside of the few occasions where pride or the preverbal 'for the sake of the kids' keep him there, he is gone. He is not into covering up anything unless he means to preserve something. Thus if a man cheats consistently and openly, it says he is done. Hence, the only time he puts up with anything untoward from the woman in is life is when blinded by something else.

We seldom do random when it comes on to matters of the heart. What I am saying is simply this, a man will cheat, put up with his wife cheating and all manner of rubbish from his wife, if he really loves her but he will not leave. When a man really loves, he becomes a fool. He might not know clearly how to express it but he literally becomes a doormat. He would rather kill the woman than lose her. This is why I am emphatic that he will not leave until a better option opens up itself to him, even if that option becomes his job or eyeing the new assistant at the office. One may ask, 'Is this not the same thing for a woman?' I would answer, 'No.' Again, a woman does not need an option, even when she loves him, she will still leave: 'I will not come back until you sort out yourself!' In most cases, however they never come back. A man on the other hand, will not leave unless the offer outside looks more convincing to him and that he no longer loves or desires his partner. This happens because love both constrains and restrains him. It does not do the same for the woman. She only stays because she respects him; he stays because he loves her more than he loves the other woman.

Hence, there is always a reason and both are looking for it. Not even 'I never love you' or 'I just want my personal space' carries water. Something is definitely wrong with the individual who thinks these are justifiable reasons to break their covenant. OK, let me again be fair, society might accept it but no way under the Sun does God accepts. Am I speaking for God or must the notion of God come up in our life experiences such as this? Yes! I am speaking as a physical voice on His behalf and yes, it is a necessity that a godly perspective be given on everyone one of our life's experiences. To be clear, His' word supports what I say. 'What God has joined together let no man put asunder' I know that this will raise the question, 'Just suppose it was not God who join them together in the first place, should they still stay together?' Well, as long as the two individual's union is in keeping with God's word and I am not talking the new one that is written to accommodate slackness and nastiness, which He God, did not ordain as His word, He joined them together. Mistakenly or non-mistakenly, it is what God expects that become the new order. Then again, God does not make mistakes. Hence, He expects us to honour our covenants and this is even when we think that our partner is the most incorrect person for us in World.

Another point I would like to make is that if we are not hold to a higher standard, such as that set out by the word of God, we will make every decision based on feelings, human wishes or the legislated rights decreed to us, which are mostly wrong in their outlay. In the realm of human reasoning, we always appear to sanction everything that God condemns. We always find justification under the guise of being modern and enlighten. This is why even though our stances have to do with us being human beings; it simply cannot come solely from the human level or perspective, for when it does, we are free to think of things that have eternal weight on consequences based upon human intellect. This is how we can end up saying that a partner was the wrong one for us.

In my estimation, a partner is only the wrong one for us if we did not know their past, their, present circumstances, their future hopes, their ideologies, their requirements from us and ultimately their characteristics before we said, 'I do'. However, if we found out or knew what type of individual they were and is projected to be before we said the 'I do' and we still went ahead and marry them, they are not wrong for us. We made a choice. Hence, we should find every way possible to honour our vows. I believe; I have the backing of the word of God on this point as well, which speaks indirectly to it, when it stated that 'The Lord will judge us for making vows and not honouring them.' In fact, the Bible declares that 'He that puts his hand to the plough and looks back is not fit for the Kingdom.' In which case, it is not whether the person is incorrect or not but one's willingness to surrender one's own self and honour one's commitment.

Just in case you think, I am saying it is OK for someone to say, 'I did not know that this is how he or she was before I got married to him or her. Therefore, I am safe to say; I married the wrong person. I am getting out', you are dead wrong. I am not saying that at all, for whatever the case, knowingly or unknowingly, God still expects us to live with our partner. God blessed marriage and He will give the grace and favour for it to work. He gives the grace because it takes patience to live with someone else, wicked or good and He give us favour so that we can endure and enjoy the fruit of our labour during and after our trials. Certainly, the individual was wicked in deceiving us but their deception did not happen overnight, it happened as we focused on the smokescreen of what we could have with them. For those who find themselves with someone who covered and disguised their flaws in order to trick them into marrying them, there is redress. However, this redress does not give anyone an 'Advance to Boardwalk and collect two hundred dollars as you pass go' ticket out of marriage. No, it does not. Why not, you may ask. Well, it still comes down to us not listening or taking the time to really investigate and learn about the individual before we got married to them.

Hence, we are not without fault, as we would like to appear. The individual was wicked yes, for making us believe that they were genuine but we are the ones who only listen to the lies they told us and ignored the advice given to us by others. We did not take the time to learn about them through the eyes of those who have had a past encounter or know their history.

Trust me when I say, never marry based on the present. Look and the past, for most of the issues that will arise in your marriage will not come from the present. Bags or skeletons hiding have a way of showing up during marriage. 'No man has ever spoken to me like this before and I have no reason to let you.' That was a voice based on her past that spoke through my wife, however, she had never married a man before who had the need to stand up to her and tell her change a behaviour that she had acquired in the past. Also, never marry a based on the future. People change and when they do, everything changes. Besides, the future is not a prediction it is the result of careful planning. If God plans it and set things into place, based on His foreknowledge of the human heart, to ensure that what He plans come through, how much more we. Therefore, man someone based on trust and faith in their character. We learn people's character by spending quality time with them learning of their past, sharing the present and whole heartedly working our future. Note that I said our future, not theirs for when we get married it is no longer my future or their future, it is our future. Again, selfishness has no place in marriage.

Look at it from the perspective of a company, if a company wants to remain viable and profitable it must seek and employ creative, dedicated and forward moving individuals. How do they do this? They ask for references before hiring anyone. In essence, they looked at past information, our school report, even though this is a poor means of judging on individual. They look at our past employment and termination history and how creative and fulfilling we have used our time and brains in the past. Not to mention; checking our online footprint. Marriage is like this, it is building the most delicate company ever, so why should we not seek to get background information or at least listen to those who have had best or worst experiences with the one we want to commit ourselves to for life? Now I know I should have listened to the ones who said and ask, 'Do you really know what you are getting into?'

Besides, no one bound us and dragged us into the marriage. Often times we fight tooth and nail to get into it. In doing so, what we fail to remember is that none of us changes overnight unless it happened via a trauma and by a trauma I mean, a violent or accidental occurrences. Therefore, for any of us to just get up and take a mental, emotional or psychological position meant that either we suffered a chemical imbalance, because of something or we thought about it long and hard and all that is now visible is something hidden in the heart long ago. We gave it time to fester before we did what we did. However, there is always a sign, a dissenting voice or a gut feeling lingering somewhere inside of us that says a storm is coming. Thus, we can never really say we did not know. What happened is that we closed our ears, eyes, brain, as well as our capacity to think logically about the information presented to us concerning the individual. In that regards, we substitute fact or plain truth for feelings and desires. Hence, it was easy for them to beguile us.

If we had looked, listened and assessed, we would have seen the flaws and then it would be up to us to decide whether we were up for the challenge of living with this individual. Moreover, if we had looked and listened and assessed and we still did not see the deception but God was our first and primary advisor we can rest assured that we will come out of it better off. We must also take comfort in the knowledge that He allowed us to go headlong into to the belly of the best. Hence, He will sustain us in it. We must always know that His will for us is that we learn lessons from our life's encounters, lesson we can use to help others in their time of crisis. Consequently, He does not have to explain Himself. That is what makes him God. However, we must know that what God does, He does well and what the enemy meant for evil, He has some great ways of turning them around for our good. Therefore, even if the devil placed the evillest of man or woman in our lives God can turn them or the circumstances around to become the greatest of blessings to us.

Note however, I am not excusing the pretender or offender, for the individual who knows how he or she is and still went ahead and married another without revealing their true self; is and was a sorrowful lot. Although I could sympathise with their varying reasons for doing so, they are without excuse and deserve anything they get. This includes their partner leaving them the 'Hell alone' or condemned to, 'Have sex with their own hands for ever' as my wife told me in a more derogatory tone. However, when such an individual's objective is complete – for in most instances, there was on underling objective for the deception – or harsh treatment that occurred in the relationship, they are not free to divorce. He or she will have to honour their commitment, for to do otherwise is to commit sin.

This is how the Bible puts it, 'If a man marries a woman and he no longer has pleasure in her, he made a mistake but he is not permitted to "put her away". If he does this, when her family protested and the woman is found to be honourable, he is to be beaten and he has to pay the price for scandalising the woman and she must still be treated as a wife.' This is why many go around discrediting the other individual when they are the ones at fault. They know that no one is really going to investigate or hold them responsible for their action, so they slander the other person and get away with it. In the context of the Bible, she must be paid double for her trouble. Paying her double for her troubles means that he has to abandon his selfish desires and become twice what she wants him to be and he cannot complain, even if she is a controlling and demanding freak. This goes for the woman as well.

This is why I maintain that the hard questions demand an answer before the wedding day, for after the wedding day, it makes no sense asking the questions again or making excuses 'they were not thought about'. If you need to ask, 'Do you love me? Will you surrender to be? How will you handle it if I get sick, lose my job or a limb? How many times per week do you want us to have sex and in what position oral or there wise? How many kids do you want? Where do you want to live or type of vehicle to drive? Or, 'Do you like my friends and how I spend my leisure time?' ask. As, asked or not asked, we have to live with the consequence of our past decision. I know many counsellors, psychologist and behavioural therapist will tell us otherwise but God said He would rather us keep silent than to make a covenant that we cannot keep.

Whichever side of the fence you fall, he or she has left and is now enjoying their new found lease on life or not and do not know how much you are hurting but that is OK, move on still. One of the most sorrowful positions we can ever take after a split is to hinge our life upon what the next individual does or does not do. We have to reroute our thinking, effort and energy into seeing where we want to go and go there, whether we feel good or bad. We cannot force anyone to love us, all we can do is genuinely love and hope that he or she will love us in return. If they do; God be praised and life is beautiful but if they do not, it is not ours but their lost.

If there was never a time when we need to see our own value and know our own worth it should be right here. One of the worst things that happen to us during a break up is a loss of our own self-worth. Either because the individual was the one who raised our awareness of our own value or what they meant or did for us resulted in our value. Whatever it was, they are gone and we lost it but it is not something we lose forever. It is still there as core values are never lost in a storm. If you can swim before, you can swim in a storm. The concern will only be for how long and how far and when God is in charge it will never be forever. Hence, it may be buried under a whole heap of hurt and pain yes but it is still there and need to be recaptured or now that we know that it exists, we need to discover it for ourselves.

Hear me and hear me well. One single individual should never determine our value or influence our drive to invest in our own selves. At all points, we must be curious, innovative, resilient and adaptive for our own self. The past was what you and others made, the present is the pain and burden of what you already made but the future is something brand new, untouched but yet influenced, always, by the past and the decision we make today. Therefore, if there is any time in our lives we cannot depend on external influence to help us regain or gain something internal it is at this time. We will have to dig deep and apply ourselves. Find our latent abilities and get to work on our charm and get out of our depressed zone and explore the World.

It might be hard to at first but find a way to live anyway. This I did by developing a depression cheat list. I called it 'The reason I did not die when she left', the original proposed title for this book. The things on this list, was what kept me from jumping over the edge and from being depressed every day when I saw things or experienced things that triggered precious memories. In essence, this list helped me to value me and the other individuals who are still in my life. It helped me to see the important people and things in my life that is worth living for. It also helped me to stick to processes and be consistent at the routine I had for my life.

I must admit that at first when I made the list, I was on autopilot and my days just pass slowly as if they were crude oil running through a de-pressurised line. Most days I would simply look at the list and put it back down. Eventually I summed up the will to start and little by little, as I moved afterwards, I found solace in the things I did and it helped me held myself together. This is why I invite you to do one for yourself. Life goes on. Full stop, life goes on.

Certainly, the experience and eventual outcome for many may differ in the end but I only have one goal in writing this book. To tell the ones who got hurt, 'Live beyond the hurt and the pain!' I know that to look at the experience with just dimmed vision is to miss the depth of the pain and I certainly do not want to trivialise your broken heart. However, know certain that if our hearts have been broken and we do not find an outlet, I can assure you, the mental institution or the grave awaits us. There is a thin line between sanity and insanity and although I do not know the scientific reason why one crosses it, I felt I almost did. I had to be giving myself reasons why I should remain level headed. Thanks be to God for my son; who become my biggest reason! I am however one of the blessed ones, for I have known of individuals who had headaches for months and some who almost go mad or perhaps I should have said gone mad.

Some people plead privacy, secrecy and anonymity when it comes to helping others by using their personal experience. I have no such inhibition, for I feel that all that happens to us; is an experience from which to grow and help others. In my writing, I am bearing my scars. This is why I am not ashamed to tell anyone who has suffered, do not die, even when all hope is lost. Why should you continue hurting when your partner is living the high life? Seldom do some of these partners know how we feel or why we keep on existing and sometime we do not know either. They bury their conscience, justify their actions and move on with their lives; do the same, move on too. They see us carrying on, because they hope that we will. After all, 'Just understand that it is not you, it's me. So move on with your life. I have to fix me. I have to make me comfortable. It's not you, bye!' 'Oh good god, you are saying all the right things but you are leaving me still' is always the cry within. You are letting me down easy but the pain of your words sting within. How do you expect me to live? You tell me!

Note however, my friend, it is not about you, so stop beating up on yourself. We all make mistakes and do rubbish but in the end we all must learn and accept that essentially it is not entirely your fault why the separation occurred. The understanding of this fact is one of the keys to recovery. Learn as well that in many instances, the individual who leave did so because they have issues, not you. They genuinely may have been fond of something about you at the start but being fond of or in love with an image, a position or a particular characteristic, does not last. Like a flower, it fades and since we are all human beings and generally return to our true nature of self-preservation, we all act in ways that are hurtful to others and sometimes our own selves. In some instances, no-one taught them how to stand and fight for anything and so what you will find out later on is that wherever they leave to go, they will replicate the same behaviour of running away when the pressure builds. This is why the divorce rate for couples marrying for the second time is so high. We are creatures of habits and in many of the things we do wrong, we are repeat offenders. We can always find ways and means to repair or fix others but we cannot fix ourselves. Essentially, unless we get help, the cycle continues, so whether we end up with someone rich and nice or someone grotesque and miserable we remain the same. Hence, I ask, you to see them through this viewpoint.

In addition to the above, some people cannot live with anyone else but themselves as it makes them feel clustered and trapped. Therefore, you being there was just complicating things and compounding their problem. Mindful, they will try to live with others and it might even work for a while but they usually find ways and means to self-destruct and destroy everything in their path.

People like these find being a Christian difficult, because it teaches monogamy and unity of relationship. To them been monogamous is not the problem, because they do want someone special in their lives, they just do not want the unity of relationship part of it which speaks of living together and all that comes with that. They would prefer a 'come over to my place and visit and go back home after a while' type of relationship.

One would ask if anything is wrong with that and although I am not quick to say yes, I must admit that it speaks to a lack of understanding of what it means to be one. We cannot become one separated half the time. It does not lend itself well for proper blending and cohesiveness. Great tasting cakes are not made by baking ingredients separately and then put them together, they have to be blended and then sent to fire. Also, even the Bible advices against it, when it said that the only time a man and his wife is not to be together in an intimate way is for the sake of prayer and fasting. The reason it gave for that advice is that it opens up the unity of the partnership to temptations from the devil. The work of the adversary brings division among people. Separation brings a snare.

I can hear a voice asking, so what would you advise service men and women or other individuals who has to go away from their partners for long periods? Well, outside of saying, to each his own or to those who can bear the strain, because they are endowed with great powers of self-control and respect for their partner, they can take the risk; I will say it is not wise.

It is not wise because it decreases both relationship and family values overtime. I will not act as though I am ignorant. We live in a real World and human conditions and need for survival forces us to do things that are not healthy for our long-term well-being and although we pretty it up and display the exceptions, we seldom highlight the norm. We do not talk about the cheating wife or husband that is at home or the sweethearts who are behaving like wives where he or she is on duty abroad. Nor do we mention the child who bears the name of the husband but actually does not belong to him or the one that is rude and uncontrollable or hates daddy and mammy because he or she is never there. How do I know this? I presently work with married seamen, who parade large picture books of all the naked women they have slept with in each port, in each country their vessel had called. I have spoken to many children who complain about daddy missing their birthdays because he had to work and oh, not to mention those who got divorced because they no longer connect with each other when they return home. Distance drove them to find alternatives. Yes, there are those who wait on the return of their partners, those who come up with ways of coping while their partners are away but they are the few. It takes a special type of human being to do this, to go against the norm and to some degree, the undertone cultural expectation and hushed accepted practice. This is why I will advise that you do not separate at all, unless it is absolutely necessary and even in the cases when you have to, make sure you plan how you will guard against giving the devil a foothold whiles you are away. The devil does wear shiny white suits and have rosy lips, broad shoulder or voluptuous breast and hips. In fact, he comes in all shape and forms, so be on the alert at all times.

This is why I do not want to say much to the one who behaved like a 'Crablouse' or the vagrant partner left behind. I know calling someone a Crablouse is derogatory but I cannot think of another suitable word right now that I want to us to describe such an individual who cheats, ill-treats or dehumanises his or her partner. To such a one, I am only saying, 'You deserve it and I hope you learn the lesson that you cannot treat people the way you do and still expect them to 'wait on you, hand and foot'. You are not God's gift to the World. Jesus is and not even He treated anyone that way!' With the same breath, I want to say to the partner that left, 'Well done, you should have left him or her sorry ass a long time ago. Now that you have done so, pick up your life and move on with it!'

Again, to the one who was left behind because you are terrible, I am only saying one more thing to you, 'Repent!' I use the word repent, for in saying all of what I have said so far, my strongest and most earnest prayer is for reconciliation. This I pray for in the good and the bad cases. I really and honestly would love for broken marriages, hearts and life, to come back together again. However, I am not naïve, this might never happen but I really want to minister to an individual who suffered the injustice of having a partner leaving them because of something they have no clue about.

I must admit that it does take a whole lot of grace and favour to overcome some of life's uncertainties and although separation might be the likely ending to a long line of problems, it is not the end to a productive life and future, in itself. It is what we do afterwards that is. This is where many of us need a little help and guidance, as we can become so overwhelmed with the separation that we forget that life goes on or it is not the end of the World.

At this point, I want to list about six reasons I did not die when she left. My hope in doing this is to highlight the fact that it hurts like Hell and that there are no easy roads to recovery but recovery is necessary. Here go the six reasons:

The first reason I want to give is that of acceptance. I know there will be days you want to be in love with someone and you want the whole nine yards but accept that it might never be with this person; ever, again. I can remember when I was moping around, someone said to me, 'Stop blaming yourself and let it go. How long do you plan to keep this up? You need to take care of yourself!' but at that time, I did not understand how they could be so callus. 'Don't you see that I am hurting, how can you just say stop blaming yourself and leave?' However, the more I moped, was the more I solicited sympathy and the more I tried to gain sympathy, was the less I took care of myself. When we want others to feel sorry for us, Heaven knows, we do some strange things! Alternatively, when we want to vilify the other individual, if I am hurting; they must hurt too, we can become so stupid. Hurting your self will not hurt anyone, especially the one who left. In reality, they do not even see you. It was not until their advice kicked in that I realised that they were right. It however took an incident to make me realise that if I was ever going to recover from my loss, the first thing I will have to do is start taking care of myself and this started with accepting what had happened and who I am.

When it all happened, as aforementioned, I felt lost and I stopped taking care of me. It was not until a co-worker said one day, 'Does anyone else noticed that Junior's two back pockets are starting to look as though they are becoming one?' To which another laughing prodded back, 'You all don't notice how he is always drawing up his pants, as though he cannot afford to buy a belt that will fit him. You know how many times I have to tell him to bore another hole in the belt so that it holds up the pants. Then again, when he draws the belt tighter; it makes the pants gather up around his waist like he is wearing someone else's pants!' I tell you, some friends will tell you how decrepit you look in private but during a time such as this some will not and it is not because they are just insensitive, we did not share our plight with them. To them it will only be a point of gossip and mockery. This was what I felt happened to me and so when they said that I was most enraged but I was more embarrassed to say a word. Any outburst on my part would simply be a case of bruised pride and saving face, for it was not as if they were not speaking the truth. They were. Being five feet eleven inches tall and weighing one hundred and thirty-three pounds, does not look too well at all.

173

It was not in my eyes and certainly not in theirs. Besides, they did not know what was going on and so they were free to say anything they wanted. That day I did not make them any wiser. I just swallowed my spit hard, laughed a deceptive laugh, went to the bathroom and washed my face as usual.

I was embarrassed but I learned from that day that embarrassment often leads to change. That day I decided to accept my faith and hobble along. It was not easy at first but the more I did it, was the less I washed my face and the more I began to eat. To ensure that I ate; I convinced two of my co-workers to order lunch for me each day. Thanks be unto the Lord, they have not failed at this, for now I am up to 145 pounds. Take it from me, a dirty or unkempt you drive people away or open you up to ridicule, thus it closes the door to greater possibilities.

Therefore, accept that they are gone and might never return. Expect them back yes but do not kill yourself over it, for in truth and in fact; they might never return. The more emphasis you place on your expectation of them returning is the more you open up yourself for trouble, for the longer that expectation goes unfulfilled is the more depression, insecurities, jealousy and resentment sets in and you end up becoming an emotional wreck. Also, accept that although you are hurting you have options, for life is not that narrow to give you one on only one tunnel to walk through. It also places no blinkers on us like horse running down a racetrack; it gives us a full view of everything and says, 'Look around, live, breathe and prosper.' Life is also never without a second chance. However that second chance lies in you finding and utilising your options in a smarter and better way than before. In fact, the only reason you feel like the breath is 'been sucked out of you' is that you have failed to see your options and thus you have failed to see the endless possibilities that lies ahead. Life sucks the wind out of our sails when we do respond to the call to utilise the other possibilities. So I say, 'look for these options, focus ON them and work on them', for herein lies your happier days.

The second reason on my list is that of playing our part in the lives of those who are still important to us. Do not starve others of their attention because one person hurt you and this goes especially for your child or children. When it all happened, my son almost became a victim. A case of, 'If you cannot catch Quaku (Harry), yu ketch im shut.' I know that her life and greatest love was wrapped up in our son and this almost became my downfall. Although I love my son, he is my World but I was almost tempted to say, 'You got what you wanted and now you are moving on but you still expect me to be a father to what you

174

wanted.' I honestly felt like all she wanted from a man was a child and she had no other way of getting him, because she feared what people would say, so she married me so that she could have a child without feeling as though she had offended God or man. She used me. Thinking this way made me really want to hurt her. God, what evil and wickedness sparked within my chest! As such, my pride and joy almost became a casualty of my broken heart. He almost became a pawn in the war of hearts!

On this wise I learned first-hand how possible it is for us to spite our children or treat them horribly because we want to hurt their partner. Statement such as, 'You remind me of your wicked father' or 'It is the same thing your miserable mother would have done' are only tips of the iceberg, for some go as far as withholding resources, quality time and affection. I thank God; He prevented me from been one of those bitter parents. Thank you Jesus!

Having this experience, I can now say that separation clouds our vision of who and what is important but we must always remember that our partner, although being the most important person in our lives, they are not the only one who deserves having us alive, healthy and strong. Our children, our parents, our friends and the list go on, plays an important role as well. Never forget that. In other words, not because of your split, no other life should be destroyed or suffer for it. A broken marriage or a broken heart should never lead to broken children or a broken legacy. I would have hurt my son and blighted my generation forever.

So, play your part in the lives of those you are responsible for and do so to the best of your ability and no matter what opposes you face, you do it, nonetheless. Never drop your hand. If you have to pick up the children, still pick them up. Do not allow them to suffer because you are suffering. I know it is hard but do it anyway. In some cases, you might feel like you are pushing water up a hill as you face resistance to your effort but do what you have to do, nonetheless.

Also, do not diminish your attendance or involvement in whatever you were involved in before the split. Do not isolate yourself. Withdrawal and self-imposed exile do little or nothing to solve or squelch the hurt. They only make you feel like the world is against you when there are genuine people around who want to see you live. Yes, many there are who will be cold and unfeeling or expect you to be your normal self all the time but get pass them and do what you can do until you can fully do what you want to do. Remember, unless you are truly guilty, no one is blaming you or is constantly looking at you and snickering. It is only a perception. 'Carry on Soldier!' If you drop your hands or drawback, you will always find justification to be negative in your attitude and greater than you will suffer for it.

My third reason for not dying was the fact that I surrounded myself with others who cared about me more than I cared for myself. In our modern era, I know we cannot trust everyone with our heart. As the saying goes 'Shaking a man's hand does not mean shaking his heart', we generally do not know what lies behind the smile or who will genuinely help during a crisis. As a child, I was taught that when we fall into a hole there are three types of individuals we will look up and see that is if, we can look up at all.

1) We will see those who are giving a blow-by-blow report of how we fell in or explaining why we must have done it. They will not know all the details but they will have on opinion and for sure, they will make it up as they go. Do you know how many times heard how I cheated, beat my wife and was unsupportive? 'And him say him a Christian,' or how many times I was give news how my wife was seen at places with man. 'Only you are a fool to put up with her.' Trust me, if you fallow them you will bleed out in the hole in which you find yourself or they will runaway every meaningful soul who would want to help. These individuals, often times, you will have to ignore, for they are not there to help but for the show. Therefore, from where you are you will have to learn how to call out help for yourself as well as instruct others to do the specific thing you want done. 'Get me out of here.'

2) We will see those who will be trying to get a view of how we look while in the hole. This set wants a memory to use later, an upper hand. 'I know your dirt. I saw you in the hole of your life. So, be careful how you behave or talk about me, as you are no better than I am. You fell and looked like this in the hole of your life.' They really do not want to help; they simply want to see how this will play out. These carry a spectator mentality. They have the talk, the oooh and the auuuh but nothing else. In fact, they will create more problems for you than you want. Without the support of officers, they needed help again cannot get to us. They will even ask a few questions 'Are you OK? Can you move?' but they will not stretch out their hand to help. After hearing me unload my sorrows many times I heard, 'Junior I would really love to help but...' The did not want to get their hands dirty. 'I know your wife and I really do not want to come between you and her.' No that was not the issue, many of them just did not want to lose her friend ship or faced her 'fastness' to her us. In the end, these be the ones who will not allow you to get pass your past. Again, I say as well, do not pay them

any attention. My grandmother would say, 'Don't waste your breath. They are not important.' and finally,

3) We will also look up and see those who will be climbing down to help us out or throwing us a rope. These individuals are not plenty and yes, they may use it against us later but at less in the time of crisis, they did not stand back and point or talk, they help. 'Come home for dinner this evening Junior' and when I got there they did not talk about my wife; they minister to me. This final set is the one we can trust. They are the ones who truly matters. They will come down to help or they are the ones with the technical skills to get others to help us. Get to know them. Trust them. They might not know everything or always have the right answers but we just have to find them or know that they are there. I will also put this in. Some of us should learn how to seek a friend before need one. I say this in light of the fact that the individuals who make up this group are individuals we did not treat like dirt when things were going 'hunky-dory' for us. As such, they know us enough to come rescue us when we are languishing at the bottom of some pit. You will not die in a hole with these individuals around.

However, be mindful that misery loves company and having people who are in the same hole as you; will only serve to push you further down into it. Know that some of these individuals are sympathetic to your pain, because some of them have been there and know how it feels to be heartbroken but watch them. This is why drunkards keep drunkard friends. We all like to swap stories with other individuals. Pity parties are great parties if you want to remain stuck. The problem with this type of behaviour is that it will only reinforce how awful our partner is, when our 'in the hole' friends are finish with us, for when they are through trying to cheer us up, they will be using points which degrade our partner. My wife is a great woman, full stop but at this time, might not be great for me. Therefore, in your bit to come out of your state of depression, watch who you ask to pull you up, for some would rather join you in the hole and echo the sentiments, 'Man wicked!' or 'Women evil!'

Also, do not allow yourself to be alone, for when you are by yourself, just the sheer force and intensity of the memories will cause depression and malevolent voices to speak to you. I know also that there are inquisitive people and some who cannot keep their mouths shut. They are always looking for a reason to gossip or gloat over how well their relationship is going base on how bad someone else's is going. Do not mind them! Surround yourself with individuals who can pour out into your spirit as you pour back into theirs. Having

177

people around you will force you to talk. In addition, it will help you to get out of your system, built up tension or hurtful feelings. Another great benefit of this is that it will get you to do the only thing you must do but do not feel like doing that of opening up and experiencing life. During this time a started, a mentor group call Brothers Connect, these young men forced me to open up.

When we open up, we give ourselves space to breathe, for things bottled up on the inside without a medium of expression, usually become the source of other maladies. Hence, what was supposed to save us kills us, because they become habits, habits of gambling, smoking, drinking, unhealthy relationships and not to mention physical and mental ailment, which are all things we do not want. Hence, I will hasten to say, do not turn to negative habits, they only make matters worse or degrade our character. I collected wines and others spirits during this time as well but at no time did I sought to drink my struggles and sorrows away. I also, worked ships at nights and in so far away place but I never turned to a prostitute to keep my company. I had a standard to uphold. Never let your standard die because someone else died.

In seeking to surround yourself with others however, I must warn you about two sets of individuals. The first is the set who will use the opportunity to lead you astray from your goals, faith and beliefs or principles. 'If you were never so high on your standard this would never have happened to you. You should have chosen someone simpler!' What do they mean by that only God knows! Another comment for example, 'If you weren't in church you could have recovered long time, because you could have found another woman who would treat you right. Boy, you know how many women out there that is dying to get a good man like you!' How do they know that I am a good man! I do not even know of that for myself. If I am a good man, the Lord will reveal it in time, so I will not be a fool and follow the wrong company to my demise. A word to the wise is sufficient: If sinners entice you do not follow them. The second set, although different from the first, can cause you great pain, perhaps not as much pain as the first but pain, nonetheless. These individuals are sympathiser and because of their 'mean well' persona, they can become crutches on which we forever lean but in really they are glory seekers. You become so dependent on them that you lose the essence of who you really are, because everyone sees them. As counsellor their ultimately motive is to say, 'I helped him or her got back on their feet when they were down and out.' Nothing is wrong with an individual getting some gratification or pleasure out of helping us back to our feet. However, it becomes

178

a problem when they forget that God and others played a part in our recovery. Or, when they begin to seek for favours from us, after our recovery and do so from a perspective of, 'Remember that I was the one who was there for you when you were...' as though their objective for helping us was to make us obligated to them. In seeking for help, just remember that some shepherds raise sheep just so that they can eat them. Therefore, my recommendation is to seek for individuals who will give you the encouragement you need to be yourself without having any expectation from you, except that of you being well. The ultimate aim in your seeking is to get better, not to become dependent or led astray.

In a time of glory seekers and 'miss leaders', I know that it might seem hard to find genuine and supportive people or individuals you do not have to pay for advice and counsel. It might even feel like there is no one who understands what you are going through and to be honest some do not. However, they are there and they care about you a whole lot. So, do not shut them out. Take off your armour for a while and let someone rub soughing oil into your wounds.

My fourth reason for not dying when she left is simply this, I got deeper involved. When we are down in a pit or caught in a storm, we can become so preoccupied or paranoid with where we are that we unknowingly entomb ourselves in it or fret to death. 'I do not know how long this is going to last, so I might as well become comfortable in my misery.' Consciously or unconsciously, we are by ourselves, saying no to everything. Instead of volunteering, we back away from responsibilities and play the 'show up after the function as started and leave just before it ends' game. We place ourselves on the backbench as it were and resign as though we have committed some eternal sin. By doing this what we do is allow a skilful spirit to take us over and so much to the point where we hire a contractor, purchase paint, fixtures and fittings and redecorate the walls of the pit until we become comfortable in it. Not to mention the storm, we throw everything of value over board and give up to the wind to take us wherever it wants to. We do so to the point where we allow our hair to become unkempt, we hardly want to bathe or eat, our house becomes rundown on the outside and on the inside it looks like a pigsty or our garden becomes over grown with weeds and some of us even lose our livelihood. We become an apparition in our own existence. We barely move in and out of our own lives, slowing or completely stopping our own progress and failing to remember that self-pity serves no purpose but to bring us shame. When we behave like this, by the time it is all over, the partner who left us, who still feels no love for us, have a reason to rejoice. However, if we cannot love ourselves enough to take care of ourselves in a pit or during a storm, might as well we stay there and die, because we really cannot love anyone else with this mentality.

However, when unforeseen things like a breakup happen to you do not stay home and become nauseating, get up and get involved. Become an even more active participant in your own life. The sidelines are for individuals who do not know how to play the game, too young to play or too old to further play, for the rest of us, the game is still on. He or she leaving has nothing to do with the suspension or cancellation of the game of life for us, live or since you have already hit the ground, run.

I was off the choir, at my church, I went back on. I held no office – I just could not take the pressure or the eyes – but I shook my self and accepted the challenges that came my way, despite how I felt. I became Youth Director. As the saying goes, 'When the tough time comes, the tough gets going.' Yes, the kingdom of my emotion and the depth of my love suffered violence but I took it by force and became me again, good old me. In the midst of it all, I gave God the glory, the honour and the worship but I also found praise for myself as well and I stopped my todays from being a repeat of my yesterdays.

This is why I will say; 'get involved in as many activities as you can.' I am not saying use this as an escape route, as this reason could be a double-edged sword. It can mask the problem. It numbs the pain but does not help use to properly deal with our emotions. Therefore, you will have to watch it and pace yourself carefully. As, being busy is not only a way to numb the hurt but it is also a way to keep you focused on what is important. It helps us to see the fact that self should never have priority over grace, helpfulness or that the right now moment and present happenings is but a stop on the road to your dream. When you have to still get up and go to work, classes, choir practice, Sunday school, pick up your child or children, help with homework, cook, wash and clean; because you have no helper, time does fly away and by the time you know it, you have a stomach to face the other person again without being angry and revengeful.

Being busy forces us to pour out ourselves into others and everyone knows that, 'He who minster to others, he himself will be ministered unto.'

This might be a difficult stop on the road to recovery but it is a necessary one; one that is not harder than life itself. Life itself is complicated without the added drama of having to smile when we want to cry or go to the office to finish a report when we would rather stay home and bury ourselves in sadness. It is at this point we will have to choose between what we would like to do and what we must do. I implore you to choose what you must do, no excuses. Many of us have always made excuses why we cannot do what needs to be done. These excuses are our way of trying to keep safe or hide our vulnerabilities but what they actually do for us instead is reinforce everything that is negative about us and keep us trapped in the 'Why is this always happening to me?' faze of our lives. On a normal basis when we do not want to do something, we make excuse but when negative things happen, we sometimes do not even have to make the excuse for ourselves others make them for us. 'Leave him alone, don't you see he is hurting,' 'I don't believe he or she has the strength to do it. How can you be so insensitive?' Hence, with the added drama that surrounds us, our excuses can be amplified and we literally have an escape clause. We will even get away with feeling as if we are alone or the worst when we compare our life to what some others are facing. However, if we truly know the depths of what others are facing, we would see that we are nowhere near. Life gives to some emotional hurt, to some physical hurt, to others psychological hurt and depends on where we are with God, spiritual hurt but we all have to deal with what we receive –good or bad. Therefore, excuses will not work. Know who you are, what you should be doing and step out and do.

Push the feeling of inadequacy aside and get involved. Develop an understanding that no matter the situation, life continues. It does not stop because you stopped, however, the longer you stop; the more difficult it will be for you to resume, as well as, for you catch up. All I will say at this point then is, grieve yes but please do not let the grieving period last too long, for life move even when we are not. In addition, there too much benefits in you from which others can learn for you to be wasting away. Hence, locking yourself up like a hermit or back-pedalling from what you used to do or found to be funny, will not help anything, it will cause you to lose you spunk. Once more, I advise you, to be careful with whom you get involved. As long as you do everything in moderation, you should be fine.

The fifth reason I did not die after she left was that I learned a skill, as well as, strengthened my passions. Life is about learning and rediscovering things. What we learn and discover, are what we are able to apply. Without learning or continuous improvement, we fail to grow and if we fail to grow, we would not have died because of the breakup, we would have committed suicide.

I had to learn that suicide is not on option. I discover that when we lose something, it is our right to find it back or if stolen, it still is our right to get it back. However, in the case where we do not get it back, we owe it to ourselves to look for another. I quit looking and making my wife's return my focus, I used the time to finish my first book – We Want You to Fly: What your parents are really trying to say. Then I went on to write – Smorgasbord – and you are reading what was next. I got up in the mornings and I exercise and began lifting weights. I must admit that this is not going too well but who cares, I am already feeling better. I also bought a Keyboard and began to learn how to play music. I converted my passion for singing and song writing into starting my group, 'Selah one Sound'. We have recorded 'Lord, I'll stay away' and 'Sovereign God' so far. I took a two-year course in Spanish and I keep getting better at it. I learnt how to paint a house and my list outweighs my need to make this point. I do not know what your passion is but if you focus on it, you can get more out of your pain than just pain. Take it from me, alone time is a good time to develop something new.

Another side to this is that sometimes in a relationship, we put off all we want to do because we are not seeking to please ourselves. We become lost in the needs of the other person, after all that is what marriage is about. We sacrifice or down play our needs and accomplishments for the good of the relationship. The Bible supports this type of behaviour: the married man seeks after how he might please his partner but the unmarried man seeks how he might please the Lord. In this circumstance, you are lord. I am not promoting idolatry or the worship of self but lord here speaks to who is important and should be given prominence in the face of the storm. It may never safe us but we are often told, 'Secure your oxygen mask or seat belt first before you assist anyone else'. This is the case of who our focus should be on when brokenness comes to visit our lives. A breakup does not change our lordship and hence should not change our desire to lead and rule and if there is anyone we should make sure we have great rule over, it is our own self. In other words, if we do not want to be like a city that is broken down and without walls, we must have restraint over our spirit. We have to tell ourselves, 'keep it together, you are important and your dreams now become your priority.' I am also not advocating selfishness or self-centeredness; all I am saying is revert. Go back to seeing what was most mportant to you before the evil winds began blowing and make them important again. Straighten out what needs straightening out and become driven in the direction that will be more profitable to you than walking around with a sulky and depressive state of mind. See and care for everyone else but live for you and the Lord Jesus Christ.

Therefore, develop your reading skills or build your vocabulary, learn to play the piano, write a book or take up ballroom dancing for that matter, just do something. Whatever you chose to develop your strength in, make sure that it is something that is exclusively and purely you. Trust me after a breakup we all need a bounce back. We need to do something for and by ourselves that will help us to reconnect with our individual self. Thus, anything that you are passionate about, it should become your focus. After all, you must gain something out of your lone time other than sleepless nights, losing weight or becoming overweight, etc.

My sixth reason for not dying when she left me was this; I maintained my faith in the risen Saviour. This I would say is the most important of all my reasons for not dying. Some things in our life happen because of what we allow or fail to allow. I did not allow my faith in God to waver for a minute. Like Job, in the Bible, I questioned everything but I reinforced my confidence in God, over and above that of self, others and economic prospect that lies ahead. Hence, in the days and nights when I could not hold myself, He held me.

It was at this time that I realised, more intently that my relationship with Him supersedes that of emotions, desires, feelings, dreams, expectations and above all, it supersedes people. After all, He is the bedrock of my life. He has my best interest at heart. This is why the principal motto for my life is, 'Jesus is the head of Junior' and in writing it, I use only one J to do so. I now see myself as connected to God and Him to me. This is why I cannot fall apart, even when my life is falling apart. I am so glad that when the bottom of life falls out, Jesus does not. This is why many of us can stand, walk and live on air.

He was there for me during my roller-coaster childhood and He has been there for me ever since. I did not acknowledge Him back in my early teens but He was there. Through this, I know that when all else fails or when everyone else leaves, He will never leave, even when I am the one at fault. I am sure He loves me even when extenuating circumstances come to say otherwise. Who else would die for a misfit or a renegade? We only love people who love us or supports us but He loves the unlovable and to the point where He died to prove it. In this regards, this reason became the lynchpin of all the other reasons. It held me together during those lonely and self-fighting days. Those days when I wished I was married but was not.

I know that there are those who do not believe in or have a supreme being who they call God but even such a one has principles and ideologies that they hold to and live by. If you are an unbeliever and although I would love to say, 'you really need to re-examine this position', I hasten to advise you; do not let go of your principles. You must have something higher than your own self and others to rely on or keep you grounded, even if it is these principles.

This type of tsunami comes in without warning and can drown everything you ever dream about, so I implore you, especially those who believe in God, do not forget your God. Hold true to Him for a threefold cord is stronger than anyone or anything else. Thus, He should be the bridge between you and all the other areas of your life. For, without Him or having faith that He will never leave us during the bad times, we will feel that it is because He has abandoned us why we are going through the predicament and we will fall into despair. It is hard when we cannot find the answer to our questions from the people around us and we might feel as though God is not talking to us either. Nothing is more hopeless. This is why we must always remember that if our faith fails, we fail and this is so because our faith is always the Alamo between our victory and self-destruction. It is through our faith we make the decision to live or die, to be happy or depressed. Our gives us value and strengthen our worth. It is always our ability to believe that things will be better and not just better but that God has our best interest at heart that brings us out. It is then, our knowledge that He is the pillar and ground of our faith that cause us to be calm in the midst of our storms. This is where the age-old hymn comes in, 'This rock is Jesus, the very one, be very sure you anchor hold and grips the solid rock'. When we know this, it causes us to prod on whatever the storm.

Having this knowledge also gives us hope and it is this hope, which makes us not ashamed or feeling that 'we are worse off than others' when others are hanging us out to dry. In essence, it safe guards our self-view and covers our pride. It keeps tell us, 'This too shall pass' or 'Tough times do not last forever but tough individuals do'. It was my faith that help me when the question was asked, 'Brother, how this happen to you?' and you have to answer. I had no answer but certainly, I had God. This is why I can say to you, 'Do not die but show the World, the devil and whoever else that you can swim, you have stamina and that it is not in yourself but the Lord.'

Besides, some things; can never be understood from a physical plane. For example, we will never be able to explain why someone who initially told us, 'I love you and will spend the rest of my life with you' just got up, walked away and forget that they ever said so. Just thinking about it makes my head hurt. On the physical plane, we see with our natural eyes, because we are physical beings. However, many of the things that we do or happen to us are not physically motivated. They are spiritually motivated. This is because we are spirits wrapped in flesh and our spirit is either predominantly good or predominantly evil and because we are under the influence of either God or the Devil, we will do things that cause others to question our motives.

This is where our thoughts come in, as our thoughts are really the manifestation of our spirit and so, depends on whom we are listening to, God or the devil; we can become either vile or a blessing. Not many of us truly know whom we will listen to during times of crisis. Only the situation will tell. At the hour of temptation, we are either going to do good things or that which is evil or disgusting. We are either going to fret to death, slaughter the other individual and then turn the gun or rope on ourselves, destroy our bloodline or we are going to get up and place a Band-Aid of forgiveness, compassion or implement a strong resolve to live our best life. I can tell you straight up that the latter things only come from an unwavering faith in God, for when we love and honestly love, these virtues are not the ones that come to mind first. What does is the devilish spirit of vengeance and if we listen, Hell is where we drag everyone else with us. However, when we have faith in God and confidence in His care for us, we see every misfortune as something working for our good. We rest in confidence that He does not give us more than we can bear and He will never allow something that will destroy us to come through the edge He has set up around us. Thus, anyone or anything that come or goes for that matter, we can handle it with Him on our side.

Hence, read the scriptures a little more, pray a little longer and a little bit more fervently, worship a little harder and endeavour to be happy. When you hide yourself in God, He hides you in the palm of His hand and nothing tears you apart although it might hurt for a while. So, I say, let the day spring of righteousness spring up in your heart and fill your heart with joy.

Chapter 9
Brighter Days

Seeing the way forward through poetry

This is the fifth year of my aloneness and I am still standing. Although I want to cry, 'I want my wife back', I am grounded in the knowledge that without pressure, water do not go up hill. My wife is under no pressure to come back. Therefore, it is my responsibility to see the way forward. Only the Lord knows how this will play out but the more I learn the wisdom of moving forward is the more I see that better is up ahead.

Hence, there is no other way I want to close this book except with a few poems. These I wrote during the period of disconnect with my wife and I think they perfectly reflect the state of mind that I was in back then and where I am now. In some way, they summarise the content of this book.

After reading this book and poetic verses, many may deduce that the answers, which I sought, were right in front of me from the beginning. Some may even go as far as to say that I completely ignored them. However, life ultimately forces us to acknowledge or accept the things we previously missed. Unfortunately, our learning and acceptance of those 'ignored answers' leave us with deeply entrenched scars. Scare that will not only be visible but also felt, as each time we fill out a document or change a particular routine it reminds us we are alone. 'Mr. Watson, who will you be naming as your next of kin?' 'Will your beneficiary remain the same as last year?' 'Will you keep the same health insurance premium as before?' 'I know it is your turn to pick up your son but you will have to work late this evening. Can you not ask his mother or someone else to pick him up?' With each answer or each explanation, we are being reminded that someone is out of place. If you are faithful and dedicated like me, 'To Hell with it' is not one of the possible answers. Hence, even after years the scares still run deep.

In order to find healing or to move on with our life, we have to pour out the poison and turn our cups upwards to God for a cleansing and a fresh outpouring.

Life is about experiences and many times those experiences cause hurt, pain, anger, bitterness and depression but these emotionally turmoil must never be treated like wine being aged in a winery. Therefore, none of our past hurts, pain or regrets should be allowed to age, for when they do, they become what others will drink from us and this must never happen. The next person who comes in touch with us, if our partner never returns or even they return, must be getting the more experienced us or the one who God as given on experience to last forever. Old things should pass away and all things, from here, be treated as new. This is why, I am thankful to God for another chance, at getting it right. As for me, I will have to accept what I can do and do what I must; this is the key to enduring emotional perplexities and overcoming them.

Air

The leaves dance at your command
As you made your way through the trees.

Although I am not seeing you
I know you are there
Closer to me than the clothes I wear.

There are two sides to this atmosphere
The pleasure and the pain
But without you, there is no life here or there.

My roots sink deeper into you
For you are the rich soil that meets my needs
Yet still others go after greed.

Your grace at Calvary
You share with sinful man
Who was trapped and scared, barren and torn apart.

Broken lives you repaired
You are ever abundant
Yet man is polluted
Running out of air.

Bedazzled

Wow! Who sent you or from whence cometh you?
Did you rise with the sun, as you set me ablaze?
On your pasture, I want to graze;
Your beauty enthralled me
Instant daydream you brought me
Love at first sight, caught me;

Flawless, though crocked a sight to behold
Can I run into your garden from the cold or take your hand for a stroll?
The crest of your neck down to your breast allures me like a moth to its death;
Star gazed, dumbstruck, tongue wagging, drooling even
I'm in luck as upon the perfume from you, my nostril is stuck;

Watching your stride, the resplendent rhythm moved me
The spirit possesses me; the jaws of love shake me
The passion of the thought of you warms my heart;
Cold sweat washed me like taking a bath
Please baby, take me, embrace me, feed me, hold me and love me while you roll
me;

Roses, jasmine, lily are the flowers of your mind
Speak to me my dear and stop time
Let wisdom flow sublime;
I am here looking at your fruits; can I touch? Can I taste?
For from whence I come nothing like you grows anywhere;
So, can we speak garble over pillows about wine and rose?
I am beside myself with joy, because you are in my life.

I Love Your Eyes

'I love your eyes,' she smiled.

'But will this be all the time?' she chides.

'When the storms rage and frown, will you still be around?'
Her question of my resolve.

'Oh my love! Does the breeze blow or the cock crow?
Do willows sing in the whistling wind? Oh yes my Love, I'll love you still.'

Why

Her response was shy, 'Why?'
'Simply, I want to be a part of your life;
Bags under your eyes and spare tyres around your waist,
I'll still want to gaze upon your lovely face;
When your breast has become long from suckling the babe
I'll still run home, to find sweet rest.'

'Stop saying that you don't mean it?'
'Baby, baby, my sweet; just give me a chance to sit at your feet.
I'll be there forever, no matter how long the sleet.
I love the spark in your eyes.'

'You are a charmer but to me this is just another lie.'
'I'll gladly prove it, as I wear the shoes of your love that fits.'
'I have heard better than this.'
'I am not promising much but I'll rest in my conviction of this:
Washing machine or wrinkled hands, house on the hill or back holly land,
Gladly I am your man; whether age ravages you or make you neat,
I want to make your life complete.'

'I wish I could make you understand that I have heard this before.
I have heard it from the bleating of the sheep
And from every suitor that comes to the door.'
'Truly, truly; I love your eyes'
'I wish you will give up trying to twist my head with another lie.
Days of wine and roses thunder and lighting, hot flashes are sure to come.'
'Yes, my midlife crisis and many uncertainties, my youthfulness will disguise.
Fitter and flat with nothing to begotten.
I am not hasty to promise what I don't have

But one promise I'll make when your hand starts to shake;
Like a shining knight to your side I will be remain
Steadfast and sure like the ancient of days;
So my love, until death do us part I'll love your yes,
Even when they have wilted and can no longer look upon this face.'

I Want to Dance with Somebody

Oh, I want to dance with somebody, with somebody who loves me. Wow that would be hot flowing with someone I can imagine in a spaghetti strap. The flow of the music would cause us to drop it; I suppose just like that. Since love is not arrogant, not turning up your nose or turning your eyes up against a blind spot, I guess we will flow just like that.

Oh, I want to dance with somebody who knows how to rock, roll and cuddle up or go for strolls, not one whose heart has grown cold, wind me up around a Maypole or behave like an old troll. This is but a dream and I will eventually come in from the cold?

Oh, I want to dance with somebody, with somebody who loves me. How would I know she loves me, would she have to take water from the moon with a spoon? Is love a feeling, a feeling of perpetual bliss, nothing can go wrong; a sense of peace not a Siren song just unbridled bliss.

In the world of dream the fascination looms that my heart will never be broken, never be sad, just happy, filled with glee and overly glad. But wake up and live before you end up in a bachelor's pad, where no spinster will unveil her bosoms glad.

The heartache, the pain, tears, the light breaks but this is the plight of those who would dare to put their heart there. Nevertheless, to have passion or be caress this is the risk that all who so wish must trifle with.

Yet I want to dance with somebody who has a firm grip, a greater understanding of the time, place where we need to be face to face as we keep life's pace. One who knows how to touch me, feel me as the rhythm moves me. One who knows how to step gently into the rat race with me without seeking to upstage me. One who through the darkest days and long nights, I can still look at the same face, the one that makes my knees shake, my lips drool, my eyes search and my ears listen with haste to hear a word, a word that applauds my warm embrace.

Oh, I want to dance with somebody, with somebody who loves me. Someone who understands my zest for life and will support me when I take on Goliath's might. One who does not question or oppose my legitimate moves to overcome the scars, broken maleness, maladies that lies on the inside. Someone who does not walk away or leave me alone on the stage of life but will see that I am on their side.

Oh, I want to dance mischievously like the wind on a bright summer's day with a crazy unselfish person who would rock my way. Someone who will move to the beat pulsating from the confidence she has in the dream I had shared. One who knows that I am not about to leave her empty and bear, as anywhere I am going I am taking her there. Someone who did not made a mistake to choose me in the first place but one who has all the confidence that although I am a little slow, I can learn all the steps that it will take the flow. I can be taught what it takes to 'make it' without faking it. Someone who knows that I can carry her there if she is just will to continuously share. Share her heart, her space and everything below and above the waist. Yes, to dance with somebody who knows how to keep me in my place while giving me space.

Oh, I want to dance with somebody, with somebody who loves me. One who moves my feet, move my life. Are you going my way or are you with me for life despite the strife? Can you hear the music of my heart? Or is it just a thought that love will last no matter what the path. I know the beats not certain but do not hide behind the curtain, hit the stage with me; for the moves I am producing is to take me a little bit further than those before me and of this I am certain.

When you have suffered as much as I have, you have to live for something, because nobody suffers so much without their life having greater meaning. So is it too late to apologise, to continue, to stir the fire that makes life worth its slice?

Don't stop dancing or perhaps stay talking as I am really hoping you can feel the beat beyond my generational crosses. I am sorry that I had stepped on your toe or trampled on your dreams but pardon me, I have never danced this way before. Then again, neither did you. That means we are both new. So, how can you accuse me of moving too slow? What do you or I know? You have your timing and I have mine but if we are going to dance together in this taciturn life we both will have to find the rhythm of a single heart, despite the pain and the strife.

Oh, I want to dance with somebody, anybody.....but then again, am I not already dancing with you! If love was a dream, I have learned that for me to know what it means, I have to dance with you and you alone; in the real world where nothing is new. I hope that by this song is through, you will know that I am only in love with you.

Take my hand and take my heart, I'll lead if you are willing to flow with a dreamer, one who is in need of a real-life partner who is not afraid to stand cheek to cheek in his corner of the one bedroom. No defence, no pretence, just the promise of a life well spent. One that is filled with music of all genres: happy, sad, melodic and wild. Use your hand to support mine, your love to hold me and your passion to direct me. Just let me know you're dancing with me and bitter song will turn to sweat as you roll with me over the cold and sleet. I got this, I got this! You must believe.

Oh, I want to dance with somebody, with somebody who loves me.

Tempers Flair

In my dreams I saw them but today they showed their K-9 for real. Years ago, long before we were wed, I saw them while lying on my bed. They were black with eyes red and at first they only walked by the side. This morning in their truest form, their colour I did not see but I felt their slobber all over me when your hands hit me.

In my dreams, I ran by this time it was too late for hell I did see. In a dream, I was warned about the pending storm but I was not too alarmed. Now I wish, I had feared those dogs, as I tried earnestly to remain calm. Peace, peace, wonderful peace but there will be none when running from these ferrous beasts.

I heard them growl and out of the shadows walk but up to this morning, I did not hear them bark. This is of course until you throw me your ring and called me a stupid ass. How did they get here? In my dream, they did not mean a thing but now I would take all the bites in the world to get away from the might of your swing.

These dogs in my dream were huge but you are a simple, beautiful thing but, oh, how your hand stings. Was it a figment of my imagination or is this the real thing? Dreams don't walk straight they say but after your temper flared, it was too late. I saw and felt everything that you hate of late and I could not finish what was on my plate. I was simple, my life in a bare and empty state.

Blackness, blackness, chasing me, dogs, black dogs, biting me; from a place they should not be. I have tried to stay out of their sight but baby, I have to come home to you at night. With their paws this long we are heading for the dumps, because we are always at each other's throat, cursing over who was wrong or who should be strong.

My ears did not hear and now my spirit fears that my name will be snared; through my spirit, you rip and tear. Running from ferocious dogs in a dream, carries no shame but how can we do this while clearing our name? You said you made a mistake when we hollered our covenant to heaven's throne. How you secretly cry for heaven's help but are your tears fake, especially when viewed from a selfish place? In the dream, I was not afraid when I ran to you in order to feel safe but now with my eyes wide open I see your hate and by extension those dogs face.

Tiptoeing, climbing walls, fences and trees, doing anything that would hurt my knees, just to avoid or not disturb those lousy flea bags but somehow I still manage to awaken them. Now it's not just at me they grab and bite, they are cutting at my offspring, my heart string. My heartache, my emotions feels like dirt and oh I pray my son will not be hurt as we pass through this larch. I must admit, sometimes it is difficult to think of him first, when on the inside, I feel so hurt and all I want to do is curse: to let out my dogs too; instead of going to church. To just let out the dogs of anger, bruised pride, insecurity and above all money plight, only to see if your dogs could match mine.

Sorry, if I stopped talking, it just that I cannot speak when I hear the sound of barking. Those dogs riling up everything of the devil inside. Those dogs barked at me from the dream of my past and the sound still echoes, so much that it causes my soul to say, 'You should have listened to those who walk this beaten path before and those who said marriage has teeth and it will bit!'

Now I agree, now I see the light. Hence, I hope we will make it through this dark and dismal night when tempers ripe and you show me how much you hate me, as each other's dogs come out to fight.

Bird Songs

'A bird in the hand is worth two in the bush,' but not when yours don't sing or keeps flopping around on a broken wing. Got this thing to hear a song but man, all it does is pick at my hands.

I did not get it for meat, although that would have been sweet to hear its bones cracking between my teeth. Just a song, any song would cheer me up and silence the fire that is burning in my chest.

The sound of the Woodpecker cracking the bark of this old oak makes me want one instead of a sparrow that neither sing in day or in the dark of night. One, just one, of the three hundred songs from the catalogue of the Nightingale would take the wedge out of my spokes and drive away all my hocus-pocus or silenced my friend's filthy jokes.

Sing Canary, sing. Oh, my sweet Canary, just take one of your thirty mini breaths a second and replenish my air supply, before I decide to get me a dog to deafen my neighbour's ear with its barking.

Fill my days with music and my nights with a dance, a cowboy song or prance. One of the forty different notes from your overtures and although some notes too high for me to hear it would still give me something to share.

My Chaffinch, please don't become bored with me and stop singing, although you have to sing the some refrain half a million times in one season. Sing, sing, SING, so the best of my rivals would run away or that my predators would become memorise each day and stay at bay.

Tell me what is important, should I stay far or should I come near, with fear. I know I called you a skylark and complained about your blizzard of notes and I also know that there were times I rattle your cage just out of joke but oh how I wish I could now hear the Woodlark's mind-numbingly and complex song that made me craze and took you in the first place.

My first love is not gone, I am still trying to hear a song and now that I can't see if you really love me, sing over these distant hills that are formed between us due to our selfish desires, poor time management and our headstrong and stubborn wills. I will know it's you, for yes, my sweet Superb Lyrebird as to my heart you still are the loudest bird call in the world.

The Bittern's call might be similar to yours and even more far reaching than the four-mile reach of the Kakapo's but my Superb Lyrebird it's never too late for me to distinguish it, for I have the sonic earring of a bat. Yes, I am blind, most of the times; so I had to develop a way of seeing you beyond the cursed side.

All this time you might be walking on the floor like the Curassows and your song might be disturbing the ground but I will listen to your buzz sound as the Savannah Sparrow or like the Zealand blue ducks. I'll find a way to get the message you are sending across the water top.

My Blue-Black Grassquit I know you had problems with the vegetation around you for oftentimes it was not enough to feed you and because you did not learn that dawn was the best time for birds to sing, to sing of the things you needed you upsets me, because I saw your timing as a misunderstanding and anger burns within when I could not provide the worms for the offspring. However, please forgive and return to singing or showing that you still have the fight within. Now, I recognise everything you did before I tried to clip your wings and muzzle the voice within and all I am saying is sing.

All I am asking is that like the Wrentit and the Bewick's Wren try to alternate the length and timing of your song both so that confusion will not pervade or stifle the atmosphere within the nest where we live or where I live at your throat or you kick me out of my part of the limb.

Although it might appear that I am not listening, why stop, I am encouraging you to sing about everything, for that is the way I will change within. Yes, it will upset me as before but I have learned from my experiences sleeping on the floor that life only changes when someone either sings the praises or drag out the carcasses.

So again, I say even though it might appear that I am not listening, sing. Sing, my sweet and don't stop I know a caged bird often don't sing, as it has no territory to protect or a mate to attract; nevertheless, pull one of your two thousand songs that exist in your catalogue my Brown Thrasher and sing.

All I ask is that you don't make it as complex as the Sedge Warbler, as again, it might annoy me. You ask for honesty, as we try to stabilise ourselves in the stormy breeze. No, you do not have mimic anybody like the Mockingbirds, Starlings, Mynahs, Marsh Warbler, Lyrebirds, Bowerbirds, Scrub-birds and

African robin-chats in order to attract me because I already want to hear you sing without the trappings.

I know it is the role of the male to sing and expose himself to everything but my Red-winged Blackbird, sing for me as the world is trying to bring me to my knees and without your songs, I can get rid of these demons that are holding back my blessings.

Help my fight, my Kite; my eagle let your screech drive fear into my enemies and turns them white. I want to be a man indeed but I am seeing too many shades and my father did not leave any clues among the weeds so help me please.

Why do we capture things and placing them in a cage or holding them in captivity is it because we love them or is it just to say I own one. I will gladly give my answer to this. I never sought to possess you. Never, a day since I met you, have I wanted to break your spirit, by being anything less than Redbreast.

As far as I know, I only want to see the best of you and for you and although we have been through the hills and valleys I still do. Oh yes, I must admit that it gives me a certain kind of prestige to know that I have you in my life but if it will stop you from singing, I will open the cage upon the re-growth of your wing, since you said you have lost it by giving me everything, so that the world can hear you sing.

You have a beautiful voice and I would hate to know that because of a selfish prince you refuse to sing.

Sing my love, sing.

Chapter 10
The Ramblings of a Broken Heart

'It one thing to say what you mean but it is another thing to mean what you said'

I feel soul-crushing pain. The honeymoon is over. The real me is here and I could not find the real you anywhere. Now, our closet is open and everyone can see our skeletons. They should have remained hidden. Now, all hell is breaking loose. The stress is getting to me and there seems to be no safe way off this ship, none that will see everyone living happily ever after.

The cold shoulder, the arguments, the misunderstandings; this is how we have come to be. Like computers, we archive every disagreement to be reused as ammunition. Why is it that our memory is so good when it comes onto the digging up of old bones but we cannot remember how to love each other? Did we love each other?

Head to feet and feet to head; that is how we sleep each night. If only preying eyes could see; this is not a marriage but a single life. My greatest fear is that our baby will grow, with a splintered soul. There is no love here, only anger, bitterness and disappointment. Not even a warm embrace to cool these bodies under the sheet. Where are the plans we once had, can't we go back to the place where we once stood, together?

A look of disgust plagues your face every time your eyes meet mine. What do I do with the love I have for you inside? I am no spring chicken, no Casanova after dark. So, I just stand, staring sadly at your form beneath the sheet; standing here, stroking the pain in my broken heart, as you sleep.

'We just grew apart!'

Oh my love, couldn't we rewind time? Should relive this life so that you my wife can really be mine? Should I gain weight, work out, grow a paunch or wear another man's face, in order to find peace in this place? You have closed off from me. I am married but singleness was never this barren.

Long forgotten is the day we tied the knot. All the smiles and the covenant seem to be forgotten. With expectant eyes, this investment made the future bright but now it is filled with impatient noise and selfish spite.

'Will you ever be good enough?' the world taunts, for I have not yet achieved the success others have flaunted. I am still learning.

'Who could have guessed that we would be like this?'

Should I be lighting a candle in the night, turning left or perhaps right? I really don't know where I went wrong; my mind keeps looping a song for freedom. I am tired of crying, of fighting these tears. How could we not last or survive the storm? How could these storms have torn us apart for so long?

I want to know the key to your heart but instead you keep telling me that I am talking fart. Really, where do I start to unfold the secret of your heart? You said I 'never wrong yet'. I know I am a man and knowing everything is not my plan but I prefer to discuss things with you, even it be to argue with you but your way is the rash way. You refuse to even save face. All I ask for is just to be a man, a man who is understood by his woman. I am begging for the love of an appreciative woman.

So, I am branded. You do not even want me to have a chance to help raise our son. However, from the first day until now, I have tried to be a married man. I come home to wash, iron, cook and clean; if only it made you glad, instead, you viewed me as less of a man. I came home late not because I was hanging out with the boys or with another 'babe'. If only you understood that I work late to put food on our plate. Then again, were you not the one who told me to take the louse job? If it was a case of me not bringing home the bacon, I could understand but now, you blame me for everything in the world that has gone.

It seems that I am always away from home, on holidays and on our baby's play days but you are helpmeet. Our child has a parent who is always around. If I am not there you are. I wish you would be patient as I hunt this meat. I wish you would support me as I hunt and gather to put food on our table and shoes on our child's feet. I wish there was patience, for one day, I will haul home more than just strips of bacon.

I don't intend to be an absentee father forever; one day I will be the ever-present dad. But no, you could not wait and now I stand here, steering singleness in the face. The solutions elude me, no answer can be found.

I never lifted a hand to hit you or to shake you to the ground. This trait existed in my progenitor before me and to my brothers it was passed down but my hands never rose to clap or to make you quiver. Now, I am the one with the shivers. I wish I knew how we got to this place. No understanding, patience or fortitude? No wrapped up with each other, living as lovers in the nude? It is what I expected when we said our wedding vows but instead you have run off, like Cinderella, without her married slippers. A single, Christian man would know how to manage a single lifestyle and could handle whatever life throws in his face but being married and living in a single state is just an outright disgrace.

*****

I got up this morning and decided that 'This is the day the Lord has made' but beyond that conviction, my heart was enormously sad. I felt like crying, like dying, like running away; like hiding, for my world just seem shattered and torn. I did not feel handsome; my pants swing around my waist. My shirt just would not stay put, in its place.

Oh but I smiled and hoped no one saw that it was fake, as I constantly wiped silent tears from my face. I looked at my shoes and they looked disfigured but that was not how I envisioned they would be. My hands felt dry but I am afraid to look at them because they would remind me that I am not fat, not rich and not bright. At least that is what I think, because I feel pressured by my plight. I can't handle the pain, turning me over and stabbing my heart, every day and every night.

But I smile; alas I smiled. I turn and opened the door for the lady at the door. I greeted her, it seemed pleasant enough. She did not deduce that I was crying and mistook it for a sparkle in my eye. Wow, she enjoyed my smile, what a sinister lie. Just the knowledge of this tore me to pieces inside.

I know that something was wrong with how I looked but I have no will power to face the mirror today or to gaze upon a face paled with bewilderment of why my life was this way. I wish there was a better way to get pass today, to get pass how low I feel, to get pass talking, to get pass living this way. I am finding it difficult to concentrate, to love the world; to love myself, to breathe, to bleed. I wish you would hug me and pour love on my insides. I wish you would smile and make me smile but you are not my wife, my lover or my friend. I wish you would help this pain to end.

'Comeback to the real world, don't let your mind stray' I heard my conscience piercingly say. It felt like a knife, cutting through my chest. After all, she was only a woman, for whom I opened the door.

To let my thoughts stray, to just open the door would have me forsaking the covenant, I vowed to God, to keep; I could not let my mind run to my heart's delight. Lust is still a sin! So, let her enjoy the warmth of a smile that covers the lowness of my mind.

She will think, 'He is a real man; not one who wants to bring me under the sheet.'

I wish there was some way to get over today without feeling this way. Am I giving up, should I cry, should I run away, should I shrink in obscurity or should I pine away: Thinking of how I allowed the warmth of her smile to lead me astray.

*****

I sat and cried silently over what you had said; knowing that I did, would not matter to you anyway. Your response would always be the same: 'You lucky, you don't have anything better to do with your tears?' Upon hearing no sympathy, something inside of me would cringe and I would become putty inside. I would break.

I wish I did not respond to what you had to say but nevertheless, the answer would always be the same.

'Yes, kill myself, for at least it would stop me from missing you this way and in doing so, I would not have to face another day living this way!'

However, verbalising such a response would only bring further distain from you; like a knife driven deep into my heart. It strengthens the hands, reaching out for me, from hell. So, I won't speak; I'll keep my distance and cry silently inside.

So, I sit and cry silently in the dark; wiping away tears that flowed from the wound inside my heart. These waters flow unabated as though my life's existence was running out through my eyes. Oh how I tried to disguise the sadness in me, by hiding behind the lies. I laughed at jokes I made up for myself, as I became silent around everyone else. I stretched the truth a little bit, remembering a better time, a time when a sparkle was in your eyes and there was no need for lies.

Hence, I speak of how well you are treating me to those who enquired about our lives but way down deep inside, I wished to kill myself and escape these lies. Everyone who looks at me sees a gentle guy; they never get to see the fragmented me inside. Constant headaches, blood red eyes and varying mood swings plague me. I periodically look at my phone to see if a friend, anyone, would send me a message, to ask me for help. I did so just to think of someone other than myself.

So, I sit and cry silently, because I constantly felt like I was no good and every happy go lucky couple who walked by, told me that I was right. I was just a simple mistake that was found out too late. I churned over thoughts after thoughts in my unable to sleep state, while something sinister played the music of shame and disgrace. My self-worth and my conviction about life, flutter between rejection and emptiness; especially when the house is empty or when I hear your voice.

I wish you were standing with me face to face but this is a wish that neither have time nor place. I feel this constant heaviness in my chest. Was this my hope of you returning? I hyperventilate as though I am running from something that was about to take my last breath, every time I think about this mess. How did I get here? What brought me to this? Why can I not shake the knowledge that I am neither your icing nor your cake? Why am I still expectant, when you have resigned to live in another place? Am I still expecting something that has long died in you? Am I still hoping that you would come back to me and it will only be a dream when I awake? Then again, I could be wrong, because to you I was just a mistake.

So, I sit and cry silently as I face my fears of living alone, rather than jumping from the top of the stairs. I spoke with the many voices, which accused me of failure. I dealt with self-pity, bruised ego, loneliness, the insufficiency of taking care of myself and I cut off utility services for which I could not manage to pay.

I ate 'dryers' from many different mothers and sisters' plate. In the midst of it all, I stopped lying to myself. I realised the woman I love, sees me as nothing. I was heartbroken. Why do I go on living this pain? Why can't I just move on, why? I guess when you truly love, you cannot quit. Yes, you have to accept the other person's wishes and the fact that fairytales are just that; tails but you cannot quit.

Yes, I told myself of all the benefits of moving on. Day in and day out, I made elaborate plans concerning what I was going to accomplish when I recovered from this but once my thoughts started straying to you, it all ends the same way, emptiness. Am I a weak man or is it that I am foolish to think that someone who never loved me and took themselves away from me will do so after so many years?

Hope is seeing to be gone. I see poorer men, less handsome men, younger and older men; men of less drive, desire, vision, strength, passion; brutal men, men who smoke, drink, womanise and lie; men of no godly focus, men who possess less than I have and men who serve the devil. They all have a woman on their arm laughing and prancing along; while I walk by, bitter on the inside. I ask, 'Why could I not be like that? What is it that I lack?'

The answer comes from the reasoning within my brain, 'Nothing! You only lack the one you've got!'

So, I sit and cry silently and move on with my sorrowful lot; smiling, as I think forward and not back.

*****

She had stopped wearing her wedding ring a year before I took off mine. When I did, the pressure of failure started plaguing my mind. She said she doesn't love me anymore and never did. This echoed within the walls of my mind. My heart melted. My spirit ran into a hole. Valentine's Day no longer means chocolate or wine as thoughts of suicide plague me. The grave told me how much it needed and missed me.

'Will you not come and fill your space in the soil? Better to die than to be living in a house of lies!' Oh, the nights I prayed and cried.

My heart was so sad and the band around my finger reminded me that I was tied to who she is: my soul mate, the one I wanted to love until I leave for the pearly gate in the sky. She was my kryptonite. I could not see any light beyond the channel of her eyes. They grew cold and dark, even when I stood to the side in order to allow her to pass. I was so madly in love with her. What was I supposed to do? I was willing to kiss even her shoes. She said it was over and that she would like me to leave her the hell alone.

Spinning this circle around my finger, reminded me of the circle around my heart and with each touch it grew tighter and maximising how much I wanted her.

'Take it off before your heart become mulch,' I hear faintly in my head.

I promised the Lord I would be faithful to only you, 'But now that things are through why should it bother you, what I do?' Tears filled my eyes but thank God for the rain that hide my tears. My head is dizzy, as I think about losing her but never for a moment did I think to cheat. My spirit misses the intimacy of you and in my heart; I have not given up on you.

From KAW to JAW 26-6-03, was off in order to wash and never went back on but nothing changed in my heart. Its absence did nothing to the sadness in my heart. I was still doing nothing but falling apart. My thumb still played with the empty spot as though it was still spinning the piece of gold. I was sad with it and sad without it; I might as well I basked in the protection gained from it.

'Restore the carat to its shaft!'

I refuse to lose the symbol that represents the place where we started. I refuse to give the impression that I am available, to be an escort or someone else's sweetheart. So great circle, go back on and remind me of the pledge.

'I will always love you, though others will come to steal my heart!'

I refuse to be a part of statistics or be considered an old fart. I will wear you across my heart for this is where you on started. I will keep this ring on my finger because it reminds me of the one I wear around my heart, the one that will not break.

So with tears in my eyes, I put on my wedding ring and told my heart, 'Stay there and be strong' but her ring, remains absent from her hand.

CPSIA information can be obtained
at www.ICGtesting.com
Printed in the USA
BVHW041111011121
620450BV00007B/114